WRITERS AND TH

ISOBEL ARMSTI
General Edi

ALFRED TENNYSON

Tennyson drawn by James Spedding, at Mirehouse, near Bassenthwaite, April 1835. Reproduced by kind permission of the Master and Fellows of Trinity College Cambridge.

ALFRED
TENNYSON

Seamus Perry

NORTHCOTE
BRITISH
COUNCIL

First published in 2005 by Northcote House Publishers Ltd, Horndon, Tavistock, Devon, PL19 9NQ, United Kingdom.
Tel: +44 (0) 1822 810066 Fax: +44 (0) 1822 810034.

British Library Cataloguing-in-Publication Data
A catalogue record for this book is available from the British Library

ISBN 0-7463-1107-9 hardcover
ISBN 0-7463-0919-8 paperback

Typeset by PDQ Typesetting, Newcastle-under-Lyme
Printed and bound in the United Kingdom by
Athenaeum Press Ltd., Gateshead, Tyne & Wear

In memory of my father

Contents

Biographical Outline

1809   Alfred Tennyson born, 6 August, to Rev. George Clayton and Elizabeth Tennyson; one of eleven surviving children. Frederick (b. 1807) and Charles (b. 1808) are older. Tennyson's father is Rector of Somersby and of nearby Bag Enderby, tiny parishes in the remote Lincolnshire wolds. George is an awkward, scholarly man, much embittered by the restriction of his life: he was effectively forced into the church after his own father, an affluent Lincolnshire lawyer, had passed his inheritance to the younger son Charles. (Charles, renamed Charles Tennyson d'Eyncourt, went on to forge a career in politics; he took over the family estate at Bayons Manor, Tealby, rebuilding the house in grandiose Gothic style.)

1816   Tennyson at Grammar School in Louth, where he is miserable.

1820   Taken away from school to be tutored by his father, whose depression and alcholism are increasing; violence over-shadows the house.

1824   Moved by news of the death of Byron, the young boy carves 'Byron is dead' into a rock.

1827   Anonymous publication in April of *Poems by Two Brothers*, including poems by Charles and Frederick as well as Alfred. Alfred enters Trinity College, Cambridge, in November.

1828   The first three parts of 'The Lover's Tale' written about this time. Arthur Hallam (b.1811), son of Henry Hallam the historian, comes up to Trinity in October.

1829   George Tennyson's violence worsens. At Cambridge, the friendship of Tennyson and Hallam deepens. Both enter for the Chancellor's Medal for a poem on the subject of *Timbuctoo*, which Tennyson wins. (He cannot bring himself to read it out in the Senate House and deputes a friend.) Tennyson is elected to the Apostles, a gifted and high-minded group which meets regularly to discuss philosophy, literature, religion, and politics. Shelley is their favourite poet.

1830 *Poems, Chiefly Lyrical* published, including 'Mariana', 'The Kraken', 'The Ballad of Oriana', and 'The Sleeping Beauty' (later part of 'The Day-Dream'). Tennyson and Hallam travel in the Pyrenees, July–September – including a meeting with members of the liberal insurgency. Tennyson later remembers their tour in 'In the Valley of Cauteretz'. Back in England, agitation for political reform is growing: ricks are set alight around Cambridge, and the Apostles join forces protecting the university from attack.

1831 Favourable reviews of *Poems, Chiefly Lyrical* by W. J. Fox and Leigh Hunt. Tennyson's father dies in March. Tennyson returns home, leaving Cambridge without a degree. Hallam publishes his essay on *Poems, Chiefly Lyrical* in the *Englishman's Magazine*.

1832 In July, Tennyson and Hallam travel to the Rhineland. Hallam is engaged to Tennyson's sister Emily. Tennyson publishes *Poems* (dated 1833) at the end of the year, including 'The Lotos-Eaters', 'The Palace of Art', 'The Lady of Shalott', 'A Dream of Fair Women'. 'The Lover's Tale' is withdrawn before publication.

1833 Writes 'The Gardener's Daughter'. Hallam dies, suddenly, of a brain haemorrhage, in Vienna, 15 September; his remains are brought back to England by sea – the passage lies behind sections ix–xvii of *In Memoriam*. Over the following months Tennyson writes 'Ulysses', 'St Simeon Stylites', 'Tithon', 'Tiresias', 'Morte d'Arthur', 'Oh! that 'twere possible', 'Break, break, break', and adds to 'The Two Voices' (begun earlier in the year). The first-written sections of *In Memoriam* date from this time, including ix ('Fair ship'), xvii ('Thou comest'), xxx ('With trembling fingers'). He also writes a number of political poems, including 'Love thou thy land' and 'Of old sat Freedom on the heights'. He begins to rework poems of the 1830 and 1832 volumes.

1834   Hallam is buried in Clevedon, Somerset (January) – the subject of section xviii (' 'Tis well') of *In Memoriam*. Later in the year Tennyson adds to 'The Day-Dream' and writes 'Sir Galahad'. He is besotted with Rosa Baring of Harrington Hall, a moneyed house near Somersby, and writes her several rosy lyrics, including 'Thy rosy lips are soft and sweet'. The frustrations of his poverty, and Rosa's enticing remoteness, would feature in *Maud* and 'Locksley Hall'. (His infatuation had cooled by the end of 1836.) Tennyson tours the Wye Valley and stops at Tintern Abbey – a visit lying behind 'Tears, idle tears' and section xix of *In Memoriam*.

1835   Tennyson stays with James Spedding at Mirehouse, the Speddings' home on Bassenthwaite in the Lake District; here he meets Edward FitzGerald, later the author-translator of the *Rubáiyát of Omar Khayyám*. Tennyson's grandfather dies in July. Tennyson writes 'Dora' about this time.

1836   Tennyson begins to fall in love with Emily Sellwood, the sister of Louisa, wife of his brother Charles.

1837   'Will Waterproof's Lyrical Monologue' and 'The Talking Oak' written about this time. The Tennyson family finally moves from Somersby rectory (commemorated in *In Memoriam*, c–ciii). They settle until 1840 in Epping Forest. Tennyson is engaged to Emily Sellwood.

1838   Rosa Baring marries in October. 'Locksley Hall' written about this time, and the English Idyl 'Audley Court', as well as, possibly, 'Walking to the Mail'.

1839   'Edwin Morris' and, probably, 'The Golden Year', written.

1840   Tennyson visits Coventry; writes 'Godiva'. His engagement to Emily is broken off: financial reasons are blamed. Tennyson's state of mind is a subject of concern. About this time (1840–1) Tennyson invests all his money in a speculative scheme to manufacture wood-carving machines.

1842   *Poems* published in two volumes in May: the first contains mostly revised poems from the volumes of 1830 and 1832, and the second new works, including 'Morte d'Arthur' with its attendant poem 'The Epic', 'The Two Voices', 'St Simeon Stylites', and 'Ulysses'. In July Tennyson attends a festival organized by a local Mechanics' Institute, memories of which would feature in *The Princess*. Apostle John Sterling publishes his appreciative review of *Poems* in the *Quarterly Review*. Tennyson travels in Ireland (September); he has become friendly with the Scottish sage Thomas Carlyle.

1843   Spedding reviews *Poems* in the *Edinburgh Review*. The Tennyson family moves to Cheltenham. After a long period of tense anxiety, Tennyson learns that his investments are all lost: he has some kind of nervous collapse, and enters a hydropathic hospital for several months.

1845   Writing 'The University of Women', later to become *The Princess*. Tennyson receives a civil list pension of £200 a year, largely thanks to Hallam's father.

1846   Tennyson travels in Switzerland with the publisher Moxon (August). There he writes 'Come down, O maid, from yonder mountain height'.

1847   Tennyson fails to write an ode for the installation of Prince Albert as Chancellor of Cambridge; he is still troubled by bad nerves. *The Princess* published.

1848   A second edition of *The Princess*. Tennyson visits Ireland with the poet and man of letters Aubrey de Vere; writes 'The splendour falls'. May–July in Cornwall on a tour of Arthurian sites.

1849   Meets Edward Lear, painter and poet, who is to become a good friend. A tour of Scotland (September). Tennyson renews his relationship with Emily Sellwood; he asks her advice about the revision of *The Princess*. Meets the poet and critic Francis Palgrave.

1850   A third edition of *The Princess*, now including songs between the narrative sections; Emily is impressed by it. *In Memoriam* published, anonymously, in May; its authorship is quickly known. Tennyson and Emily marry in June. Following the death of Wordsworth, Tennyson appointed Poet Laureate (November).

1851   Tennyson adds the 'weird seizures' passages to *The Princess*, now published in a fourth edition. A son is stillborn in April (see 'Little bosom not yet cold'). Tennyson tours Italy with Emily (July). *In Memoriam* reprinted; a seventh edition of *Poems* appears, dedicated 'To the Queen'.

1852   Tennyson publishes a number of political poems in

periodicals (including 'Hands All Round!' and 'Britons, Guard Your Own'). Hallam Tennyson born in August. *Ode on the Death of the Duke of Wellington* published (November).

1853   A tour of Yorkshire and Scotland (July and August). In Edinburgh he writes 'The Daisy', remembering the Italian tour of 1851. The family moves to Farringford, an ample house on the Isle of Wight (November). Tennyson leases it for three years, and buys it in 1856. Frequent visitors include Edward Lear, Tennyson's lines to whom ('To E.L., on his Travels in Greece') are published this year in the eighth edition of *Poems*.

1854   Lionel Tennyson born in March. Tennyson writing *Maud*. 'The Charge of the Light Brigade' (December).

1855   Honorary degree from Oxford. Tennyson publishes *Maud, and Other Poems*, including (besides the title poem) 'The Brook', 'The Daisy', and 'Will'. Friendly with the Brownings, John Ruskin, and Jowett, the classicist and theological controversialist. (Tennyson's lines 'To the Master of Balliol' are addressed to him.)

1856   Writing Arthurian poetry.

1857   'Sea Dreams' written; published in *Macmillan's Magazine* in 1860.

1859   'Riflemen Form!' published in *The Times*. The first four of *Idylls of the King* published: 'Enid', 'Vivien', 'Elaine', and 'Guinevere'. 'The Grandmother' published (as 'The Grandmother's Apology') in the periodical *Once A Week*.

1860   'Tithonus', a revision of 'Tithon', is published in the *Cornhill Magazine*. Prince Albert asks Tennyson to sign his copy of the *Idylls*. Tennyson and Palgrave discuss the contents of an anthology of English poetry (August). Touring Cornwall and the Scilly Isles (August–September).

1861   Tennyson writes 'Northern Farmer, Old Style', the first of his Lincolnshire dialect poems. Palgrave's anthology, *The Golden Treasury*, much influenced by Tennyson's advice, published (July), dedicated to Tennyson. With his family, Tennyson tours the Pyrenees, revisiting Cauteretz (August–September), where he writes 'In the Valley of Cauteretz'. They are in the company of the poet Clough, who is shortly to die. Tennyson begins 'Enoch Arden' (November).

1862   A new edition of *Idylls* (February), dedicated to the memory of Prince Albert, who had died the previous year. Received by the widowed Queen at Osborne House: she expresses gratitude for *In Memoriam* (April). Travelling in Derbyshire with Palgrave (August).

1863   Working on 'Aylmer's Field' throughout the year (begun in July 1862).

1864   Meets Garibaldi (April). *Enoch Arden* published (August); it includes, beside the title poem, 'Aylmer's Field', 'Tithonus', and 'In the Valley of Cauteretz'. It is an immense success: by the end of the year 60,000 copies have been sold.

1865   Tennyson's mother dies (February). Holiday in Belgium and Germany (August–September).

1867   Writes 'The Higher Pantheism' (December).

1868   Work begins on Aldworth, a second home near Haslemere: the architect is a friend, the Arthurian author James Knowles. 'Lucretius' published in *Macmillan's Magazine* (May).

1869   Work proceeds on Aldworth. *The Holy Grail and Other Poems* published (December, but dated '1870'), including 'The Coming of Arthur', 'Pelleas and Ettarre', and 'The Passing of Arthur', as well as 'Lucretius', 'The Higher Pantheism', and other recent poems.

1872   Hallam Tennyson goes up to Trinity, Cambridge. *Gareth and Lynette* published (October). A new edition of Tennyson's *Works* (1872–3) gathers together all the *Idylls of the King* (except *Balin and Balan*, written in 1874), with a new epilogue addressed to the Queen.

1874   Emily's health collapses. She is unable to continue dealing with Tennyson's correspondence, which is by now enormous. Hallam abandons his studies to take up the burden (September).

1875   Tennyson occupied with the staging of *Queen Mary*, the first of several historical plays.

1876   *Queen Mary* premièred; soon withdrawn. Writes and publishes his next play, *Harold*, and begins work on a third, *Becket*.

1879   Death of his brother Charles (April). 'The Lover's Tale' finally published (May).

1880   Tennyson about to stand for the Rectorship of Glasgow University; but, on learning that he is being presented as the Conservative Party candidate, steps down. Emily by this time an invalid. *Ballads and Other Poems* published (November).

1881   Tennyson's play *The Cup* running at the Lyceum theatre.

1882   'To Virgil' published in the journal *The Nineteenth Century* (September). *The Promise of May*, another play, produced.

1883   Visits Denmark with Gladstone (September). Tennyson accepts the offer of a barony (December), having earlier turned down a baronetcy several times.

1885   Publishes *Tiresias and Other Poems* (November).

1886   Lionel Tennyson dies returning from India (April), later commemorated in Tennyson's 'To the Marquis of Dufferin and Ava'. *Locksley Hall Sixty Years After* published (December).

1888   In the autumn, badly ill with gout and rheumatic fever; his doctor finally declares him better the following May.

1889   Publishes *Demeter and Other Poems* (December). Hallam Tennyson takes his father's place as a pall-bearer at Browning's funeral.

1892   Tennyson dies at Aldworth, 6 October; buried in Westminster Abbey, 12 October. Emily too ill to attend. *The Death of Œnone, Akbar's Dream, and Other Poems* published, 28 October.

1893   *Becket* a hit at the Lyceum, Henry Irving in the title role. Hallam Tennyson works on the *Memoir* of his father.

1896   Emily Tennyson dies, 10 August.

1897   *Alfred Lord Tennyson: A Memoir by his Son* published.

Preface

This is a short book about a large subject: how Tennyson's imagination dealt with his lyric gift. I have said something about all of the major poems; but I have not tried to be comprehensive, nor have I set out to give a full account of Tennyson and his times. Instead, I have looked at the stylistic life of the poems, keeping in mind throughout what I take to be the crucial matter of Tennyson's *verbalism* (Walt Whitman's excellent word), and describing the role which that extraordinary facility plays in his poetry – a role played out across a wide variety of genres and purposes. That other kinds of question might be pursued, of an ideological kind perhaps, I certainly do not deny; but the matter of verbalism strikes me as peculiarly pressing for any sympathetic reader of Tennyson – his confidence in its vast capacity, his scruples about its proper limits – and it may well encompass many of those other possible questions too. It will be apparent that I am indebted particularly to those critics who have, in one way or another, addressed just this concern: Isobel Armstrong, John Bayley, Eric Griffiths, and, especially, Christopher Ricks.

Some thoughts about *In Memoriam* first stirred in an essay about elegy contributed to *A Companion to Victorian Poetry*, edited by Richard Cronin, Alison Chapman, and Antony Harrison (Blackwell, 2002); and a few of the points I make about Tennyson and Wordsworth had their first trial in a paper given at the International Tennyson Conference (Lincoln, 2001), and subsequently published in the *Tennyson Research Bulletin*. An earlier version of Chapter 1 formed a lecture delivered to the Tennyson Society in 2002: I am most grateful to the Society both for its invitation and for the kindness of its audience. Something like a Tennysonian character, this book has long been pending, and I warmly acknowledge the editorial patience of Isobel Armstrong and Brian Hulme. It was finally completed while I was on a period of study leave from the University of Glasgow that was funded by the Arts and Humanities Research Board: I am much indebted to both institutions for their generosity. I have learnt a lot about Tennyson from the conversation of Richard Cronin; and I should thank especially Nicola Trott for her insights and encouragement.

Glasgow, Oxford
May 2004

Abbreviations and References

All quotations from Tennyson's poetry are taken from *The Poems of Tennyson*, ed. Christopher Ricks (2nd edn; 3 vols.; Harlow: Longman, 1987), abbreviated as 'R'. As many readers will be using the one-volume paperback redaction – *Tennyson: A Selected Edition*, ed. Christopher Ricks (Harlow: Longman, 1989) – I have given for each poem cited the number it is allocated by Ricks (which is the same in the full and in the redacted edition) rather than the page number (which obviously differs). For the convenience of those using the full text I have given, in brackets, the number of the relevant volume. Thus: 'R. (i). 73' means poem 73 – 'Mariana', as it happens – which is in the first volume of the big edition. In that case, and in the case of most of the major poems I shall be speaking about at length, the poem is in the paperback edition as well. Where it was necessary to say so, I have cited *In Memoriam* as *IM* and *The Princess* as *P.*, followed by section and line number.

Items in the bibliography have been given full publication details. I have not included there all the texts from which I have quoted, which would have made it unwieldy. For texts cited in the notes, place of publication should be understood as London unless otherwise stated.

I have used the following abbreviations within the text:

CH   John D. Jump (ed.), *Tennyson: The Critical Heritage* (London: Routledge & Kegan Paul, 1967)
IR   Normal Page (ed.), *Tennyson: Interviews and Recollections* (London: Macmillan, 1983)
HL   *The Letters of Arthur Henry Hallam*, ed. Jack Kolb (Columbus, OH: Ohio State University Press, 1981)
HW   *The Writings of Arthur Hallam*, ed. T. H. Vail Motter (New

York: MLA, 1943).

The Letters of Alfred Lord Tennyson, ed. Cecil Y. Lang and Edgar F. Shannon, Jr. (3 vols.; Oxford: Clarendon Press, 1982–90)

M.   Hallam Tennyson, *Alfred, Lord Tennyson: A Memoir by his Son* (2 vols.; London: Macmillan, 1897)

Introduction

'Finest Verbalism'

> He left his episode and on he went
> Like one that cuts an eight upon the ice
> Returning on himself.
>
> (Tennyson)[1]

Most critics of Tennyson come sooner or later (and better sooner
than later) to the matter of Tennysonian language, the
extraordinarily sumptuous, sheerly mellifluous noise of it: his
early critics called it his 'luxuriance'; and many then, and since,
have regarded it mistrustfully. Matthew Arnold, much taken but
not taken in, discerned the luxuriance most clearly:

> The essential bent of his poetry is towards such expressions as –
>
> > Now lies the Earth all Danaë to the stars;
> >
> > O'er the sun's bright eye
> > Drew the vast eyelid of an inky cloud;
> >
> > When the cairned mountain was a shadow, sunned
> > The world to peace again . . .

Such lines (Arnold goes on to give more) exemplify a poetic
disposition towards the 'heightened and elaborate', which
Arnold considered a far lesser thing than chaste Homer's
'natural thoughts in natural words'.[2] Walter Bagehot also
thought Tennyson's art unnaturally 'ornate', similarly evasive
of the actual fact: 'Nothing is described as it is, everything has
about it an atmosphere of *something else.*' R. H. Horne too saw,
or rather heard, 'a poetical dialect', the sheer sound of which
was somehow its own self-enchanting end – 'Nay, he will write

1

_m with nothing in it except music, and as if its music everything, it shall charm your soul' (*CH* 285, 155). No wonder perhaps that by 1930, in *Seven Types of Ambiguity*, William Empson should appear so bored by Tennyson's 'simple and laborious cult of onomatopoeia', and no more drawn to the idea, equally Tennysonian, 'that sounds are valuable in themselves'.[3] Some years later, he nicely exemplified the sort of problem to which that idea might give rise by quoting Tennyson's line 'Far-folded mists, and gleaming halls of morn' – where 'halls' (as Empson thought) had a disastrous and inadvertent cosiness, making you think of the men playing billiards in the entrance hall of the big house: 'The word is only there for the vowel sound and the line feels mouldy.'[4]

A good deal of the criticism, then and since, has turned on the thought that the self-delighting opulence of Tennyson's characteristic poetical dialect – its 'mouthability', in Ricks's word[5] – is more than merely mouldly, but somehow dubious, even a *problem*, of a moral and quite possibly a political kind – as though the luxuriance of the idiom were engaged in avoiding something ('an atmosphere of *something else*'), perhaps covering something up. It does not soothe misgivings much that Tennyson himself often seemed immensely proud of a purely sonic gift, as though sound were the untroubled victor in any war with sense. He long remembered the admirably rolling line he had come up with when 8 years old: 'With slaughterous sons of thunder rolled the flood' – 'great nonsense of course, but I thought it fine' (*M*. ii. 93). It was not with any great confessional humility, you imagine, that he once 'confessed that he believed he knew the quantity of every word in the English language except perhaps "scissors"'' (whatever that means).[6] And it was praise for precisely that sort of super-nicety of musical judgement which he seemed especially to value in responses to his work – as when he recollected, 'Archbishop Trench . . . was the only critic who said of my first volume, "What a singular absence of the 's'!"'' – praise wittily full of the sibilants it deplores (*M*. ii. 231, 286).[7] ('I'd almost rather sacrifice a meaning than let two s's come together', he once said.[8]) He was famous for his ringing readings, 'lingering with solemn sweetness on every vowel sound' (*IR* 58), and once finished his much-criticized *Ode on the Death of the Duke of Wellington* with the

2

commentary: 'It is a great roll of words, the music of words . . . People do not understand the music of words' (*M*. ii. 386). That music he had long understood. The only thing he gained from his awful school, he told his son, 'was the memory of the words, "sonus desilientis aquae"' (*M*. i. 7), a phrase that was so good partly thanks to Tennyson, since Ovid actually wrote 'ex alto desilientis aquae' – 'it is evidence of the auditory quality of his imagination', as Dwight Culler nicely observes, 'that in his memory he imported the sound (*sonus*) of the water into the phrase'.[9] The younger Yeats once lamented the bad Victorian habits that 'so often extinguished the central flame in Tennyson';[10] but he did not dispute that there *was* a central flame, and it burnt with the conviction that there was a music of words – that 'words alone are certain good', as Yeats himself put it. James Knowles recalled of Tennyson: 'As a single line he said he knew hardly any to exceed for charm "Of Abbana and Pharphar, lucid streams". . . "Poetry", he would say at such times, "is a great deal truer than fact"' (*IR* 93).

Christopher Ricks once nominated as the best criticism of Tennyson a remark by Walt Whitman: 'Tennyson shows more than any poet I know (perhaps has been a warning to me) how much there is in finest verbalism' (*CH* 349–50).[11] The special discrimination of Whitman's remark lies in its well-mannered concession of the dangers of excess ('perhaps has been a warning') alongside its superlative recognition of genuine excellence ('*finest* verbalism'); and its critical fruitfulness begins with the question that it leaves open: well then, how much *is* there 'in' it? One suspicion might be: not much – that the fine sounds are more or less all there is – that the poetry is, as a contemporary satirically said of *Maud*, 'a little like the foam without the wave' (*CH* 190). The most intelligently sceptical response to his mannerism (because, like Whitman's remark, it admires what it suspects) is the great letter by Gerard Manley Hopkins about the 'Parnassian' mode in poetry – those passages when a masterful stylist, such as Tennyson, relies too much on his capacity superbly to sound like himself: 'he is, one must see it, what we used to call Tennysonian' (*CH* 280). But W. H. Auden's is the comment critics usually quote in this sort of context: 'he had the finest ear, perhaps, of any English poet; he was also undoubtedly the stupidest' (although Auden belatedly acknowl-

3

ᴧne stupider).[12] Chesterton makes much the same point ᴧt the Tennysonian style, with the confidence of a man whose own style fits him perfectly: 'he had much more power of expression than was wanted for anything he had to express. He could not think up to the height of his own towering style.'[13] Aldous Huxley took a dim view of Tennyson's mental equipment, but warily conceded that he 'knew his magician's business'.[14]

But worse than empty-headed, perhaps all this verbalism might have something very definite concealed within it: the art might actually be up to something, something unsavoury. Part of Bagehot's uneasiness at Tennyson's high ornateness was the inkling that it was covering up something rather low: in *Enoch Arden* (which inspired Bagehot's remarks) is not all the preambulatory finery really trying to keep at bay the thought that Enoch makes a living by selling fish? And, at the protracted crisis of the poem, beneath 'the gorgeous additions and ornaments with which Mr Tennyson distracts us', does there not lurk the 'dismal act of a squalid man' (*CH* 285, 290, 291)? Well, literary notions of what is dismal and squalid change with the generations; but the suspicion that the finery of the verbalism is a kind of aesthetic disguise is still a live critical instinct. Kate Millett's account of *The Princess* remains a rousing example of such detection: the dazzling 'heap of shining lyrics' that she describes evidently plays its part in the poem's aesthetically evasive tactics – 'the cloying sweetness, the frenetic sentimentality, all conspire to hide the fact that this is only candy-coated sexual politics'.[15] (It is hard not to agree that something troublingly evasive is indeed going in *The Princess*; and it is only a partial defence to say that it seems to have troubled Tennyson too.) The disreputable hidden thing need not be gender, of course; it might be imperialism; or class. Alan Sinfield, for a more recent (and influential) example, says that Tennyson's art is (among other things) 'in the service of a wider project, calculated to help Europe handle its own ideological problems, and especially those associated with its domination of the rest of the world'; further, that it is collusive with 'classic capitalism'; and that such political collusions are effected largely by Tennyson's tendentiously aesthetic deployment of '[t]he elaborate diction, the obtrusive syntax and the intense effects of sound and rhythm' – 'the full Tennysonian battery' – in fact, the 'poetical magic', that whole way of using words that is 'always more like that of music than ordinary language'.[16]

Ordinary language would be preferable. When the reaction against Tennyson set in, toward the end of the nineteenth century, 'elaborateness' was often prominent on the charge sheet (as A. C. Bradley records[17]); but complaining critics had always complained especially about Tennyson's 'aversion from the straight-forward and strong simplicity of nature and truth' (the objection made by Christopher North (*CH* 52)). For T. S. Eliot or Auden – to each of whom, though in very different ways, 'The poetry does not matter' (in Eliot's phrase) – Tennyson's sumptuous verbalism was just the kind of romantic enchantment that should most be resisted. And much recent ideologically minded criticism, like its unacknowledged modernist forebears, begins with the same desire not to be taken in, but to be disabused – to free poetry from the spell-binding aesthetic authority attributed to it by the literary avant-garde in which Tennyson came of age. Tennyson's friend Arthur Hallam said reverently in his review of Tennyson's *Poems, Chiefly Lyrical*, that 'poetry is a sort of magic' (*CH* 38); the disenchanted modern critics I have in mind seek instead the wholly unmagical things that the poetry leaves unsaid, or only barely says, or unwittingly lets slip. Such a habit of mind sets the distracting drapery of verbalism against the really *real* meaning in an abrasively oppositional way: 'The magic of Tennyson's poetry . . . facilitates a claim of sagacity,' says Sinfield, in an exemplary moment of principled suspicion, 'The tricks are excellent, but we need to read the fine print.'[18]

Ever since Harold Nicolson's biography of 1923, critics have liked to think of Tennyson as a man divided in two, a superficial public face and a dark private interior;[19] and much recent ideological criticism might be seen as an ingenious twist on that traditional sense, making of its doubleness a duplicity. In Sinfield's Marxist approach, as much as in (say) Eve Kosofsky Sedgwick's deft and celebrated feminist reading of *The Princess*, a poem is made to yield up its covert *true* intention, raised from the private depths like the troubling and formative experiences of a patient under analysis.[20] Adversarial criticism of this kind needs to assume (for its own ends, and often quite knowingly) that its object is more simple-minded than it really is – which is

5

usually a matter of finding it more single-minded than it really is: however intricate the poem's manifest verbal complexity, deep down its subconscious meaning usually turns out to be more or less straightforward, and more than less deplorable. (Oddly enough, then, if such adversarial critics go astray, it may not be because they are too adversarial, but rather because they are altogether too respectful, in a curiously old-fashioned way, and look to the poems under their scrutiny for meanings of the most coherent and unified kind.) But, instead of seeing the intricate verbal life of the poetry as a distraction from what's *really* going on – the cogent compulsions of ideology, which the author either cannot cognize or cannot wholly conceal – we might do better to assume what Isobel Armstrong has called, in a far from unsympathetic response to the adversarial school, 'a more generous understanding of the text as struggle'.[21]

The point feels as though it has an instinctive rightness when it comes to Tennyson, anyway, whose poetry is repeatedly drawn to poetic forms that openly enact or emulate dispute and struggling indecision of one kind or another: an early poem is exemplarily entitled 'Supposed Confessions of a Second-Rate Sensitive Mind Not In Unity With Itself' (R. (i). 78). Perhaps no one better fulfils Arnold's memorable description of the poetic spirit of the age as 'the dialogue of the mind with itself'.[22] Tennyson thought (*IR* 157) that one of his best critics was Richard Holt Hutton, who finely recognized in his poetry 'that comprehension of grasp, that deliberate rejection of single strands of feeling, which always distinguishes him';[23] and it is in what Sinfield calls the 'tricks' ('the elaborate diction, the obtrusive syntax and the intense effects of sound and rhythm') that such comprehensive intricacies are bound to lead their local life. Eliot began his great essay on *In Memoriam* with due regard for Tennyson's 'complete competence'; and maybe it is hard not to feel with Martin Dodsworth that Eliot's words, while meaning well, actually imply a sort of 'shallow brilliance', a concession of verbal proficiency not so very far from Sinfield allowing that the tricks are indeed excellent. But a little later in that essay Eliot offers rather better tribute, pausing to deepen his earlier praise, and giving the best single piece of advice to Tennyson's readers: 'Tennyson's surface, his technical accomplishment, is intimate with his depths.'[24] (The insight is related

6

to a more encompassing Eliotic truth: 'we cannot say at what point "technique" begins or where it ends.'[25]) Attending to the technical accomplishment need not, that is to say, require sidestepping the commitments and responsibilities of politics or morals, Tennyson's or our own, as the adversarial critic might allege; but it may prove a salutary way of sidestepping an undue single-mindedness about what they are likely to be. All the print is 'the fine print'.

The complicatedness of 'feeling' that Hutton discerns is not an alternative to some purer rigour of 'thought' (as in, say, 'political thought'), something that might be set out plain and square in ordinary language, if one chose. It is, rather, the most capaciously self-aware, often self-disputatious, expression of what it is that is *being* thought; and the intricate elaborateness of Tennysonian verse does not, at its best, work to obfuscate or distract – although it is often conscious of the possibility of obfuscation and distraction – but works rather to elaborate intricacy. Eric Griffiths writes characteristically well about this: 'Tennyson is thought to be preoccupied with word-music, with fondling, as it were, the bodies of words, to the exclusion or detriment of responsible thought . . . But Tennyson thought *in* melody.'[26] He had thoughts outside melody too, of course, and kept himself well-informed about the many ideological and doctrinal crises of the age, which could rouse him to passion; but he was in no important sense a *thinker* about politics or religion or philosophy, in the way that Gladstone was, or even Browning or Hopkins was.[27] In conversation, especially as a grand old man, his more weighty announcements and portentous remarks are frequently funny, only sometimes on purpose. He once declared to the poet and diarist William Allingham (who has the best stories): 'I could not eat my dinner without a belief in immortality. If I didn't believe in that, I'd go down immediately and jump off Richmond Bridge'; and after asking why Allingham was laughing so much, he could only add, bleakly, 'in such a case I'd as soon make a comic end as a tragic' (*IR* 28). To William Knight he was very lofty about what needed to be done, philosophically speaking:' "I want to know how we are to unite the One with the Many, and the Many with the All . . . For my part," he said, "if I were an old Greek I should try to combine the doctrine of Parmenides with that of Heraclitus" '

7

(*IR* 182) – a disarming metaphysical tip, as Professor Knight may have thought.

Sometimes such blunt-fingered speculation made it into his poetry, the metrical statement of a wise position, and when it does it mostly sounds dismally far from wisdom: 'God is law, say the wise; O Soul, and let us rejoice, | For if He thunder by law the thunder is yet His voice' ('The Higher Pantheism', R. (ii). 353, ll. 13–14). The inadvertent comedy of plodding complacence in those lines was satirized most beautifully by Swinburne: 'God, whom we see not, is: and God, who is not, we see; | Fiddle, we know, is diddle: and diddle, we take it, is dee.'[28] The pat assurance that Swinburne's nonsense expertly sends up there alerts us to the honestly unassured quality of thought that Tennyson's lyricism worked, more characteristically, to liberate from the gruff assertiveness of his table talk. W. F. Rawnsley's recollections nicely intimate the all-important relationship in Tennyson between a vocation to sing and an occasion to think.[29] 'The *sound* of a line of poetry (for poetry, to be fully understood, should be read aloud) was very much to him . . . In speaking of Browning, he once said to me: "I don't think that poetry should be *all thought*: there should be some melody"' (*IR* 21): not *all thought*, then, but not *all* melody either.[30] As it happens (and unlike Browning) Tennyson actually had no ear for music: 'he was by nature shut out from it', he said, something that saddened him, since he thought music 'expresses what can't be expressed in words' (*IR* 114; and cf. *M.* ii. 394). Odd, reflected a memoirist, that one 'whose every line was music, cared so little for it except in poetry' (*IR* 90): an entirely commonplace remark, no doubt; but just possibly more suggestive, if the implication is that a Tennysonian sort of musicality worked, in its own way, to get 'expressed in words' what might more normally elude them – the poet discovering his peculiarly enabling medium in the interplay between the beautiful noise of 'melody' and the inflections of a thoughtful voice. Some such view seems suggested in Arthur Hallam's prescient review of *Poems, Chiefly Lyrical* anyway. Hallam thought Tennyson a poet of 'sensation' rather than one of 'reflection', a poet gifted with an ear of 'fairy fineness': such a lyrical disposition did not *exclude* thought from his verse, to be sure, but it did mean that 'the elevated habits of thought [are] *implied*' – which was 'more impressive, to our

8

minds', as Hallam loyally, and shrewdly, insisted, 'than if the author had drawn up a set of opinions in verse' (*CH* 42).

Hallam sets 'habits of thought' against 'opinions in verse': an interest in the mind's dynamics supercedes the attraction of credal certainty. When Hutton praised Tennyson's rejection of 'single strands of feeling', it was in the course of acclaiming him as a poet unable to write a 'mere wail of agonising doubt without shedding some glimpse of faith'. Hutton observed the contesting elements constituting a virtuously unquiet mind, and Eliot was making out much the same contention, though with a different emphasis, when he said of *In Memoriam*: 'Its faith is a poor thing, but its doubt is a very intense experience.'[32] For both those readers, the poem's faith and hope are entwined in doubled strands of feeling, as they repeatedly are in the movement of Tennyson's verse:

> There lives more faith in honest doubt,
> Believe me, than in half the creeds.
>
> (*IM* xcvi. 11–12)

By Tennyson's standards, that is a subdued piece of word music, although the delicately organized staccato effect of unelidable consonants ('in honest doubt') sweeps with great effect into the expansive chiming 'ee's of 'Believe me' and 'creeds', as the mind gains some purchase upon disbelief and its impediments and moves towards more harmonious spiritual ease. Still, it is not quite the bolstering aphorism it might have been: certainly not the well-pointed sentence that (as Ricks notes) Tennyson marked in the margin of Bailey's *Festus* – 'Who never doubted never half believed'; but something made at once more heartfelt and less certain by the interrupting phrase, with its insistent weight, 'Believe me'. Philip Larkin once complained of Tennyson that 'his lines seem to hover awkwardly between speech and verse'; [32] but what can sometimes be an awkwardness can prove at other times an enriching strength (as is finely shown, for that matter, by Larkin's own verse, the intense lyricism of which frequently sounds, too, as though something almost being said). In the best Tennyson, the aural dimensions of a spoken idiom often complicate, or enrich, the aesthetic authority of the verse's sonorities: Eric Griffiths writes about this most beautifully in *The Printed Voice of Victorian Poetry*. In the lines from *In Memoriam*, for instance, Tennyson's 'Believe me' sounds at once as a claim of conviction ('believe me, *I* know what I'm talking about'), and also a plea to be believed ('you *must* believe me'), an appeal that admits the very real possibility of a reader's frank incredulity about faith on these terms, life on this knife's edge. A determination to think well about the tenuousness of belief is complicated by the presence of a countering thought: for 'Believe' to follow so hard upon 'doubt' acts out in the turning of the line a turning of the mind upon itself. The verse expresses a kind of moderation or reserve about its own spiritual claim, registered in its honest avoidance of an expected hyperbole ('than in *all* the creeds'): what might have promised to be a useful piece of wisdom to live by, itself a homely but profound sort of creed, turns out to be something at once less than that and a good deal more – not a 'creed' (a statement of what one believes) but, perhaps, half a creed (what one half-believes). If *In Memoriam* is 'what he had to say on religion', as Jowett reported, then what he had to say is intricately and inwardly articulated, writing 'myself to myself' (*M.* i. 325, 173).

The philosopher Henry Sidgwick saw in the alternating existence of *In Memoriam* a witness to 'the whole truth . . . that assurance and doubt must alternate in the moral world in which we at present live' (*M.* i. 304). Religious assurance and doubt is what *In Memoriam* has mostly in mind, of course; but beliefs of all kinds might enjoy the advantages of such self-interrogation, what Coleridge admired in Shakespeare as 'the flux and reflux of the mind'.[33] (Whitman recognized among Tennyson's exemplary verbalist habits 'doublings upon himself' (*CH* 350).) A comprehensive paraphrase of the *In Memoriam* lines, allowing for their full implication, would not be arrived at quickly, because the truth of their desire to believe is entwined with a truthfulness about how they mistrust too. 'That's the swift decision of one who sees only half the truth,' FitzGerald once heard Tennyson say of a decisive acquaintance (*M.* i. 37).[34] As we shall see, Tennyson's poetry often dwells, contrarily, on indecisiveness and on decisions deferred, lingeringly, uneasily, sometimes scoldingly; Allingham once attentively noted 'a peculiar *incomplete* cadence at the end' when Tennyson read a poem (*IR* 58). Poems that might seem nevertheless to have arrived at a decision or denouement often spurred him to devise sequels that carried them on. Of *In Memoriam*, for example, he said, 'I think of adding another to it . . . showing that all the arguments are about as good on one side as the other, and thus throw man back more on the primitive impulses and feelings' (*IR* 96) – not that 'the primitive impulses and feelings' held out much promise of a final answer either. 'He was sometimes described as advancing opposite opinions at different times,' his son Hallam conceded in the *Memoir*, mustering a defence that is touchingly idealizing: 'from his firm sense of justice he had a dramatic way of representing an opinion adverse to his own in a favourable light, in order that he might give it the most generous interpretation possible' (*M.* i. 185). (Hutton noted Tennyson's tendency 'to over-express any morbid thought or feeling he wishes to resist' (*CH* 370).)

The absence of intellectual certitude which Hallam seeks to cast a virtue was certainly not always greeted that way by the critics: 'we have the idea of a poet . . . who is not in a fixed attitude', fretted R. H. Horne, 'not resolute as to means, not determined as to end' (*CH* 165); 'His genius is bold, but is waylaid at almost every step by the timidity and weakness of his temperament', said George Gilfillan;[35] 'he must, by continual study and meditation, strengthen his intellect', advised J. S. Mill (*CH* 96). But the false notes usually sound, sometimes poignantly, just when Tennyson is trying to sound more resolute, determined, bold, and strong than he properly is. He believed, a lot of the time, that he was not the sort of person who could come – as many people whom he much admired evidently could – to the fixity of an attitude, not about religion nor about many other things; and this was something to be ashamed of sometimes, but occasionally something not to be so uneasy about too. One problem with Wordsworth, Tennyson said, was that he was 'too one-sided to be dramatic' (*M.* i. 278); and when the protagonist in 'The Two Voices' wishes to scold, one term of disapproval readily comes to hand: ' "O dull, one-sided voice," said I' (*R.* (i). 209, l. 202). Tennyson was highly esteemed by his fellow Apostles, the intently cerebral discussion group he joined while an undergraduate at Trinity College, Cambridge: he was thought of as 'the Poet of the Apostles' (*M.* i. 131); but he could not face reading to the company the philosophical paper that the society's rules officially required,

11

as though instinctively suspecting his thoughts to be out of place as long as they were to be cast as a thesis, and cast out of his melody. (That is why a kind of self-mocking satire is occasionally implicit in the vigorously single-minded *ex cathedra* judgements of the ageing sage: 'I should consider that a liberty had been taken with me if I were made simply a means of ushering in something higher than myself' (*M*. ii. 474) – a *liberty*?) Sometimes he could be bullishly anti-intellectual about all this: he must have enjoyed telling the Master of Balliol, 'I hate learning' (*M*. ii. 463). At other times, he could be brusquely self-deprecating: 'I am so glad to know you', stammered the Duke of Argyll at their first meeting; 'You won't find much in me – after all,' Tennyson replied (*M*. ii. 513).

One of the things that a poet might most fruitfully hold in honest doubt is poetry itself. Eliot praised in Tennyson 'the sense of confidence that is one of the major pleasures of poetry';[36] but a large part of what most productively communicates itself from the stirring depths to the accomplished surface is – far from a 'sense of confidence' – the characteristically modern thought that 'technical accomplishment', the 'finest verbalism', which Whitman recognized and so many have distrusted, is – well, no, actually *not* enough, and that the resources of poetry should be put to some more serious purpose or *use* than being merely *art*. Isobel Armstrong has astutely remarked that in Tennyson, as in several other Victorian poets, 'the sheer verbalness of poetry is foregrounded';[37] and this verbalness can be a source of misgiving as well as of pleasure, doubt as well as assurance. Modern criticism's mistrustful regard for the Tennysonian dialect here replicates Tennyson's own frequent disquiet. Ezra Pound, busy forging a literary revolution, sought to exclude from verse 'every *literaryism*, every book word' – in short, all 'Tennysonianness of speech';[38] and suspecting literariness in much the same spirit, though to rather different ends, Alan Sinfield says, 'Magic does not guarantee wisdom', and he writes in purposeful critique.[39] But such a sentiment is really an eminently Tennysonian one (though not the only Tennysonian one). A sign of Tennyson's scepticism about his native gifts of verbal magnificence is the nagging scrupulousness he felt about getting the facts right, not poetically right but *really* right (no question here that poetry is

12

'a great deal truer than fact'). E. F. Benson adroitly made appropriate noises over the mistake about railways in 'Locksley Hall' (which imagines not railway tracks but 'grooves' (R. (ii). 271, l. 182))): 'A fine line of poetry was worth more than the truth about the railway line.'[40] That strikes a practically *symboliste* note – as when Yeats defended the ornithology in one of his poems by protesting an exclusive concern with the peahens of Indian poetry, and a complete lack of interest in the birds of the poultry yard. But it was not the note of Tennyson, who felt obliged to acknowledge and explain the error, once it was pointed out. He never printed his poem 'Anacaona', according to Hallam in the *Memoir* because, although he 'chose words which sounded well', the natural history turned out to be wrong (*M.* i. 56); and even errors that would not be detected, as faulty natural history might just be, troubled him immoderately. 'My father was vexed that he had written "two and thirty years ago" in his "All along the Valley" instead of "one and thirty years ago", and as late as 1892 wished to alter it since he hated inaccuracy': his son persuaded him to keep in that apparent error, largely because it was 'more melodious' (*M.* i. 475 n.). Tennyson's 'material is derived not from the world of Nature, but from the world of Art', said a devout critic (*CH* 450); but, when literary sources were identified, the poet would often insist vehemently on the real-life origin of his observations (*IR* 71; *L.* iii. 238–40).

That kind of uneasiness or queasiness about the authority of art, and about the challenges that might be made to it, are all-important to the Tennysonian effect, for the 'complete confidence' that Eliot acclaimed is not always what strikes us most about Tennyson's poetry: not that it is often positively *incompetent*, of course – Hopkins found 'each verse a work of art, no botchy places, not only so but no half wrought or low-toned ones, no drab, no brown-holland'[41] – but that it is not always at ease with its competence. Ricks best describes the highly distinctive effect I have in mind here when he mentions 'the conflict which is often felt in reading Tennyson, the conflict between confidence in his extraordinary expertise and faint uneasiness about the extent to which the expertise is verbal or purely verbal'.[42] A reader of Tennyson as good as W. David Shaw feels moved '[t]o allay this uneasiness' and argues his way persuasively;[43] but some sense of uneasiness is often not a thing to assuage but a crucial ingredient in the way the poetry gets to work on us. No great poem is so movingly unsettled by its own verbal dexterity as is *In Memoriam* (unless it is *Four Quartets*); no poet edges his work into the world with such cautious uncertainty and exposed wariness of purpose as Tennyson does 'Morte d'Arthur' or *The Princess*. He often spoke with ostentatious contempt of his own works (though not of *Maud*, of which he was very protective), especially to FitzGerald: 'you can't hate it more than I do'; 'My Book is out and I hate it and so no doubt will you' (*L.* i. 204, 281). That, like his occasionally desperate vulnerability before the critics – '*I do not wish to be dragged forward again in any shape before the reading public at present*' (*M.* i. 145) – might imply a horror about being made public: an anxious self-consciousness, perhaps, about lacking fixed and manly attitudes, rather as Keats grew anxious to write poetry 'which cannot be laugh'd at in any way'.[44] Tennyson told a friend: 'If I had to choose life over again . . . I wouldn't be a poet, I'd be a pachyderm . . . a thick-skinned fellow with no nerves' (*IR* 156).

The unallayed suspicion that something is lacking or awry – the hall-mark awareness of a poetry somehow incompletely at one with itself – this underlies much of the best Tennyson, without, at its best, undermining it. So, when readers find unadmitted meanings lurking in the depths of the poetry, they are, I think, genuinely on to an important part of the Tennysonian effect; but casting that secrecy as a matter of denial or aesthetic occlusion seems to me to be coarsening the extremely involved relationship in Tennyson between eloquence and reticence, assertiveness and unspokenness – between a passionate faith in lyricism and unshifting doubts about it. Swinburne was very sharp about this, and not quite unsympathetically: 'Lord Tennyson is so ostentatious of his modesty, so unsparing in his reserve . . .' (*CH* 339). The memoirists describe a man who combined an exuberant taste for positively exhibitionist recitation and display with determined taciturnity in company and an often obsessive desire for privacy; and the poetry too is drawn between a superbly performative music and an acute sense of the heart's inarticulacy.[45]

That sounds a solemn music; and sometimes it is solemn; but the self-consciousness about poetic proceedings which this imaginative predicament inspires can inspire a sort of humour, as well as anxious introspection. What Eric Griffiths cleverly says about the speaker of *Maud* captures an experience often felt when reading Tennyson, I think, one that naturally lends itself to the comical because it turns around a puzzle about seriousness: 'we are constantly having to decide how seriously to take what we read him saying, to decide whether he is "only" being poetical.'[46] Chesterton said: 'We cannot help feeling that Tennyson is the Englishman taking himself seriously – an awful sight';[47] but that is an unusual failure of alertness on Chesterton's part. Jowett thought Tennyson 'always lived in an attitude of humour' (*M.* ii. 461 n.), and Tennyson's good friend Knowles spoke most tenderly about his temper:

> There was a great abundance of playfulness under the grimness of his exterior, and as to humour, that was all pervading and flavoured every day with salt. It was habitual with him, and seemed a sort of counteraction and relief to the intense solemnity of his also habitual gaze at life in its deeper aspects, which else would almost have overwhelmed him with awe. (*IR* 89)

The 'struggle' that Armstrong makes out, and the 'conflict' felt by Ricks, can find themselves cast as the 'counteraction' of a highly idiosyncratic brand of Tennysonian comedy – one sign of a self-awareness about the powers and charms of verbalism that a resolved ideological criticism, vigilant for single-mindedness, is disposed to miss. I am not ambitious to propose Tennyson as a humourist exactly, though that was what his travelling companion Locker-Lampson called him (*M.* ii. 68) and he was not alone in thinking so;[48] but the immense importance of his work to the poetry of Edward Lear (a good friend and one of his most instinctively brilliant critics) does suggest a connection of some kind with comedy, if comedy of an oblique variety.

This little book does not attempt to cover Tennyson's entire career, nor does it proceed chronologically: readers wishing to follow the poet from Lincolnshire to the Isle of Wight and from Louth School to the House of Lords should consult one of the several excellent biographies and works of criticism I have put in the bibliography. Instead, I have tried to write an essay that takes Eliot's observation to heart, and, paying due attention to the 'technical accomplishment', seeks throughout to connect the pleasures of that accomplishment to the profundity of the 'depths'. (Eliot enjoys, perhaps, a special affinity with Tennyson, but Tennyson's contribution to twentieth-century poetry generally was immense: my epigraphs from Eliot and Auden might hint at some connections between the Victorian Laureate and literary modernity, but a proper study obviously belongs elsewhere.)

The first chapter begins with an unignorable aspect of the accomplishment: the extensive use that Tennyson's poetry makes of repetition. The mixture of eloquence and inarticulacy that stirs in so much of his poetry might be expected to find a natural idiomatic haunt in repetitiveness: for what could be more ostentatiously virtusoso than the poetic audacity of repeating (as in Macbeth's 'And with some sweet oblivious antidote | Cleanse the stuff'd bosom of that perilous stuff | Which weighs upon the heart'); and yet what could be more surely 'a mark of poetic collapse' (in Derek Attridge's words) – 'the very sign of banality and formula of boredom . . . a scandal, a stone of stumbling' (in Kathleen Lea's) – than repeating?[49] Of course, repetition and its opposite – doing things again and being unable ever to do them again – these are important features of normal existence as well as of poetic language, as Tennyson was aware; and besides offering a medium hospitable to the ambiguities of his creative temperament, the repetitive texture of his poetry also sustained and confirmed Tennyson's unrelenting fascination with ideas of recurrence and return in life. An unadmiring Stephen Dedalus, in Joyce's *Ulysses*, coined the dismissive name 'Alfred Lawn Tennyson'; but unadmiring need not mean exactly unimpressed, and Stephen's pun invokes 'lawn tennis', a game, after all, composed largely of returns, or attempted returns – for which suggestion we might be grateful.

The reiterative disposition I am attributing to Tennyson nurtures the poetry of stasis and suspension that many of his best readers have remarked and enjoyed; but he accepts a vocation as a poet of immobility with some reluctance: in fact, as though by reaction, he invests an immense amount of energy in the countering thoughts of progress and advancement. (Eliot says: 'he was opposed to the doctrine that he was moved to accept and to praise'.[50]) Chapter 2 describes the complicating ways in which his diverse understandings of progress influence his verse: I mean the (to him) 'progressive' ideas that he dutifully, public-spiritedly seeks to incorporate into his art, and for which his high-minded contemporaries often applauded him. I also mean the formal 'progressiveness' of narrative – of storytelling, to which he devoted many poems, but for which, as Eliot rightly said, he 'had no gift at all';[51] and that is the subject of my third chapter. *The Princess* and the *Idylls of the King* both show the impress of Tennyson's lack of a gift; but having no gift can sometimes be a kind of gift; and he writes at least one great extended piece of anti-narrative storytelling: *Maud*, which frankly breaks the normality of narrative sequence into disjointedness and perplexing inconsequentiality. The impulse to progress comes into its most intimate and fruitful alliance with the counter-impulse to regress in the state of mourning, and in its formal poetic enactment, elegy. That is why, I shall be saying, *In Memoriam* is his greatest poem, along with some of the other poems occasioned by Arthur Hallam's death, unquestionably the central event of Tennyson's life: 'One can hardly conceive the overwhelming impression made on a mind like Tennyson's by the loss of a friend who was more than all the world to him', said Jowett (*M*. ii. 464). I seek to describe the centrality of *In Memoriam* in Chapter 4.

The focus throughout remains quite close, and I thought to take the opportunity of a brief Coda to imply a fleeting wider perspective. Namely, that we might understand the contested life of Tennyson's lyricism, my subject throughout, historically: as an aspect of his relationship with his immediate predecessors, the great Romantic poets. (Which leaves much to be said, of course, but I hope it says something: I aim to return to the subject elsewhere.) 'Romanticism' – to hypostasize an abstract noun for the moment – bequeathed to Tennyson's generation an immensely lofty idea of Art, empowering the aesthetic with a wonderful autonomy and grandeur; and Tennyson, like many of his contemporaries in one way or the other, found the idea irresistible – and yet somehow unsustainable too. His resistance to the idea of 'Art' was, in part, nervily ethical: the expectation that artistry be set to do good public work troubled any claim that art might make to a special inward kind of self-justifying delight. But resistance was also due, no doubt, to a yen after 'a sort of counteraction' (in Knowles's phrase) – for another, counteracting, aspect of Romantic thought invested the *un-*aesthetic world, ordinarily exisiting outside art, with an intense if paradoxical sort of literary allure; and Tennyson inherited that as a possible vocation for poetry too. Much of his most compelling poetry consequently experiences a dual loyalty, drawn at once to both varieties of Romantic creativity, existing about the uncertain boundary between art and non-art. 'The Palace of Art' is his fullest and most self-conscious exhibition of such post-Romantic dilemmas, a poem that dramatizes his predicament in a marvellously indecisive choreography of Tennysonian turning and returning, turning to and turning away; and I end with some words about that.

1

Returns

> You say I am repeating
> Something I have said before. I shall say it again.
> Shall I say it again?
>
> (T. S. Eliot)

This chapter is about the resourcefulness with which Tennyson said things and then returned to say them again. Poets and critics have often thought repetition fundamental to the way that poetry normally gets about its business; but its presence in Tennyson is more than exemplary. For Tennyson was peculiarly preoccupied, in mutually complicating ways, by the ideas of change (its dreadful inescapability, its redemptive progressiveness) and of changelessness (its stultifying paralysis, its wonderful immutability); and that involved preoccupation led him to find in repetitiveness one of his richest poetical resources. Of all kinds of verbalism, repetition surely feels the most purely *verbal*, most innocently lyrical: 'But my kisses bring again, bring again, | Seals of love, but seal'd in vain, seal'd in vain.'[1] At the furthest remove from a normal semantic act, such repeats appear the hall-mark, rather, of what Auden once called the 'absolute gift' of music. But (as I tried to say in the Introduction), music and meaning are always crossing paths in Tennyson poems. Repeating something might, for example, evoke a claustrophic inability to move on; but equally it might create a luxuriant sense of dwelling ease; and, at its most peculiarly Tennysonian, it might manage to do both at once.

Of course, imagining styles of changelessness hardly exiles the thought of change: the stayings-still of repetition are always likely to incite the question that stirs in so much Tennyson, 'Is this the end? Is this the end?' (*IM* xii. 16). With each repeat in a succession of repetitions, your anticipation of its ending grows stronger, while your suspicion that it might yet continue grows tenser: imagine the first audience of *King Lear* listening to the old man cry, 'Never, never, never, never, never'. Tennyson's studies in reiterative immobility typically brace themselves for alteration, often occupying a suspended moment just before kinds of catastrophe, 'Deep in forethought of dark calamities, | Sick of the coming time and coming woe' ('Pierced through with knotted thorns of barren pain', R. (i). 190, ll. 2–3). Tennyson loved *Clarissa* for being one of 'those great *still* books' (*M.* ii. 372); but the immense narrative lethargy of Richardson's novel gathers its power from an ever-looming act of devastating violence. Doubtless lots of poets, like people at large, are attracted by doom: the young Tennyson's circle seems to have felt itself peculiarly involved in pressing calamity (I shall adduce some reasons for that in the next chapter); but Tennyson's investment in the idea was of a different order. Herbert Tucker has written with great insight and style about Tennyson's interest in the inevitable and the predetermined, though whether this prompts what Tucker calls a 'poetry of aftermath' exactly is a nice point: Tucker himself finds in Tennyson 'an awareness of a threat from beyond, a sentence of doom that was nearing its period' –which suggests, perhaps, less a genius for aftermath than one for *pending*.[2]

He was certainly drawn by the thought of things hanging (*pendeo*: to hang, hang down, be suspended) and about to fall – like the magnificent bird in his fragment, 'The Eagle' (R. (i). 199). (Compare the suspended animation of these lines from 'The Lover's Tale', poised while they await their verb: 'her words, syllable by syllable, | Like water, drop by drop, upon my ear | Fell' (R. (i). 153, i. 564–6).) A more numinous sense of foreboding waningly enlivens the *Idylls of the King* once the poem begins to sense 'A doom that ever poised itself to fall' ('Merlin and Vivien', R. (iii). 469, l. 189). In the first version of 'A Dream of Fair Women', Tennyson imagined suspension as a choice vantage point for poetry, picturing the Poet pendant above the world like an aeronaut 'Selfpoised, nor fears to fall' (R. (i). 173, n.). On his deathbed his Shakespeare lay open at favourite lines from *Cymbeline*: 'Hang there like fruit, my soul, | Till the tree die' (*M.* ii. 428). We can often find his own poetry sustaining the poised, tensed predicament of things which, like that soul, are about to have been – like the old year in 'New Year's Eve', 'Almost, almost, almost gone' (R. (ii). 268, l. 9): Ricks memorably christens this Tennyson's 'art of the penultimate'.[3] One of the earliest surviving poems we have, 'Armageddon', announces in stiffly visionary mode that lifelong passion: the poem is pitched on the brink of no return, dwelling with impressive vagueness 'on the vast | Suspense of some grand issue' (R. (i). 3, iv. 33–4) – which is where the poem ends. Such an ominous sense of temporality often roused Tennyson to mythical heights, like that; but it could inspire work in a more human register too. He had a strikingly recurrent interest in a particular narrative of recurrence: the situation of someone returning to a familiar scene to find it (and perhaps himself) still the same and yet altered utterly. In such a plot, the necessary entanglement of personality with time, the interlacing of things changed with things unchanged, naturally emerges with a special intricacy. It is a dramatic circumstance for lyric that Tennyson inherited from Wordsworth, another poet deeply drawn by the thought of being 'destined to live, | To be, to have been, come, and go' (*The Prelude* (1805), vii. 402–3); and I end this chapter with some words about what Tennyson found in his predecessor in the poetry of returnings.

Writing in the idiomatic privacy of his notebook, Gerard Manley Hopkins vividly suggests the importance to poetry of 'repetition, *oftening, over-and-overing, aftering* . . . speech wholly or partially repeating the same figure of sound'.[4] Hopkins makes the point wholly his own, but something like it has been repeatedly discovered by poets and their readers, in very different styles. To go back to an English beginning, Puttenham's *Arte of English Poesie* (1589) advises: 'first of all others your figure that worketh by iteration or repetition of one word or clause doth much alter and affect the eare and also the mynde of the hearer, and therefore is counted a very brave figure both with the Poets and rhetoriciens'; and Puttenham goes on to list seven varieties, including (as his honest English paraphrases put it) the 'counter-turne', the 'Eccho sound', the 'cuckowspell' and the 'doubler'.[5] But it need not be merely a word or a phrase that is repeated: other patterns of repeating occur through metre and stanza form, through the recurrence of refrains, burdens, or wheels ('O, how the wheel becomes it!' Ophelia says); and the repeating of sounds in rhymes, within lines and at their ends, and in patterns of assonance and alliteration. The linguist Jakobson made the point in an abstract way when he declared the 'fundamental' element of poetry to be *'parallelism'*;[6] F. W. Bateson once arrived at the same truth through the *OED*;[7] a theoretically minded contemporary might put it differently again ('the iterative process is constitutive of the artistic work').[8]

Well, all true no doubt, and quite probably rather banal; anyway, surely altogether too encompassingly true to look of much help when it comes to discriminating the business of particular poems. And yet, perhaps, the truism has a special pertinence to the case of Tennyson, for no other great English poet seems drawn quite so powerfully, so repeatedly, to the poetic resource of repetitiveness.[9] His gifted friend and early reviewer Arthur Hallam bore admiring witness to the repeated returns of verse in one of his favourite poems, 'Recollections of the Arabian Nights', 'by the recurrence of which, as a sort of mysterious influence, at the close of every stanza, the mind is wrought up, with consummate art, to the final disclosure' (*CH* 44); and the sway of repetition's mysterious influence, and its elusive but powerful relationship with finality, are mainstays of the Tennysonian universe. I am not, I should say at once, being at all original in saying so: Tennyson is one of the star turns in the little handbook which the Victorian critic Alphonso Smith dedicated to repetition in poetry;[10] and a French professor once devoted an entire zealous book to Tennyson the repeater, enumerating hundreds of instances.[11] But I think there is still something to say about it: I am taking heart (and more) from Martin Dodsworth here, who once suggested that 'no satisfactory view of Tennyson's achievement can afford not to take this characteristic repetitiousness into account'.[12] I think that very true, and agree too that it is not merely a matter of style. Or rather, it is a matter of style that quickly leads us into deeper concerns: for (following Eliot's axiom) the repetitiveness of the Tennysonian surface is intimately involved with the poetry's most abiding and deeply felt preoccupations, about time and change, the fear of change and the desire for it.

One repetitive place to begin might be with a line Tennyson himself especially liked – 'The mellow ouzel fluted in the elm' (R. (i). 208, l. 93), the distinction of which he held to lie largely in its miniature orchestration of recurrence. 'The richness of the bird's note is expressed by the "u" sound in two consecutive words, and the "el" in two other words gives a liquid tone which makes the line perfect', as W. F. Rawnsley reported (*IR* 22). Sonic patterns of recurrence like that are habitually at work: there is, for instance, nothing left idling acoustically speaking in the line, 'Tears, idle tears, I know not what they mean' (*P*. iv. 21). The 'i' of 'idle' promptly recurs as the pronoun 'I' (so that what gets repeated is not just 'tears' but 'tears I'); 'know' and 'not' are close-knit alliteratively, while the vowels follow a gentle modulation from the subdued moan of 'oh' to the 'o' of 'not', repeated in 'what'; and as the line ends, with 'mean', the vowel sounds faintly in tune with its opening word, 'Tears'. Tennyson was a poet of beautiful noise whose lines often set about describing beautiful noises, and then the gorgeously enactive appropriateness of their consonants and vowels can lull by a fine reiterative excess. The famous (perhaps notorious) example would be 'The moan of doves in immemorial elms, | And murmuring of innumerable bees' (*P*. vii. 206–7); but the habit sometimes feels ubiquitous, and its effects are often marvellous, so good that you smile:

> Dry clashed his harness in the icy caves
> And barren chasms, and all to left and right
> The bare black cliff clanged round him, as he based
> His feet on juts of slippery crag that rang
> Sharp-smitten with the dint of armèd heels –

> ('Morte d'Arthur', R. (ii). 226, ll. 186–90)

That such alliterative wonders ('bare black cliff clanged') could become a tic was something of which Tennyson was quite aware, incidentally, and he even regarded the gift as something to keep an eye on: 'when I spout my lines first, they come out so alliteratively that I have sometimes no end of trouble to get rid of the alliteration', he told his son (*M*. ii. 15).

The effect of repetition might promise to be one of the most innocently self-delighting lyricism ('Then hey nonny nonny, hey nonny nonny!'[13]) – the 'musical reduplication' that J. M. Robertson identified in Tennyson (*CH* 434). Repeats of such a kind promise to function as a verbal marker, indicating that this is poetry you are hearing, rather as a radio announcer periodically reminds you of the station you have tuned to. To say so makes repetitions sound like one of the 'new combinations of Language' that Coleridge once declared justified by 'Poetry . . . as *Poetry* independent of any other Passion'[14] – the autonomous artistic realm of 'poetry as poetry' is what Tennyson himself typically has in mind when he refers to the 'music' or 'word-music' of poems. But Coleridge also stipulated another, contrary, criterion for poetical language: 'every phrase, every metaphor, every personification, should have it's [*sic*] justifying cause in some *passion* either of the Poet's mind, or of the Characters described by the poet.'[15] Much of Tennyson's poetry might be seen leading its life under the simultaneous sway of those rival justifications, the 'poetical' and the psychologically revelatory (self-revelatory, or revelatory of a dramatic character). No doubt much the same could be said of all decent verse;[16] but perhaps the tension between the two justifications noticeably intensifies in writing after the great Romantics (like Coleridge), who had created 'poetry as poetry' as a vocation it had not been before – but whose creative interest in realistically representing the diverse life of the human consciousness was quite as great as their commitment to the autonomy and self-sufficiency of the artwork. The musical and the dramatic met in the notion of the *Lyrical Ballads*, the hybrid genre invented by Wordsworth and Coleridge; and that fruitful conjunction of opposites evidently inspired Arthur Hallam (who knew his Wordsworth and Coleridge well) to see something similarly innovative in Tennyson's verse: 'a new species of poetry, a graft of the lyric on the dramatic, and Mr Tennyson deserves the laurel of an inventor, an enlarger of our modes of knowledge and power' (*CH* 48).[17] For a small instance: that the first line of 'Tears, Idle Tears' ends in 'mean', returning in sound to its opening word, 'tears', making perfect the line's charmed lyrical circle; but, within *The Princess*, this lyricism is informed by a dramatic situation, and the line's inability to progress also enacts acoustically its introspective speaker's powerlessness to move on emotionally.[18]

The repetitive texture of Tennysonian verse at its most fine-grained is often involved with repetition of a much more obvious kind. I mean the sorts of effect categorized by Puttenham (all of which might no doubt be exemplified by Tennyson's works) in which whole words or phrases recur. In such repetitious devices, the poet says something, and then returns to say it, or something very like it, once again, or twice again; and the possible dramatic implication of such effects ranges enormously. Peter Conrad finds a connection between Tennyson's repetitiveness and his sense of abysmal meaninglessness;[19] but you might also attribute recurrence to plenitude, not futility, 'the very abundance of joy that is found in the pleasant utterance' (*CH* 202): repeats sound in Tennyson diversely, from excited resound, to *sotto voce* confirmation, to stagnating immovability, to monomaniacal obsession, to wondering tongue-tiedness, to remorseless inescapability. A case of samples:

Tears, idle tears, I know not what they mean

(*P.* iv. 21)

The woods decay, the woods decay and fall

(R. (ii). 324, l. 1)

For I'm to be Queen o' the May, mother, I'm to be Queen o' the May.

(R. (i). 168, l. 4)

Break, break, break,
On thy cold gray stones, O Sea!

(R. (ii). 228, ll. 1–2)

With honour, honour, honour, honour to him,
Eternal honour to his name.

(R. (ii). 309, ll. 149–50)

And come, for Love is of the valley, come,
For Love is of the valley, come thou down
And find him

(*P.* vii. 183–5)

Birds in the high Hall-garden
When twilight was falling,
Maud, Maud, Maud, Maud,
They were crying and calling.

(R. (ii). 316, i. 412–15)

Come into the garden, Maud,
For the black bat, night, has flown,
Come into the garden, Maud,
I am here at the gate alone;

(R. (ii). 316, i. 850–3)

25

Proputty, proputty, proputty – that's what I 'ears 'em saäy.
Proputty, proputty, proputty – Sam, thou's an ass for thy paaïns

(R. (ii). 344, ll. 2–3)

And the list might easily be extended – the Arthurian blank verse alone would supply a catalogue of reiterative effects, that being in large part what the advertised 'faint Homeric echoes' amount to ('The Epic', R. (ii). 225, l. 39).[20]

> Until King Arthur's table, man by man,
> Had fallen in Lyonnesse about their Lord,
> King Arthur: then, because his wound was deep,
> The bold Sir Bedivere uplifted him,
> Sir Bedivere, the last of all his knights . . .

('Morte d'Arthur', R. (ii). 226, ll. 3–7)

(It is hardly informative, in any obvious way, to tell us that the Lord of King Arthur's table was King Arthur; nor to remind us, after only two words' interval, that it is Sir Bedivere who is picking him up.) As I shall be saying later, the *Idylls of the King* frequently resort to weightily incantatory repeats, staying the verse against the narrative, and (so you might think) defeating one prime point to writing in unrhymed lines – an intrinsic advantage of blank verse being, as an eighteenth-century critic put it, precisely its liberation from rhyme's 'perpetual returns of similar impressions [which] lie like weights upon our spirits'.[21] But Tennyson sometimes contrives to make even unrhymed verse weightily return:

> the Prince and Enid rode,
> And fifty knights rode with them, to the shores
> Of Severn, and they past to their own land;
> Where, thinking, that if ever yet was wife
> True to her lord, mine shall be so to me,
> He compassed her with sweet observances
> And worship, never leaving her, and grew
> Forgetful of his promise to the King,
> Forgetful of the falcon and the hunt,
> Forgetful of the tilt and tournament,
> Forgetful of his glory and his name,
> Forgetful of his princedom and its cares.

('The Marriage of Geraint', R. (iii). 466, ll. 43–54)

The storyteller is growing forgetful of his duties too: the *Idylls* repeatedly run into reiterative sand like this. Puttenham would recognize that as 'the figure of *Report* . . . when we make one word begin, and as they are wont to say, lead the daunce to many verses in sute';[22] and such reiterative verbal choreography is often set within larger-scale repetitions of chorus or refrain or 'burthen', so that not just individual lines or runs of lines but entire poems often turn about something said over and over. As in 'Œnone', reviewing which an exasperated Croker, in the *Quarterly*, counted (it is an underestimate) the refrain '*sixteen* times repeated' (*CH* 74):

> O mother Ida, many-fountained Ida,
> Dear mother Ida, harken ere I die.
>
> (R. (i). 164, ll. 22–3)

(Yet how delicately 'I die' fails quite to reiterate 'Ida', a disappointed repetition that makes a dying fall.) Croker was not alone in being annoyed by Tennyson's reiterative habits: Robert Graves grew quite as fed up with the repeated refrain in 'The Ballad of Oriana', the meaningless jingle of which stood plainly revealed, he thought, once you replaced it with the phrase 'bottom upwards' and found it made sense just as well.[23]

> They should have stabbed me where I lay,
> Oriana!
> How could I rise and come away,
> Oriana?
> How could I look upon the day?
> They should have stabbed me where I lay,
> Oriana –
> They should have trod me into clay,
> Oriana.
>
> (R. (i). 114, ll. 55–63)

A 'disgraceful suggestion', thought Larkin.

When Whitman chose a representative line to illustrate Tennyson's 'finest verbalism' he unerringly opted for one based upon the repetition of a repetition: 'And hollow, hollow, hollow, all delight' (*CH* 350, quoting R. (iii). 475, l. 37)) – a line that, as Ricks nicely observes, is itself the repetition of a phrase Tennyson had first written some years before.[24] As that example of self-echoing suggests, repetitiveness was a cast of mind as well as a figure of choice:

As when we dwell upon a word we know,
Repeating, till the word we know so well
Becomes a wonder, and we know not why . . .

('Lancelot and Elaine', R. (iii). 470, ll. 1020–2)

(Lines that themselves sympathetically interlace words and sounds.[25]) One of Tennyson's earliest memories was of inducing a kind of 'waking trance' by repeating his name, 'two or three times to myself silently, till all at once, as it were out of the intensity of the consciousness of individuality, the individuality itself seemed to dissolve and fade away into boundless being' (*M.* i. 320). In boyhood, a milder but related kind of mystical transport came to him from reiterating a reiterative mantra: 'the words "far, far away" had always a strange charm for me' (*M.* i. 11); and it seems, in retrospect, happily prophetic of a lifetime's enthusiasm that, in his earliest surviving letter, the boy should single out for praise Milton's line, 'O dark, dark, dark, amid the blaze of Noon' (*L.* i. 2). Palgrave remembered his liking especially the refrain to Sidney's 'Only joy, now here you are': 'Take me to thee, and thee to me: | No, no, no, no, my Dear, let be!' (*M.* ii. 503). Asked, in his last days, what his favourite hymn was, he replied: 'I like Heber's "Holy, Holy, Holy" better than most' (*IR* 191). His own poems often grew from repetition: sometimes, as I have already said, they were built upon acts of self-borrowing (an observation first made by Sir Charles Tennyson, and handsomely corroborated by Ricks[26]); sometimes, repetition was a method of composition. 'My father's poems were generally based on some single phrase like "Someone had blundered",' Hallam Tennyson tells us, 'and were rolled about, so to speak, in his head, before he wrote them down' (*M.* i. 268). Tennyson tells that story about 'The Charge of the Light Brigade' too: 'the line kept running in my head, and I kept saying it over and over till it shaped itself into the burden of the poem' (*IR* 24). He was a great performer of his poems, of course, and, while it is normal to say that to recite a poem is 'to read or repeat' it (*M.* ii. 324), for Tennyson 'repeat' sometimes acquired an additional significance: ' "Oriana" Tennyson used to repeat in a way not to be forgotten at Cambridge tables,' said FitzGerald (*M.* i. 48), implying in 'used' something more than a one-off turn; and such repetitive habits of performance are doubtless related to the repetitiousness that was so crucial to the works' original imagining. One of the more unsettling entries in Lady Tennyson's devoted journal runs, 'He read a good deal of "Maud" again';[27] he once read that poem to Jane Carlyle 'three times in insistent succession'.[28] So, when writing about *The Princess*, T. S. Eliot hit upon a genuinely Tennysonian criterion of excellence, even though it was one he felt obliged to withhold from *The Princess*: 'it is a poem which we must read, but which we excuse ourselves from reading twice.'[29]

Given his sensitivity to the multiple charms of duplicated noise, it is no wonder that echoes should ring so impressively throughout Tennyson's auditory world. Some Shakespearianish juvenilia addressed to the owl echo themselves with merry self-reference:

> Thy tuwhoos of yesternight,
> Which upon the dark afloat,
> So took echo with delight,
> So took echo with delight,
> That her voice untuneful grown,
> Wears all day a fainter tone.
>
> (R. (i). 82, ll. 2–7)

The mature poet conjured such playfulness into, for instance, the reflective pause of onomatopoeic mastery at the end of 'The Golden Year':

> high above, I heard them blast
> The steep slate-quarry, and the great echo flap
> And buffet round the hills, from bluff to bluff.
>
> (R. (ii), 276, ll. 74–6)

(Tennyson said: ' "Bluff to bluff" gives the echo of the blasting as I heard it from the mountain on the counter side, opposite to Snowdon': 'the whole gist', recorded an acquaintance, 'was in his pronunciation of the word "bluff," twice repeated . . . a sort of quick propulsive effort, as though throwing the word from his mouth'.[30]) Naturally, you feel, a Tennyson hero cannot better imply the depth of his attachment than by adducing the way he made his beloved's name echo: 'at eve and dawn | With Ida, Ida, Ida, rang the woods' (*P.* iv. 412–13); nor can a better Tennysonian fame be imagined than remaining forever the

29

subject of unending reverberation: 'No stone is fitted in yon
marble girth | Whose echo shall not tongue thy glorious doom'
('Tiresias', R. (i). 219, ll. 131–2). Echoes normally feature in *Maud*
as a mark of the speaker's monomania ('And Echo there,
whatever is asked her, answers "Death"' (i. 4)), and the verse
frequently resonates with his infatuation ('Birds in our wood
sang | Ringing through the valleys, | Maud is here, here, here'
(i. 420–2)); but at one point the noises tintinnabulate with a
subtler effect:

> 'Tis a morning pure and sweet,
> And a dewy splendour falls
> On the little flower that clings
> To the turrets and the walls;
> 'Tis a morning pure and sweet,
> And the light and shadow fleet;
> She is walking in the meadow,
> And the woodland echo rings;
> In a moment we shall meet;
> She is singing in the meadow
> And the rivulet at her feet
> Ripples on in light and shadow
> To the ballad that she sings.

(ii. 171–83)

The stanza rings with echoes as the woodland does, words and
rhythms replicating themselves in a whirl of self-exciting
insistence. The thrilled expectation of encounter is mentioned
('In a moment we shall meet'), only to be tantalizingly deferred
by a near-return to an earlier line ('She is walking in the
meadow'), as though dallying, but then hope is finally indulged,
in sound, when 'rings' belatedly meets up with its long-sought
rhyme (in 'sings').

Echoes catch a Tennysonian genius so comprehensively
because they embody both reiteration (an echo repeats its
original) and changefulness (an echo decays away); and this
stanza unobtrusively registers a more forlorn part of the
speaker's mind by having 'meadow' experience a beautifully
managed echoic falling-off, from 'meadow' to 'meadow' to
'shadow', the stanza's one off-rhyme. As it happens, the whole
stanza (itself part of a section of *Maud* that revivifies a lyric, 'O
that 'twere possible', written long before) rings with an echo of

30

a poem from *The Princess*, 'The splendour falls on castle walls', which also entwines the idea of an echo's faithful recurrence with the idea of its successive falling away: 'Blow, bugle, blow, set the wild echoes flying, | Blow, bugle; answer, echoes, dying, dying, dying' (*P*. iii/iv. 5-6). The grammar begins to grow subtly dislocate in that couplet's second line, the firmness of injunction ('Blow, bugle, blow') falling off into a dissipating trail of sounds, the syntactical grasp loosening. (Benjamin Britten's setting of the song in the cycle *Serenade* catches this movement in sound most beautifully, the second line drawn out into a lingering diminuendo of repeated *dying*s.)

The poetic credentials of repetition feel very primitive: oral literature, like the ballad, tends to be heavily repetitive (Tennyson knew many ballads by heart (*M*. i. 48)); and possibly it feels infantile too, the sort of thing you might expect a man to have grown out of. It is apparently true that children resort spontaneously to patterns of repetition if you ask them to make verses (but not if you ask them to tell you a story).[31] Maybe Auden had that thought somewhere in mind when he called Tennyson 'the great English poet of the Nursery' – speaking, as John Bayley once happily observed, 'with the knowingness of the man who recognises his obsession commenting on the man who doesn't'.[32] The nursery in this case, needless to say, is not a place of nurture and recollected pleasure, but the origin of recurring trauma and damage: 'In no other English poet of comparable rank does the bulk of his work seem so clearly to be inspired by some single and probably very early experience,' says Auden.[33] (If a stupid poet, as Auden has it, then perhaps 'stupid' in the root sense of 'stunned, benumbed, or fixated by obscure early sorrow': so says Gerhard Joseph.[34])
    Auden nicely exemplifies his sense of Tennysonian fixation with a quotation from a stanza of *In Memoriam* which itself says something over again:

> So runs my dream: but what am I?
> An infant crying in the night;
> An infant crying for the light:
> And with no language but a cry.

(liv. 17–20)

31

(Sound contributes there to the sense of something unshiftably forlorn about the 'I', as a pervasive 'i' rhyme practically freezes the verse into the immobility of *AAAA*, and 'I' finds itself additionally landlocked within the internal repetition of 'crying'.) My attention in this book is not primarily biographical; but it is too important a truth about Tennyson's poetry not to remark the imprint upon it of (in Larkin's desolate phrase) 'violence | A long way back'. A clearer idea of the profound unhappiness of his early years, dominated by the violence and drunken misery of Tennyson's disinherited father, began to emerge in Sir Charles Tennyson's fine biography of 1949, and has been confirmed by several later *Lives*; the *Memoir* by Tennyson's son is loyally reticent, as usual, but contains one haunting phrase in which you can glimpse a distress behind the speculative discretion of a double negative: 'I think that their childhood . . . could not have been in the main unhappy' (*M*. i. 5). (Ricks tactfully brings the biographical evidence to bear on the poetry in the early chapters of his study.)

Auden's association of Tennyson with the repetition of infantile experience gathers strength, I take it, from *Beyond the Pleasure Principle*, where Freud describes the plight of a patient unable to bring repressed memories to full consciousness, and so unable to achieve any curative purchase upon them: 'He is obliged to *repeat* the repressed material as a contemporary experience instead of, as the physician would prefer to see, *remembering* it as something belonging to the past.'[35] Certainly Tennyson was often obsessionally troubled, 'really ill, in a nervous way' (*IR* 6), as FitzGerald put it, in a pre-Freudian age. The nerves sometimes flash into the letters, especially those before he married: 'The perpetual panic and horror of the last two years had steeped my nerves in poison' (*L*. i. 222), he told FitzGerald, who had some years before described him 'reverting for a moment to the great sorrow of his own mind' (*M*. i. 152). Carlyle memorably reported to Emerson 'a man solitary and sad, as certain men are, dwelling in an element of gloom, – carrying a bit of Chaos about him, in short, which he is manufacturing into Cosmos!' (*IR* 16). Nor does Hallam Tennyson attempt wholly to conceal from the *Memoir* the monotonous unhappiness of his father's early life, when '[t]he current of his mind . . . ran constantly in the channel of mournful memories and melancholy forebodings' (*M*. i. 165). Auden's impatience with such incapacity is brisk: 'there was little about melancholia that he didn't know; there was little else that he did';[36] but many more sympathetic readers have similarly felt something 'morbid' about Tennyson's poetry – 'at least in the sense that it grows from morbid feelings in the poet himself', as Martin Dodsworth qualifies the claim.[37] And that makes a nice qualification, because it makes the morbid feelings a kind of raw material to be handled ('manufacturing into Cosmos!'), and not something more simply determining: Tennyson's lyricism was not the hapless victim of his unhappiness; but, rather, it found in the repetitiveness of despondency a subject matter and one imaginative home.

'Mariana' (R. (i). 73) is the first masterpiece of Tennyson's art of repetition, and the best poem in *Poems, Chiefly Lyrical* (1830). In Shakespeare's *Measure for Measure*, Mariana is abandoned by her intended, Angelo, but he eventually turns up and ends the play marrying her. Tennyson's poem extricates her from the consequentiality of that plot, or of any other plot, consigning her instead to the immobilised perpetuity of a state of mind – Hallam's review called such states 'moods of character' (*CH* 42). As the reviewer Fox recognized, 'Mariana' portrays a sort of day in the life, moving 'through the circuit of four-and-twenty hours'; but, as he also saw, this is a life that is no life to speak of, for whatever happens Mariana has 'but one feeling', and 'again and again we feel, before its repetition, the coming of the melancholy burthen' (*CH* 29). (Tennyson was much occupied by the thought of a being in time but not properly alive: the speaker of an early poem laments, 'I never *lived* a day, but daily die, | I have no real breath' ('Perdidi Diem', R. (i). 128, ll. 4–5).) The critic Humphry House once cleverly said that Tennyson was 'one on whom the consciousness of time bore like a burden';[38] which is just what it does here (as Ricks says).[39] 'He cometh not'; but the refrain saying so comes again and again, the poem returning with sad inevitability to a burden, within which the words return upon themselves, as though the hope of verbal innovation had disappeared with other hope, and all inventiveness were spent:

33

> She only said, 'My life is dreary,
> He cometh not,' she said;
> She said, 'I am aweary, aweary,
> I would that I were dead!'

(ll. 9–12)

The poem endures what 'The Miller's Daughter' calls a 'weary sameness in the rhymes' (R. (i). 162, l. 70): as Mariana wears out her language ('aweary, aweary'), so the narrative voice empathetically finds itself in dead ends of its own, tautologically going over the same ground ('she said; | She said'). As in 'Oriana', an apparently interminable recurrence evokes the plight of a crisis that will not reach a catastrophe: 'O breaking heart that will not break!' (R. (i). 114, l. 64).

The structural recurrence of Mariana's refrain is accompanied by subtler acts of repetition, gently insinuating a claustrophobic sense of limited resources (the poplar is mentioned three times, mosses twice); and the vocabulary feels somehow confined too, treading in its own footsteps as though for lack of linguistic room: 'athwart' comes twice (an excellent synonym for 'across' in so thwarted a universe); 'blackened' in 'blackened waters' (l. 38) fails to move significantly beyond the 'blackest' moss of the first line; the 'thickly' of the second line recurs uninspirationally in 'thickest dark' (l. 18) and then again in 'thick-moted' (l. 78). Sounds are converging here too: 'gray-eyed' and 'rounding gray' (ll. 31, 44) scarcely stray far from the melancholy ambit of 'grange'; sunbeams, in this 'moated' place, seem doomed to be 'thick-moted' (l. 78). The opening of the second stanza, in particular, is a wonder of poetry with nowhere to go:

> Her tears fell with the dews at even;
> Her tears fell ere the dews were dried;
> She could not look on the sweet heaven,
> Either at morn or eventide.

(ll. 13–16)

The lines set out with dreary evenness a routine of unaltering despair; the deftness of an off-rhyme ensures that the 'heaven' (which she cannot see) feels like it does not properly belong in this linguistic world; while 'eventide' not only accomplishes its expected rhyme with 'dried', but harks back to 'even' as well,

34

creating a doubly binding perfect rhyme and a kind of sonic doldrum.

So Tennyson's accomplished monotony keeps artful company with his heroine: 'repetition is found in uttering grief, as when there is no more to say;'[40] but in fact the poem is not wholly without change, for a rising subterranean panic breaks out into the intensification of the last stanza – 'Oh God, that I were dead!' (l. 84). That makes for a kind of ending, but of the most tentative or provisional kind, and certainly no climax: it is what she says *whenever* the sun goes down (ll. 77–9). There is no reason, really, for the poem ever to end: Mariana's lover not coming is not an element of a plot as it was in Shakespeare, but the condition of her whole existence, 'in the nature of her being itself', in John Bayley's words – rather as waiting is for the tramps in Beckett's *Waiting for Godot*, a play also set in a world in which there is nothing to be done.[41] In the perpetuity of her victimhood, which ruins but does not finally destroy her, Mariana even acquires an unexpected sort of tenacity, rather as Beckett's tramps do – a secret obduracy of purpose caught in the fine line that closes a lyric which Tennyson wrote around the same time: 'The world will not change, and her heart will not break' ('Song [I' the glooming light]', R. (i). 85, l. 22).

Tennyson implied as much by writing a sequel, published in *Poems* (1832), called 'Mariana in the South' (R. (i). 160). He asks elsewhere, in a fraught poem called 'Love and Duty': 'Of love that never found his earthly close, | What sequel?' (R. (ii). 279, ll. 1–2); and 'Mariana in the South' implies that the sequel is but more of the same. Her desolation is unchanged whatever new elements a landscape might offer to furnish her consciousness with symbols for it. (Hallam wrote to a friend: 'it paints the forlorn feeling as it would exist under the influence of different impressions of sense' (*HL* 401).) 'Mariana in the South' also repeats a refrain, using an off-rhyme (moan/morn) to insinuate the same trapped and broken spirits as her English namesake endured:

> But 'Ave Mary,' made she moan,
> And 'Ave Mary,' night and morn,
> And 'Ah,' she sang, 'to be all alone,
> To live forgotten, and love forlorn.'

(ll. 9–12)

This Mariana is a good deal more talkative than is the first one – the paradoxical effect of which is to communicate rather less of her desolation; she also has Catholicism to complicate her death wish and despair. But the Marianas are alike in being imprisoned, each in what the Prince of *The Princess* calls 'the muffled cage of life' (vii. 32), and neither is quite inured to the gaol of herself. Tennyson seems to have thought this the picturesque case of a quite general state of affairs: many of his finest poems would dramatize a condition in which existence is possible only within constraints that make it unendurable. 'Man is free, but only free in certain narrow limits', he darkly told an admirer, 'They are like the cage of a bird' (*IR* 109; cf. *M*. i. 319). ('Fatima' recreates Mariana's pent state in a sexy East: 'My whole soul waiting silently, | All naked in a sultry sky' (R. (i). 163, ll. 36–7). 'Rosamund's Bower' replays it in mediæval England: 'He comes no more' (R. (ii). 281, l. 12).)

The scenery of 'Mariana in the South', as a reviewer duly noted, is 'in keeping with her heart' (R. (i). 160, headnote); and other reviewers admired in the earlier poem too the way that Tennyson used the objects in the surrounding landscape as an oblique way of intimating Mariana's being, as though the verse were in some analogical relationship with its refrain, as the vehicle to the tenor of a metaphor. Mill prominently praised Tennyson's 'power of *creating* scenery, in keeping with some state of human feeling; so fitted to it as to be the embodied symbol of it'; and Hallam also singled out the 'vivid, picturesque delineation of objects, and the peculiar skill with which he holds all of them *fused*, to borrow a metaphor from science, in a medium of strong emotion' (*CH* 86, 42), a Tennysonian cast of mind that he knew from other works too. (Hallam reportedly much admired a poem that began 'Thy soul is like a landskip, friend' (R. (i). 136) and that went on to made a formal analogy of it.) Tennyson seems habitually to have thought of characters and casts of mind as being like landscapes and terrains – and vice versa, for that matter: 'A known landskip is to me an old friend,' he wrote winningly to his fiancée, 'An old park is my delight, and I could tumble about it for ever' (*M*. i. 172).[42] And, of course, every reader grasps that the moated grange and its environs are, in some way, indissolubly at one with the state of Mariana's mind; still, as Denis Donoghue says, 'Mariana and the landscape are not one and the same', as they might be in a more straightforward poem;[43] and the separateness is important. (Much of *In Memoriam* will occupy itself with the same imponderable relationship between the suffering self and the natural scene, insisting on their disconnection while entertaining the thought of their sympathetic concurrence.) For Mariana's despair does not hold exclusive imaginative jurisdiction over the poem: much of the work's weirdly unsettling power lies in the enigmatic relationship it maintains between the verse and the refrain – in the contrast between the accretive relish of Tennyson's descriptive magnificence ('The blue fly sung in the pane' (l. 63)) and the stalled inarticulacy of his central character. Unlike Tennyson, Mariana has really nothing much to say, and what she does say is soon emptied of significance by its deadening reiteration: no matter what glorious picturesque details each verse proffers, Mariana for one remains quite unimpressed – 'She only said'. Tennyson was moved in several places by the idea that (as a sonnet puts it) 'all the infinite variety | Of the dear world will vary evermore', while 'One only thought I have, and that is death' ('Sonnet [Alas! how weary are my human eyes]', R. (i). 185, ll. 11–12, 14); and it is the blunt inconsequentiality of such a state that, as it accumulates in 'Mariana', begins to acquire a subterranean sense of comedy: that so fine a poetic performance should associate with so unconvivial a subject! Isobel Armstrong implies the dark humour submerged in the poem when she observes the refrain's growing flavour of *non sequitur*.[44] Tennyson would go on to develop the latent power of such poetical inconsequence.

Leigh Hunt singled out for criticism Tennyson's 'excessive fondness for repeating a lyrical "burthen"' (*CH* 128): as 'Mariana' shows, one reason why a poet might want to make a repeated chorus feel remorselessly inescapable is the desire to create precisely a sense of burdensomeness. (Edward Lear, Tennyson's friend and his astute reader, also understood the power of reiteration to insinuate an inescapable bind:

> There was an Old Man who screamed out
> Whenever they knocked him about;
> So they took off his boots, and fed him with fruits,
> And continued to knock him about.[45])

Tennyson was vividly aware of the connections possible between a repetitive music and a state of mind:

> Then as a little helpless innocent bird,
> That has but one plain passage of few notes,
> Will sing the simple passage o'er and o'er
> For all an April morning, till the ear
> Wearies to hear it, so the simple maid
> Went half the night repeating, 'Must I die?'
> And now to right she turned, and now to left,
> And found no ease in turning or in rest;
> And 'Him or death,' she muttered, 'death or him,'
> Again and like a burthen, 'Him or death.'

('Lancelot and Elaine', R. (iii). 470, ll. 889–98)

A poem written before 'Mariana', 'Unhappy man, why wander there', had already used a burden to similar (though lesser) effect: 'I heed not season, place, or time, | They're all the same to me' (R. (i). 52, ll. 15–16). That manages to sound curiously chipper about being trapped in the world which your mind forges for you, where 'Mariana' evokes the studied hysteria of a living death 'without hope of change' (l. 29). Still, there is a rum kind of consolation in the thought that, in death, one might 'Lie still, dry dust, secure of change' ('To J.S.', R. (i). 183, l. 76); and while Mariana's psychological entombment is dreadful in an obvious way, it also appears to impel a kind of perceptual richness, intensifying normal experience into something rich and strange (Tennyson admits 'sad and strange' (l. 5)). Like the roses in Eliot's 'Burnt Norton', her broken shed and the mosses and the rest clearly have 'the look of flowers that are looked at'.[46]

Tennyson was sharply conscious of the awfulness of Mariana-feeling: of an 'earthy spirit' trapped in 'an eternal prison', when, within the dynamic life of nature, 'all low things range | To higher but I cannot change' ('From the East of life joybeams did strike', R. (i). 184, ll. 13, 16, 23–4). And yet, appalling though the thought may be that nothing will ever change, it may be no less dreadful to think that *everything* is *bound* to. Heightened states in which nothing alters feature in many of Tennyson's poems as precarious fantasies of positive delight – something that helps explain the scarcely secret delight that Tennyson takes in the absorbing detail of Mariana's dismal locale (which he might have tumbled about for ever) while experiencing so much fellow-feeling with her paralysis. Tennyson was exercised from his earliest verses by the thought that chief among time's unchanging burdens was the thought that nothing remains unchanged; and he evidently felt much more deeply than one might usually feel a logical paradox the paradoxically unchanging truth that 'All truth is change' ('Οί ῥέοντες' (R. (i). 122, l. 4)), that 'All things will change' ('Nothing will Die', R. (i). 93, l. 38), that the world is 'full of strange | Astonishment and boundless change' ('Chorus', R. (i). 101, ll. 9–10). Something not so unlike the kind of endless recurrence endured by Mariana might serve to free you from what Tennyson calls, in his Cambridge prize-poem 'Timbuctoo', 'all shocks of Change, | All on-set of capricious Accident' (R. (i). 67, ll. 25–6).

'The Sleeping Palace', from 'The Day-Dream' (R. (ii). 241), a poem of great self-deprecating charm, lightly recasts Mariana's 'dreamy house' (l. 61) as subject to a wonderful spell: the plants are 'creeping' as before (l. 45), but they now serve as part of an impenetrable hedge to safeguard a palace where 'all things in their place remain, | As all were ordered, ages since' (ll. 53–4). Part of Mariana's desolation was that 'Old voices called her from without' (l. 68); but here the noise of the 'varying year' scarcely registers in a house where 'the life is stayed' (ll. 1, 18):

> Faint murmurs from the meadows come,
> Like hints and echoes of the world
> To spirits folded in the womb.

(ll. 6–8)

In this other world, the maiden has a 'constant beauty' in a winningly literal way, kept in a sleep which sounds something like death: 'The fragrant tresses are not stirred | That lie upon her charmèd heart' ('The Sleeping Beauty', ll. 15, 19–20) – 'She sleeps', Tennyson repeats (ll. 17, 21, 23). Unlike Mariana's absent lover, the maiden's suitor shows up, a foxy Prince, whose kiss ensures the charm is 'snapt'; time then crashes back with jovial exuberance ('And sixty feet the fountain leapt' ('The Revival', l. 8)) and some nicely prosaic business ('My joints are somewhat stiff or so' (l. 26); and then Tennyson's interest promptly lapses. In Keats's 'The Eve of St Agnes', which looks like a source for the poem, the lovers' dangerous escape is a matter of some narrative tension; Tennyson's lovers slip away quite effortlessly into the sunset:

> And o'er them many a flowing range
> Of vapour buoyed the crescent-bark,
> And, rapt through many a rosy change,
> The twilight died into the dark.
>
> ('The Departure', ll. 21–4)

That casts 'change' in its rosiest light; but the poem has already struck a more sceptical note about the Prince's achievement in releasing 'the long-pent stream of life' ('The Revival', l. 15) – 'Come, Care and Pleasure, Hope and Pain, | And bring the fated fairy Prince' ('The Sleeping Palace', ll. 55–6). Fated, indeed, but not exactly fêted in the Tennysonian universe: in an inconclusive 'envoi', the poet ruefully reflects,

> Well – were it not a pleasant thing
> To fall asleep with all one's friends;
> To pass with all our social ties
> To silence from the paths of men . . .
>
> ('L'Envoi', ll. 3–6)

The ambiguity there is amused: 'To pass to reclusive silence, while keeping all our chums with us' is no doubt the proper emotion to entertain; but how pleasantly solitary is the thought, 'To pass to silence, with all our social ties passing away as we go'.

'The Day-Dream' is far from unusual in conjuring over a state of being in which life is happily pent, a 'quiet dream of life' ('Requiescat', R. (ii). 341, l. 6): Tennyson repeatedly pictures luxurious geographies, great palaces of immobility, glittering cityscapes (like Timbuctoo), existing with magical self-absorption outwith the depredations of normal circumstance. (Camelot, in the *Idylls of the King*, is the last in the line of these special urban spaces.) Of the *Poems, Chiefly Lyrical*, Hallam especially liked 'Recollections of the Arabian Nights', another poem of somnolent inactivity, which lingeringly amasses sumptuous incidental details, until you realize that the incidental details are what the poem is really about, and that the immanent sense of narrative direction, climaxing in the ultimate glimpse of Al-Raschid himself (R. (i). 83, l. 153), is merely a ruse. The Tennysonian charm of the palace is that nothing happens: certainly, nothing depends upon the final sighting (in the source tale, the thought of encountering the Caliph is terrifying).[47] The description of the palace grounds draws on Coleridge and on Shelley; but it is idiosyncratically Tennysonian too, establishing a perfumed poetic idiom and an exotic style of park design that would both become hallmarks:

> Thence through the garden I was drawn –
> A realm of pleasance, many a mound,
> And many a shadow-chequered lawn
> Full of the city's stilly sound,
> And deep myrrh-thickets blowing round
> The stately cedar, tamarisks,
> Thick rosaries of scented thorn,
> Tall orient shrubs, and obelisks . . .

(ll. 100–7)

A Persian beauty makes a timely appearance, but not to much effect: the bookishness of this spicy orient gives its eroticism a slightly forlorn air, more the dutiful fulfilment of a genre's demands than anything remotely amorous. (The same is true of an earlier poem, 'Thou camest to thy bower, my love' (R. (i). 40).) What seems more truly the source of Tennysonian passion is the gorgeous sameness of the poem's catalogue-stanzas, and the recurrence of its refrain: he might have agreed with Kierkegaard, the century's most suggestive (and enigmatic) thinker about the subject, that 'repetition is a beloved wife of whom one never tires. For it is only of the new one grows tired. Of the old one never tires'.[48]

The repetitiousness of 'Recollections of the Arabian Nights' plays harmlessly with its bogus moment of narrative climax, but other Tennyson poems of garden and palace brace their charmed stillness against the pressing possibility of events with more purpose. The Cambridge prize poem, 'Timbuctoo', followed the poet's aspirational spirit from 'the slime | Of this dull world' to the 'Unutterable buoyancy and strength' that accompanies his vision of the transcendent sparkling city (R. (i). 67, ll. 146–7, 155):

> Seest thou yon river, whose translucent wave,
> Forth issuing from the darkness, windeth through
> The argent streets o' the city, imaging
> The soft inversion of her tremulous Domes,
> Her gardens frequent with the stately Palm,
> Her Pagods hung with music of sweet bells,

41

> Her obelisks of rangèd Chrysolite,
> Minarets and towers?

(ll. 225–32)

The precarious grandeur of the pleasure dome from Coleridge's 'Kubla Khan' ('The shadow of the dome of pleasure | Floated midway on the waves') is never far away from these miraculous urban sites, and with it comes Coleridge's cultivated sense of mysteriously imminent demise: 'Ancestral voices prophesying war!' These lines from 'Timbuctoo' reverberate darkly too with the impossible heterocosm conjured up terribly by Othello: 'If heaven would make me such another world | Of one entire and perfect chrysolite,' he swears, with Desdemona already murdered, 'I'ld not have sold her for it'. Sure enough, the vision of Timbuctoo is no sooner achieved than it is about to be lost: the presiding spirit tells Tennyson that 'the time is well-nigh come | When I must render up this glorious home | To keen *Discovery*' – at which point the imaginary city will dwindle into the 'huts' that are really there, 'How changed from this fair City!' (ll. 238–40, 245). (Much the same thing happens in the posthumously published 'In deep and solemn dreams': 'what darkening change' (R. (i). 132, l. 55).) 'Timbuctuoo' was written up from an earlier poem 'Armageddon', so thoughts of terminal disaster were always mixed up with its fantasies of glittering permanance; but the sense of 'all things creeping to a day of doom' generally stirs in much early Tennyson ('The Mystic', R. (i). 96, l. 40). Great cities are often falling, and prophecies of such disasters frequently uttered: he wrote with great vigour about the Fall of Jerusalem and the Fall of Babylon; he impersonated a druid foretelling the fall of Rome, and he recounted a bizarre vision of future woes vouchsafed to Charles of Sweden, in which 'the nations shall quake, | And the thrones fall down' (R. (i). 34, 46, 18, 49, ll. 95-6). Camelot is doomed from the start too.

'The Kraken' (R. (i). 113), a delightfully lugubrious fantasy, is similarly drawn toward thoughts of future apocalypse, but, in the meantime, indulges a monstrous idyll of changelessness, which ends not with a falling but a waking up: the uncomely Kraken is a Sleeping Beauty.

> Below the thunders of the upper deep;
> Far, far beneath in the abysmal sea,

> His ancient, dreamless, uninvaded sleep
> The Kraken sleepeth . . .

(ll. 1–4)

The poem is just close enough to a sonnet to awake the possibility of the purposeful turn of mind that normally characterizes that form; but returning, not turning, is what thoughts of this submarine place properly do: 'Far, far beneath', the Kraken redundantly 'sleepeth' a 'sleep', while about him immobile rhymes and near-rhymes (height/light/polypi/lie/die), and one recurring rhyme (deep/sleep), circle round upon themselves. The Kraken heedlessly occupies a bizarre marine version of the Tennysonian garden, with 'many a wondrous grot and secret cell' – like the garden of the Hesperides, it is an enchanted space apart that is perilously maintained by the power of singing well, as the daughters of Hesperus sing:

> The golden apple, the golden apple, the hallowed fruit,
> Guard it well, guard it warily,
> Singing airily,
> Standing about the charmèd root.
>
> .   .   .   .   .
>
> If ye sing not, if ye make false measure,
> We shall lose eternal pleasure,
> Worth eternal want of rest.

('The Hesperides', R. (i). 169, ll. 14–17, 23–5)

What that poem does not include, but what its use of the legend cannot exclude, is the knowledge that the apples are indeed stolen (by Hercules). Another lovely little song, 'A spirit haunts the year's last hours' (R. (i). 86), is set in a garden nearer England, but one similarly haunted by a pressing sense of change. Tennyson superbly discovers a Keatsian ripeness in the well-nigh final (but not quite the final) moments of the garden's life:

> My very heart faints and my whole soul grieves
> At the moist rich smell of the rotting leaves,
>   And the breath
>   Of the fading edges of box beneath,
> And the year's last rose.
>   Heavily hangs the broad sunflower
>   Over its grave i' the earth so chilly;
>   Heavily hangs the hollyhock,
>   Heavily hangs the tiger-lily.

(ll. 16–24)

Here, you imagine, a listener would have heard the 'peculiar *incomplete* cadence at the end' that Allingham noticed when the poet read (*IR* 58): how deftly Tennyson contrives the metrical possibility of an 'And' at the beginning of the last line (a word to make an end of a list) only to pass it over, leaving the reader with a pause to voice instead, and the poem drifting to a beautifully irresolved rallentando, mindful of an end but not quite ended, left hanging. The last lines return upon the breathily alliterative phrase 'Heavily hangs' (your breath would steam in the air) and pace themselves with great calm (the lingering epithet 'broad' is perfectly chosen); and they are themselves a repeat, since they form the refrain we have already met at the end of the first stanza: their time-biding repetition lulls the rich autumnal decay to a standstill, without quite excluding graveyard thoughts of a final wintry dissolution.

One likely source for Mariana's reiterated 'ballad-burthen music' ('The Daisy', R. (ii). 311, l. 77) was Wordsworth's 'The Thorn' (from *Lyrical Ballads*), the speaker of which several times reports the repeated lament of Martha Ray: 'Oh misery! oh misery! | Oh woe is me! oh misery!' In connection with that poem, Wordsworth supplied a note which sought to defend its repetitiousness, explaining with a fine critical intelligence

> why repetition and apparent tautology are frequently beauties of the highest kind. Among the chief of these reasons is the interest which the mind attaches to words, not only as symbols of the passion, but as *things*, active and efficient, which are of themselves part of the passion. And further, from a spirit of fondness, exultation, and gratitude, the mind luxuriates in the repetition of words which appear successfully to communicate its feelings.[49]

Wordsworth implies finely the sort of transition through which words might go as they gather by reiteration an imaginative interest in their own right, conjured from the normality of symbol into mysteriously defamiliarized '*things*', making you stop to wonder at them; and his last sentence happens to describe very beautifully a Tennysonian sort of luxuriance, though not one always simply associated with fondness, exultation, or gratitude ('Dear mother Ida, harken ere I die').

FitzGerald remembered Tennyson taking a dim view of Wordsworth's repetitive lyrical ballad: 'There was no end of

44

"This Thorn" in the piece that bears the name: "such hammering to set a scene for so small a drama"' (*M*. i. 152). That Tennyson should have exemplified so finely Wordsworthian reasons for repetition makes it all the more interesting that he should take against Wordsworth's own practice, not only in 'The Thorn' but also in the Wordsworth poem that seems to have meant most to him: 'Lines Written a Few Miles above Tintern Abbey on Revisiting the Banks of the Wye during a Tour, July 13, 1798'. Frederick Locker-Lampson records him saying (in 1869), 'You must not think because I speak plainly of Wordsworth's defects as a poet that I have not a very high admiration of him. I shall never forget my deep emotion the first time I had speech with him. I have a profound admiration for "Tintern Abbey"' (*IR* 176). As it happens, Locker-Lampson then heard him criticize the poem in some detail: it goes on too long, for one thing; and, for another, Wordsworth's literary tact failed him in it, especially in the opening paragraph, in which 'the word "again" occurs four times in the first fourteen lines' (*M*. ii. 70). As indeed it does (my italics):

> Five years have passed; five summers, with the length
> Of five long winters! and *again* I hear
> These waters, rolling from their mountain-springs
> With a sweet inland murmur. – Once *again*
> Do I behold these steep and lofty cliffs,
> Which on a wild secluded scene impress
> Thoughts of more deep seclusion; and connect
> The landscape with the quiet of the sky.
> The day is come when I *again* repose
> Here, under this dark sycamore, and view
> These plots of cottage-ground, these orchard-tufts,
> Which, at this season, with their unripe fruits,
> Among the woods and copses lose themselves
> Nor, with their green and simple hue, disturb
> The wild green landscape. Once *again* I see
> These hedge-rows, hardly hedge-rows, little lines
> Of sportive wood run wild . . .

(Tennyson even corrected the poem in Locker-Lampson's copy, to remove its diffuseness and repetitiousness.[50])

A defence might well be mustered for the recurrence of Wordsworth's wording, since the lines turn precisely about the idea of recurrence: 'again' sounding again sounds a keynote for the whole intricately self-revisiting paragraph ('Five . . . five . . . five'; 'hedge-rows . . . hedge-rows');[51] and so establishes in the texture of the opening lines the wider situation of the poem. (How discreetly fine, as well, that a poem which lives to keep down pressing thoughts of a loss – 'other gifts | Have followed, for such loss, I would believe, | Abundant recompense' – should begin by dwelling on the pleasurable half-thought of 'a gain'.) But that Tennyson *noticed* the prolonged sequence of 'agains' is more important than the justice of his verdict.[52] For not only was repetition one of his own most distinctive poetic resources (as I have been saying through this chapter), but repeating the word 'again', in particular, served him superbly well on several occasions; and when it did, it served as the local stylistic embodiment of an imaginative interest in things returning, or in returning to things. For instance, 'The Losing of the Child', a song written for the third edition of *The Princess* though in the event not used, shows a willingness to exploit such underlining self-reference far beyond the well-spaced recurrence of the word in Wordsworth's lines:

> The river left the child unhurt,
>   But far within the wild.
> Then we brought him home again,
> Peace and order come again,
> The river sought his bound again,
> The child was lost and found again,
>   And we will keep the child.

(R. (ii). 290, ll. 15–21)

'Again' is confirmatory and resounding there, returning buoyantly to announce and then to confirm a happy return (the tense of the last line leaps to the prospective as though in glad sympathy). Tennyson's attraction to the Arthurian cycle was doubtless due, in no small part, to the returning that lies at the heart of its idea (as it does at the heart of its Tennysonian idiom): Arthur is so enticing a prospect because he is a king who, like the child in the *Princess* lyric, will buoyantly come *again*. In the 'Epic' pendant to 'Morte d'Arthur', the verse charmingly confirms the thought of Arthur's coming again by organizing an echoic chorus, thus enabling 'come again' to come again too:

> and all the people cried,
> 'Arthur is come again: he cannot die.'
> Then those that stood upon the hills behind
> Repeated—'Come again, and thrice as fair' . . .
>
> (R. (ii). 226, ll. 295–8)

Hutton was typically shrewd to emphasize Tennyson's enthu-siasm for 'the mystic presage of a glorious return' (*CH* 377).[53]

There is an obvious pleasure inherent in having come again, of all phrases, the phrase 'come again'; and the echo is fittingly jubilant; but coming again in 'Tintern Abbey' is a more fruitfully ambiguous business – and comes nearer to a more typical Tennysonian use too. Building on the slight foundation of (among others) William Lisle Bowles, whose sonnets of senti-mental return to childhood scenes had first inspired young Coleridge, Wordsworth's great blank verse lyric of returning effectively inaugurates a literary tradition, in which the speak-ing voice encounters, in memory, an earlier self and discovers itself to be the same and yet different. Back again in the place he was five years before, Wordsworth discovers he is the same, but not the same, person that he was five years before:

> And now, with gleams of half-extinguished thought,
> With many recognitions dim and faint,
> And somewhat of a sad perplexity,
> The picture of the mind revives again.

As Mr Bloom says forlornly in *Ulysses*, Joyce's great reworking of the Wordsworthian memory poem – it is other things too – 'Me. And me now'.[54] A replication, yet a diminishment: it is the imaginative logic of the echo, of which Wordsworth was a laureate to rival even Tennyson – as in 'Yes, it was the mountain Echo', in which the echo answers back to Wordsworth's shouting cuckoo, 'Like her ordinary cry, | Like – but oh, how different!'

That a person may be at one with his former self but different too, his self single and yet multiple, perennial and unchanging as well as mutable and episodic, was one of Coleridge's chief philosophical fascinations; sometimes an absorbing anxiety, but sometimes a source of sprightly fun – as in his fondness for the Irish 'Bull', *I was a fine child, but they changed me*.[55] Coleridge discusses that particular Bull in chapter four of *Biographia*, a

47

chapter about Wordsworth and the *Lyrical Ballads*, which is (like much in that apparently wayward book) really no coincidence; for what Coleridge casts there as a metaphysical crossing of 'I's finds a different sort of existence in his friend's 'Tintern Abbey' (published in *Lyrical Ballads*), where it appears as a passionately felt imponderable: 'I cannot paint | What then I was'. (Much of *The Prelude*, Wordsworth's large-scale autobiography, works to stave off, without quite successfully resisting, the thought: 'I was a fine boy, but they changed me' – 'they' being, from place to place, Cambridge University, the picturesque, French politics, Godwinian theory.)

'Tintern Abbey' mattered to Tennyson because it was about recurrence and difference, change and the unchanged, his central subject; and it set that preoccupation at the heart of personal identity. Walking in the New Forest, Tennyson wrote home to his wife: 'my soul was not *satisfied*, for I did not meet with any so very large beech as I had met with before – but I, the man, I, myself, rejoiced, in spite of past I's, in the beeches and have resolved to stay till Monday' (*L.* ii. 125–6) – a play between the 'I, the man, I, myself' and its 'past I's', a play of continuity yet discontinuity, which feels eminently Wordsworthian. Tennyson had always found the subject compelling. As a boy he had singled out from Milton's *Samson Agonistes* the hero's lines describing how thoughts 'present | Times past, what once I was, and what am now' (*L.* i. 1); and memory had early suggested itself as a poetic subject, in first attempts as not much more than an occasion for clichéd regrets ('Why present before me | Thoughts of years gone by'), but the interweaving of pastness and presentness within a double self are perhaps already implicit even there ('I stand like some lone tower | Of former days remaining' ('Memory', R. (i). 5, ll. 5–6, 65–6). He remained not unimpressed by the 'Ode to Memory' he published in *Poems, Chiefly Lyrical* (R. (i). 84): its sense of memory as 'Artist-like' and of the mind as 'many-sided' is properly Wordsworthian (ll. 92, 116), though the Shelleyan melodramatics do it no favours ('O strengthen me, enlighten me! | I faint in this obscurity' (ll. 43-4)). The more ragged, but felt lines of 'Memory [Ay me!]', which Tennyson did not publish, sensationalize a Wordsworthian sort of ambivalence: 'Blessèd, cursèd, Memory' (R. (i). 126, l.5).

What stirred him in 'Tintern Abbey' was not merely an evocation of mutability, but the intricately dual evocation of the 'permanent in the transitory', an intermingling that he found encapsulated in the line 'Whose dwelling is the light of setting suns' (M. ii. 70); and Tennyson's greatest single response to Wordsworth's example was his own best blank verse lyric, 'Tears, Idle Tears', from *The Princess* (iv. 21–40). He did not mention 'Tintern Abbey' explicitly when he described that poem's genesis, but he clearly implied his mindfulness all the same: it 'came to me on the yellowing autumn-tide at Tintern Abbey, full for me of its bygone memories'. He said, too, that it expressed much the same emotive paradox that moved in Wordsworth's poem: 'It is the sense of the abiding in the transient' (P. iv. 21–40 n.); and the phrase finely catches a telltale Tennysonian ambivalence: the verbal noun implies both a pious confidence – '*that which* abides in the transient, the eternal in the temporal' – and a less assured sense of a self somehow inhering in time – '*how it is* to abide in the transient, to reside within wasting change'. Eric Griffiths has best described the doubleness of the self, transient yet persistent, evoked by 'Tears, Idle Tears', and suggests its connection with Wordsworth's temporal imagining in 'Tintern Abbey' of 'dead selves and their relation to the current self'; and he draws suggestively upon Arthur Hallam's philosophical essays to describe 'the knowledge of pastness within one's self' that Tennyson's poem discovers. Hallam's essay 'On Sympathy' describes beautifully such an encounter with one's 'past I': 'There is pleasure, in so far as it is a revelation of self; but there is pain, in so far that it is a divided self, a being at once our own and not our own' (HW 138).[56] Hallam's essay purports to be associationist in its philosophy of mind, and it draws on the philosopher Hartley in a wholly orthodox way for its time. But its central assertion, 'that the soul exists as one subject in various successive states', maintains just the paradoxical conviction of the abiding *oneness* of the multiple self that had famously led Coleridge to abandon Hartley. Tennyson, too, deplored the associationist thought that the 'I' was *merely* an accumulation of transient experiences, simply 'a bundle of sensations' (M. i. 317): something, an 'I myself', stayed unchanged.[57]

'Tears, Idle Tears' has a hesitant sort of lyricism: it is a lyric; but, as Tennyson himself implied (M. i. 253), its blank verse lacks the rhymes people instinctively listened for (at least, what rhyming does go on shuns the publicity of line-endings). It is, you might say, a chastened lyric: Tennyson raises the auditory prospect of confirming rhymes that come again, but only to obstruct it – quite the opposite of the ebullient comings-again in 'The Losing of the Child'. The return upon itself that the first phrase enacts ('Tears, idle tears') is forlornly unprogressive, quickly establishing a moving pattern of self-circling incapacity. Where Wordsworth's poem finds in deepness a mysterious source of confirmation ('something far more deeply interfused, | Whose dwelling is the light of setting suns'), Tennyson finds an obscure profundity that resists explication ('Tears from the depth of *some* divine despair') or demands renewed attempts to refine meaning: 'deep as love, | Deep as first love' ('not lazy hypnotic repetition . . . but precise memory arising – following on – from emotion', as Jonathan Dollimore says well[58]). As with many of Tennyson's most deeply felt poems, the power of 'Tears, Idle Tears' partly derives from its proximity to inarticulacy ('I know not what they mean'), an attribute he recognized himself: 'It is in a way like St Paul's "groanings which cannot be uttered"' (*IR* 92).[59] For the main body of the poem is a sequence of defeated analogies for something wholly elusive: the feel of a life presided over by a pressing but indefinite absentness; and the comparisons offered round upon themselves with broken reiteration (Fresh as . . . Sad as . . . So sad, so fresh . . . sad and strange as . . . So sad, so strange'). The hesitancy of the poem's eloquence emulates the reticence of its spiritual claim: 'Tintern Abbey' works with heroic strenuousness to affirm a sense of continuity between past and present ('*Therefore* am I still | A lover of the meadows and the woods, | And mountains' (emphasis added)); 'Tears, Idle Tears' has to make do with much less hope than that (even). Where Wordsworth's poem moves towards a benedictive address to another (his sister), Tennyson's speaker remains alone; and the optimistic faith in the 'permanent in the transitory' that Tennyson found stirring in Wordsworth's poem has a darker Tennysonian revoicing in the sudden tonal intensification of his last line: 'O Death in Life'.

The 'setting suns' of 'Tintern Abbey' are reimagined in 'Tears, Idle Tears' as an insistent but undemonstrative succession of sunrise and sunset and sunrise, infusing the poem with a pervasive sense of change's ubiquitious agency. Still, permanence of a subdued kind does accompany the otherwise overpowering sense of transience: for, of course, the poem has a refrain, which, while it registers the passing of things, does so repeatedly, with all the tenacity of a Tennysonian burden – 'the days that are no more'. Tennyson was long passionate about the phrase 'no more'. (That is another look back to 'Tintern Abbey', which hopes to brave out pastness: 'That time is past, | And all its aching joys are now no more, | And all its dizzy raptures. Not for this | Faint I, nor mourn nor murmur'.) As a young man, Tennyson had begun a little lyric, 'Oh sad *No More!* Oh sweet *No More!* | Oh strange *No More!*', and ended it, 'Surely all pleasant things had gone before, | Lowburied fathomdeep beneath with thee, NO MORE!' (R. (i). 57, ll. 1–2, 7–8). The last-moment recasting of the tag as the name of an allegorical figure works clumsily; but it already implies the way that a Tennysonian sense of absence can be so powerful as to exist like a living presence – which is what the later lyric's turn to 'Death in Life' does so much more profoundly. In a characteristically Tennysonian way, the phrase itself, 'the days that are no more', brings to mind the perplexing presentness of the past that it elegizes as lost. An unremarkable enough phrase, to be sure, but a kind of wonder accrues to Tennyson's use of the phrase through repetition; and it is importantly different from, for instance, the 'dear, dead days beyond recall'.[60] The eighteenth-century poet Shenstone had singled out the 'singular pathos' of the phrase 'no more', a singularity which he saw lying in its double-vision, 'reminding us at once of past pleasure, and the future exclusion of it';[61] and his dual-awareness of pastness and futurity brings us someway near what's going on. W. David Shaw usefully reminds us of Tennyson's mastery of paralipsis, 'the rhetorical trope that, in pretending to pass over a matter, tells it most effectively';[62] James Richardson calls this a poem's 'unsaying of the very detail it seems to present' (as in, 'Unlifted was the clinking latch').[63] A paraliptical negative, such as Wordsworth's 'Not for this | Faint I, nor mourn nor murmur', cannot but arouse some thoughts of what it is that is not happening or what it is that is not there. Just so, Tennyson's negative grammar confers an existence on 'the days that are' (a full iambic stress insists on *are*) before resigning them to oblivion ('that are no more'), in a readerly interplay of presence and non-presence which emulates the elusive but insistent life of recollected absent things. The days are 'beyond recall, yet alive – tantalizingly vivid and near'.[64] Things 'that are no more' do not disappear from view so much as enter a new, paradoxical, Tennysonian kind of perpetuity: 'No more by thee my steps shall be, | For ever and for ever' ('A Farewell', R. (ii). 265, ll. 3–4).

Several Tennyson poems follow in the footsteps of 'Tintern Abbey' and other Wordsworthian revisit poems (like 'Yarrow Revisited', which we know Tennyson admired too (M. ii. 421–2)). 'The Dell of E——' (R. (i). 9), an otherwise unremarkable piece of juvenilia, shows how early Tennyson was drawn to the plot: revisiting a characteristically Tennysonian ecological niche of wandering streams and incense-bearing breezes, 'Long years' afterward, the speaker predictably finds a desolated scene ('man's rude hand had sorely scathed the dell' (l. 30)). That is simple enough in recording loss; later poems of return explore revisits and changefulness with rather greater subtlety: the dramatic monologue 'Tithonus' (R. (ii). 324), for example, works a remarkable variation on the theme. The speaker, granted the immortality he craved, but not eternal youth, is always the same yet dreadfully mutable; while the dawn, ever 'returning on thy silver wheels' (l. 76), reminds him continually of his own changefulness:

> with what another heart
> In days far-off, and with what other eyes
> I used to watch – if I be he that watched –
> The lucid outline forming round thee . . .

> (ll. 50–3)

(The whole mysterious burden of personal identity is caught in the wondering aside, 'if I be he that watched'.)

'Tithonus' began (as 'Tithon') in the shocking aftermath of Hallam's death, after which one all-important thing could never be the same. Another poem, 'In the Valley of Cauteretz', perhaps the most tender example of Tennyson's poetry of revisiting, records his impressions of the country he had visited years before in Hallam's company, and to which he had now come again:

All along the valley, stream that flashest white,
Deepening thy voice with the deepening of the night,
All along the valley, where thy waters flow,
I walked with one I loved two and thirty years ago.
All along the valley, while I walked today,
The two and thirty years were a mist that rolls away;
For all along the valley, down thy rocky bed,
Thy living voice to me was as the voice of the dead,
And all along the valley, by rock and cave and tree,
The voice of the dead was a living voice to me.

(R. (ii). 326)

He had never been happier than during his first visit (*L.* ii. 94), and his return was something of an anti-climax: 'it had become a rather odious watering-place, but the hills wore their old green, and the roaring stream had the same echoes as of old' (*L.* ii. 327). Like all Tennyson's poetry about returning, it is about the way the self changes through time, and the way it stays true too; and it builds upon an unstated analogy between the self in time and the persisting life of a running stream, developing the Tennysonian paradox that the self, like a stream, remains a single thing while forever changing, abiding in the transient. That time flows on, that the original experience is unrepeatable (you cannot step in the same stream twice), this is sadly obvious: as the remorselessly vivacious stream says in 'The Brook', 'men may come and men may go, | But I go on for ever' (R. (ii). 313, ll. 33–4). But the poem's hypnotic reiterations seem set on recurrence; and that deep need is not left quite unfulfilled. The eighth line, with its adroitly hesitant metrical stumble ('to me was as the voice of the dead'), fondly proposes a likeness ('was *as* the') between the stream now and the stream of memory; and the culminating line takes that analogy over, turning it round, and confirming a simile into a truth, with a renewed firmness of metrical purpose: 'The vóice of the déad was a líving voíce to mé' (not 'was *as* a'). What unites the poet's speaking self and his recollected self, different by 'two and thirty years' though they be, is their common love for Hallam: the phrase 'All along' sounds the length of the poem, describing the poet's physical progress up the valley; but also suffusing itself by that insistent reiteration into the temporal dimension of the poem ('all along' as 'throughout, continuously'). It is as though the poem is half-voicing a thought too private to be

53

brought to the surface, something at once implied and concealed by the insistent repetitions of the poem: a thought like 'All along I have loved you'. You really could not have a better exemplification of Eliot's axiom, that the Tennysonian surface 'is intimate with his depths'.

One variant on the return narrative that Tennyson found especially compelling was the return home that discovered it to be no home at all.[65] Again, perhaps Kierkegaard is our best guide to what is going on in such a story and what its connection with repetitiveness might be. The narrator of his *Repetition*, convinced that 'He who wills repetition is matured in seriousness', attempts to replicate the enjoyable episodes of his past life, only to find himself disappointed, and doomily convinced that, in reality, '[t]here is no such thing as repetition':

> My home had become cheerless, precisely because it was the reverse of a repetition, my mind was unfruitful, my troubled imagination was engaged in transmuting into the delights of Tantalus the memory of how richly the thoughts presented themselves on the former occasion, and this rank weed of memory strangled every thought at birth... The only thing repeated was the impossibility of repetition.[66]

Aware of such disappointment, the Lotos-eaters, happily immobilised in their enisled tranquillity, regard the thought of a return trip with lazy abhorrence:

> all hath suffered change:
> For surely now our household hearths are cold:
> Our sons inherit us: our looks are strange:
> And we should come like ghosts to trouble joy.
>
> (R. (i). 170, ll. 116–19)

'Tears, Idle Tears' had likened the days that are no more to 'remembered kisses after death' (l. 36), meaning, of course, 'kisses remembered after the loved one is dead', but, especially coming so soon after the deathbed scene of the third verse, the bizarre sense flickers across the line (as Griffiths nicely observes) 'as kisses you remember after *you* are dead'.[67] Analogously, Tennyson's revisit poems often entertain the thought that returning home makes you like a visitant from beyond the grave. Such a plot provides a narrative occasion for Tennyson's persistent feeling of a death-in-life: as of one who might

> year by year alone
> Sit brooding in the ruins of a life,
> Nightmare of youth, the spectre of himself . . .
>
> ('Love and Duty', R. (ii). 279, ll. 11–13)

The Lotos-Eaters think themselves spectres of themselves, as though home had remained most fully alive and they had grown dead: as, of course, in a characteristically Tennysonian way, they richly are, in the sense that their island life of unchanging ease is a delicious kind of annihilation – 'Give us long rest or death, dark death, or dreamful ease', they sing (l. 98), as though uttering synonyms rather than ultimatums. (It is a Kierkegaardian point: 'Complete repetition, then, is death or – if one prefers – eternity . . . both being, however, beyond life and beyond narrative'.[68]) Tennyson went back to the thought in *In Memoriam*, meditating the threat to 'domestic peace' that would attend the appearance of those who had 'past away' (the euphemism is tenderly evasive in the imagined circumstances); and yet despite such risks, the wish for Hallam to return is irresistible, 'Whatever change the years have wrought, | I find not yet one lonely thought | That cries against my wish for thee' (*IM* xc. 20, 13, 22–4). That is sad in its wishfulness and, like *In Memoriam* at large, distinguished by a strong-hearted diffidence that eludes self-pity (Tennyson's *thought* would be lonely; the thought that *Tennyson* is lonely is present but not advertised).

'Enoch Arden' (R. (ii). 330) is Tennyson's most simply desolate narrative of coming back from the grave. As in 'The Lotos-Eaters', the grave in question is the spicy stasis of a Tennysonian Arcadia, an exotically barren geography of reiterative splendour (Enoch is stranded on the island waiting for some passing ship to find him and carry him home again):

> The blaze upon the waters to the east;
> The blaze upon his island overhead;
> The blaze upon the waters to the west . . .
>
> (ll. 590–3)

Once home, Enoch learns that everyone has believed him dead (they are wrong, but his wife Annie is not wrong to say of him, 'I shall look upon your face no more' (ll. 212)). Describing his response to the news, Tennyson numbingly uses the word 'again' again, as though the verse were stuck on the word, dismally haunted by the proper coming-again of happy restitution, which, as Enoch and we know perfectly well, is not going to materialize:

> when she closed
> 'Enoch, poor man, was cast away and lost'
> He, shaking his gray head pathetically,
> Repeated muttering 'cast away and lost;'
> Again in deeper inward whispers 'lost!'
>
> But Enoch yearned to see her face again;
> 'If I might look on her sweet face again
> And know that she is happy.'

(ll. 708–15)

The tangle of identity and difference, of what is the abidingly the same again (his love) and what contingent and wholly altered, is there the stuff of high pathos; and it leads to a one-sided recognition scene of more than merely melodramatic power, because it brings into play the emotive paradoxes of change and changelessness that Tennyson always found so compelling. In Enoch's absence, Annie has remarried; Enoch returns, unseen, and like a ghost, a situation that inspires a flash of Tennyson's old art of repetitiousness, as well as the use of a favourite phrase:

> Now when the dead man come to life beheld
> His wife his wife no more, and saw the babe
> Hers, yet not his, upon the father's knee . . .

(ll. 754–6)

Enoch's whole sad tale was precipitated by a contingency – what Tennyson calls 'a change, as all things human change' (l. 101); and sheer change is the unfeeling engine of the poem's domestic tragedy. But dismal as the attempt to come home again in such changeful conditions is likely to be, Tennyson evidently regards the alternative island life of exotically repetitive changelessness with weary horror. That implies a different movement of his mind and a quite distinct attitude towards change; and that is the subject of my next chapter.

2

Making Progress

Ears poise before decision, scenting danger.

(W. H. Auden)

Despite his aptitude for staying put, Tennyson often felt a duty to progress. An abstract idea of progress was a part of the *Zeitgeist*: like many intellectuals of his time (the lingering dog-days of Enlightenment perfectibilism) Tennyson entertained a stirring but hazy faith in the general thought of advancement. ('No idea perhaps occupies a place in his poems so central as that of the progress of the race', was how it struck one contemporary (*CH* 326).) Progress was inextricably tied up with contemporary improvements and scientific discoveries – 'As we surpass our father's skill, | Our sons will shame our own' ('Mechanophilus', R. (i). 197, ll. 21–2) – but could easily assume a compellingly vague universality and become a cast of mind: *OED* defines a telling Victorian sense of 'future', 'A condition in time to come different (esp. in a favourable sense) from the present', as though onward were almost necessarily upward.[1] Thackeray was refreshingly sardonic about it all: ' "Bless railroads everywhere," I said, "and the world's advance[''']'.[2]

Nothing was safe from what Tennyson himself called 'the great progress of the age'.[3] W. J. Fox, for example, launched his review of *Poems, Chiefly Lyrical* with the cheering reflection: 'It would be a pity that poetry should be an exception to the great law of progression that obtains in human affairs; and it is not . . . progressiveness is merely a consequence from, a sort of reflection of, the progressiveness of [man's] nature' (*CH* 21). No aspect of the nineteenth-century spirit is likely to strike us as more offputtingly bumptious. Chambers's *Vestiges of Creation*, which Tennyson knew, interpreted evolutionary history as a

57

long sequence of providentially ordained improvement;[4] and Tennyson approved of attempts to project that sense of incremental advancement into futurity, such as that he found in the naturalist Wallace, who showed that 'man has a prospective brain' (*IR* 109). Tennysonian progress at its most outspoken is often, redeemingly, at its most giddily cosmic or mystical, imagining immense and impersonal time schemes of advance: 'Move upward, working out the beast', *In Memoriam* counsels, to little conceivable effect (cxviii. 27).

But if Tennyson was, as Gladstone said, 'too intimately and essentially the poet of the nineteenth century to separate himself from its leading characteristics, the progress of physical science and a vast commercial, mechanical, and industrial development' (*CH* 248), then part of that representative power lay precisely in the instinct that repeatedly led him indeed to 'separate himself' from any such forward strides. Hallam Tennyson nicely catches the division of impulses I have in mind, when he recalls his father's responsiveness to nature: 'he felt a rest in her steadfastness, patient progress and hopefulness; the same seasons ever returned; the same stars wheeled in their courses' (*M*. i. 312). Such vacillation – between the restfulness of sameness and the aspiration to progress, patient or otherwise – shapes much of Tennyson; and this chapter is about the way his verses diversely assume that contradiction, shaped by a wavering rhythm that equivocates between the obligation to move forward and the desire to stay still. The sense of progressiveness, embraced and put in question by his poetry, need not be on so numinously vast a scale as Hallam's example; it might be a more humanly proportioned awareness of 'the need of going forward, and braving the struggle of life' (*M*. i. 196). 'Blessed be those that grease the wheels of the old world', he told Spedding, 'insomuch as to move on is better than to stand still' (*L*. i. 120). Or, as the poem 'Youth' more wearily puts it: 'Yet well I know that nothing stays, | And I must traverse yonder plain' (R. (i). 223, ll. 53–4).

One expression of this formative hesitancy is conservatism: the politics expressed in Tennyson's public poems embody the same emotive pattern, poised uneasily, as I shall presently be saying, between a reformist taste for change and an unshifting fear of change. The political poems are only one example of

Tennyson's argufying verse evading more straightforwardly single-minded attempts to persuade. A normal argument, for example, might hope reasonably to progress to its conclusion, a task that many of Tennyson's poems appear to set about. J. S. Mill says: 'all writing which undertakes to make men feel truths as well as see them, does take up one point at a time, does seek to impress that, to drive that home'.[5] But single points are forever finding themselves complicated by second thoughts and revoicings in Tennyson's discursive verse: he realized an alternative kind of intellectual vocation to Mill's, in poems that dwell in states of doubt and indecision, successfully resisting anything like the firm push to solution that might seem such an argumentative poem's whole *raison d'être*. The double-voiced inward conversations of vacillation did not only beset him, Hamlet-like, but fascinated him too: the poems, most typically, bide their time, deferring the conclusion towards which they ostensibly incline by dwelling within irresolved minds. (Tucker says neatly of Tennyson's spokesmen that 'they exhibit determination rarely and suffer it often'.[6]) A Tennysonian character like Mariana exists in an impotence so habitual that the possibility of action scarcely arises: she 'does not act, but is continually acted upon', as Wordsworth disapprovingly said of Coleridge's Ancient Mariner; and such passivity may indeed be deplorable. Elsewhere in Tennyson, decisions do get made; but when they do they regularly precipitate disaster; and when resolute characters and men of action appear in the poems, their willed single-mindedness is typically regarded with the deepest misgivings, as though decisiveness were a sort of delusion or even madness. There is often a coincidence in Tennyson between muscular commentary on the state of things and an atmosphere of possible insanity – which is 'not the right medium', as a contemporary critic reasonably remarked, 'through which to view the world for serious purposes' (*CH* 189).

The idea of progress requires you to think well of change; and Tennyson's politics revolve about an indecisiveness over change. 'Stagnation is more dangerous than Revolution. But *sudden* change means a house on sand,' he said in old age (*M.* ii. 339); but some such pattern in his politics was established long before, in the excited and anxious atmosphere of liberal hope and pressure for reform in early 1830s Britain; and (unlike Wordsworth's, say) his politics remained largely constant, or so his habits of self-borrowing would suggest.[7]

The period leading up to the Reform Bill of 1832 was immensely turbulent, with much social unrest in Britain and in Ireland, and uprisings across Europe, including one in Spain, in which Tennyson and Hallam played a small role, supporting a misconceived liberal insurgency led by General Torrijos.[8] The leading Apostle, John Sterling, 'prime mover of the conspiracy', had fierily looked forward to revolution when an undergraduate, and espoused the utopian prospects of human perfectibility.[9] That was extreme for the group, and Sterling's politics soon moderated after university, when he fell into Coleridge's circle; but a general commitment persisted in what his fellow Apostle William Donne praised (in Hallam) as 'forwardness' of thought (HL 514). However, even that nebulous notion of prospectiveness, enlightened by 'an untiring faith in the undefeated energies of man', was accompanied by deepening trepidation and dismay, especially after the Spanish revolution quickly collapsed.[10] 'Do you share in the general despondency of wise and good men at the present aspect of the world?' wrote Richard Chenevix Trench to Donne, in December 1831, 'I live in the faith of a new dispensation, which I am very confident is at hand; but what fearful times shall we have to endure ere that! We must pray earnestly not to be swept away by the great torrent';[11] and, a few weeks later, he wrote again, 'Hallam, Blakesley and myself, and one or two others, sit like a congregation of ravens, a hideous conclave, and croak despair, which however does not prevent us from smoking a multitude of cigars, and drinking whatever liquor falls in our way' (HL 514). The morose humour does not disguise a genuinely burdensome predicament; and, under the millennialist influence of the Scots preacher Irving, Trench came to see things as positively apocalyptic: 'we are fallen on the last days.'[12] Hallam was not immune to such diffused millennial feeling, gloomily mindful of 'the tempests of the days that are coming' (HL 512): 'The country is in a more awful state than you can well conceive,' he wrote from Trinity College (HL 387), in the autumn of 1830, when protesting agricultural labourers burnt ricks around Cambridge; nor was he alone in being prepared for the worst – Wordsworth happened to be visiting the University, and his table talk was similarly dismal, 'furiously alarmist, nothing but revolutions, reigns of terror' (*M.* i. 72). The liberal enthusiasm of the Apostles, excited by Spanish rebellion, promptly swung behind the defence of the University – a shift of alliance the irony of which was not lost on the wry and humane James Spedding: 'visions of broken heads & arms, scythes & pitchforks disturbed the purity of our unselfish contemplations, & the idealisms of our poetical imaginings'. (It was a false alarm anyway: 'the threatened army did not make the threatened attack,' Spedding reported, 'very much to my satisfaction & the disappointment of the more adventurous spirits among us'.[13]) Besides social unrest, looming parliamentary reform was also troubling the circle: 'I confess myself much alarmed', wrote Trench, not long back from trying to help a revolution on its way, and barely reconciled to the Reform Bill 'from the considerations of its inevitableness, and its necessity'.[14] When the Bill was finally passed in 1832, Hallam's pessimism deepened: 'The country is in jeopardy hourly increasing' (*HL* 722).

Culler says of the group, 'it is difficult to say whether they were radical or conservative';[15] and some sense of the difficulty seems to have troubled the Apostles themselves. The apparently stark discrepancy between doomy reaction and Apostolic forwardness was not lost on Hallam anyway: in a poem, he tried to brave out any charges of inconsistency:

> Oh falsely they blaspheme us, honoured friend,
> Who say the faith of liberty is gone
> Out of our slavish bosoms . . .
>
> .   .   .   .   .
> There is no change . . .

(HW 104)

A droll account of the Cambridge events by two other members sought to smooth over inconsistencies more chirpily:

> We loved the past with Tory love,
> Yet more than Radicals we strove
> For coming years of gold.[16]

But Hallam had already described himself forlornly as 'one of strong passions, irresolute purposes, vacillating opinions'; and the sense of ideological disorientation evidently grew over-powering: 'I have been perplexed lately with some of these odious politics,' he wrote to Emily Tennyson (later his fiancée) (*HL* 354, 426). When Trench returned to England from the Spanish fiasco, Hallam feelingly wrote to him, 'I do not wonder you should feel these misgivings and backward yearnings of mind' (*HL* 411): some such tussle between forward and backward yearnings of mind seems to have become the defining temper of the set. 'In good truth', a sadder and wiser Trench reflected, 'one cannot make a concordance either of the universe without us, or within, and we only set ourselves a-jarring and bring our contradictions into more open day by the attempt'.[17]

For them all, a reformist's pleasure that the times were changing went along with an oppressive fear that the times were changing; and Tennyson shared that mixed feeling.[18] He had thrown himself vigorously into the defence of Cambridge, while, according to his son, 'he largely sympathised with the labourers in their demands' (*M*. i. 41). He supported the Anti-Slavery Convention and Catholic Emancipation, and 'from first to last . . . preached the onward progress of liberty' (*M*. i. 42); but he wrote to his aunt after the Reform Bill, 'the future is so dark in the prospect', nervously distrustful of 'Reform (not the measure, the passing of which is unavoidable) but the instigating spirit of reform which is likely to subsist among the people long after the measure has past into a law' (*L*. i. 69). And accordingly, the political poems that Tennyson wrote in the late 1820s and early 1830s (not all of which were published at the time) are dedicated to the twin propositions that change is good – 'power that still should change and fleet | Had festered in the hands of few' – and yet that change is bad, if there be rather too much of it – especially, say, were it left to those 'Still changing, whom no change can please' ('Hail Briton!', R. (i). 194, ll. 31–2, 53). The recurrent violence of political change in France stands behind much of the fear: as an old man he dreaded 'a universal French Revolution' (*M*. ii. 339), but as a very young man he was already fascinatedly repelled by stories of the mob's macabre savagery (in 'Come hither, canst thou tell me if this skull' (R. (i). 50)); and gruesome scenes from 'ever-murdered France' remained in his thoughts (e.g. 'Aylmer's Field', R. (ii). 337, ll. 760–8). Revolutionary violence appears as a grisly parody of progress, as an uninspired epigram of later years, addressed to Paris, made to quip: 'How often your Re-volution has proven but E-volution | Rolled again back on itself in the tides of a civic insanity!' (R. (iii). 433, ll. 3–4). Parisian progress manages merely to regress (to savagery), which is what happens to England at the end of the *Idylls* ('and all my realm | Reels back into the beast, and is no more' ('The Passing of Arthur', R. (iii). 475, ll. 25–6), reversing the properly E-volutionary course.

When Tennyson tries to sound chipper about progress he often thinks about spring (perhaps with Shelley in mind: 'If Winter comes, can Spring be far behind?'): the way it 'Makes all things new' and stirs the poet to 'Ring little bells of change | From word to word' ('Early Spring', R. (i). 200, ll. 2, 29–30). But when, in 'The Progress of Spring', he looks forward to what he flatly calls 'new developments', what he is really approving is the evolutionary gradualism of the season's 'process', like that of a seed growing into the plant it always contained within itself (R. (i). 193, ll. 94, 106) – what he calls, in 'Hail Briton!', 'seasonable changes' (l. 151). Such new developments have the advantage of scarcely constituting anything strictly *new* at all:

> The state within herself concludes
> The power to change, as in the seed,
> The model of her future form,
> And liberty indeed.
>
> ('I loving Freedom for herself', R. (ii). 238, ll. 17–20)

The manuscript has 'within herself contains': 'concludes' adroitly slips the passing idea of curtailment into all this talk of growth – happily paused by the line-ending – in contrast to the revolutionary 'cycles of disastrous change' that we hear about a few lines later (l. 31). ('And this is my delight to live and see | Old principles still working new results' ('The constant spirit of the world exults', R. (i). 145, ll.3–4).)

Tennyson never sounds hugely convincing when he hymns 'fertile change and wide variety' ('The constant spirit', l. 2): 'This Earth is wondrous, change on change' one poem of this period bravely begins (R. (i). 201), but it soon turns to fly fantastically off to the moon rather than stay earthbound. Still, seasonable change is (as Trench thought the Reform Bill) inevitable and necessary: the emotions are wonderfully entangled. Armstrong describes a 'peculiarly radical conservatism, which dreads change and sees its necessity';[19] and if this sounds a familiar combination, then it is because its paradoxical conjunction – admitting alteration while devoutly wishing that things stay much the same – replays in political terms the mysterious coincidence of difference and continuity within the self that I spoke about (in Chapter 1) in Tennyson's self-discovering poetry of return:

> Meet is it changes should control
> Our being, lest we rust in ease.
> We all are changed by still degrees,
> All but the basis of the soul.
>
> ('Love thou thy land, with love far-brought', R. (ii). 235, ll. 41–4)

That stanza feels as though it begins with a large admission: an odd sardonic energy twists the expected 'rest' to 'rust'; but the third line, while appearing merely an amplification of the original sentiment, introduces an obtrusive ambiguity: 'still' means 'constant, continual' (as in 'I'm still standing'), of course, but the verse does not quite exclude an awkwardly oxymoronic sense, 'remaining in the same position' (as in 'I'm standing still'). (It is remarkable how often, when describing *change*, Tennyson should be drawn to include the word *still*, as though obliquely to register the double movement of his mind on the subject. Examples from just the last few pages: 'power that still should change and fleet', 'Still changing, whom no change can please', 'Old principles still working new results'.) The last line, as though heartened by that possibility, then turns from allowing ubiquitous alteration ('All') into affirming continuity after all. 'All but' sounds modestly concessive, but 'basis' reserves for changelessness something fundamental – as in Hallam's insistence 'that the soul exists as one subject in various successive states'.

To conceive of a society as being (properly) something like a person, as Tennyson does in that poem, is to take up a particular sort of politics. If we need to give Tennyson's implicit position a label, Culler's suggestion of 'a slightly liberalized version of the thought of Burke' will do well enough;[20] but perhaps more useful is what T. S. Eliot wrote, with perceptive fellow feeling, about the emotive paradox at the heart of Tennyson's politics:

'conservative, rather than reactionary or revolutionary', the politics of a man who 'believed explicitly in progress, and believed implicitly that progress consists in things remaining much as they are'.[21] (And belligerently *just* as they are, if the threat of change is desperate, as when the refrain of 'English Warsong', stridently intent on defending the realm against the French, sticks recalcitrantly with 'England' unchanged: 'Shout for England! | Ho! for England! | George for England! | Merry England! | England for aye!' (R. (i). 116, ll. 7–11).) Eliot describes a classical conservativism – not, I mean, the modern free-market ideology that goes under that name – a political disposition mistrustful of individualist innovation, and preferring instead the individual's submission to deeper movements of transhistorical community: 'Where Freedom slowly broadens down | From precedent to precedent' ('You ask me, why, though ill at ease', R. (i). 195, ll. 11–12). Like much conservative thought, it tends to make the idea of good individual agency feel very mysterious, or perhaps self-contradictory: Roger Scruton's *The Meaning of Conservatism* exemplifies the enigma I have in mind with characteristic penetration. He describes how someone who acts in a conservative spirit 'acts from tradition'; wilfully to choose a different idea to guide your actions, one that 'does not belong to tradition', leads to 'the emergence of the individual from social life, and the first glimpse of the empty solipsism that waits outside'.[22] (Another example of the paradox would be the relationship between tradition and individual talent in Eliot's literary thinking.) The ideal is change without initiative, progress without disruption; things different, yes, but somehow still the same too. The informing riddle of it is that the individuality of decision is really defensible only when it is spontaneously surrendered up to some greater, impersonal agency, like 'Freedom' perhaps.[23] The psychology is intricately mystifying; volitional action acquires a kind of taint. At his most dutifully buoyant, Tennyson protests (too much): 'There lives a power to shape our ends | Rough-hew them as we will!' ('I loving Freedom for herself', ll. 55–6); but any such confidence is hardly vindicated by *Hamlet*, to which he alludes, and its pious certainty that action is irrelevant before the benevolent sway of providence is certainly not endorsed by Tennyson at large. He does not dwell much on such conservative perplexities; but that

65

an imponderability about the rectitude of action and the business of coming to decision should lurk within his emotive politics is scarcely a coincidence: for it is the central subject of so much of his poetry.

'Eminently', said John Forster of Tennyson, 'he is worthy to be the poet of our time'; and the age's burden was not light, as a contemporary review made clear: 'Let Mr Tennyson reflect that, having "the gift of poesy", a strange responsibility devolves upon him.'[24] That poetry should devote itself to the ends of sweetness and light, easing its readership from what Arnold called 'The hopeless tangle of our age', was a heady Messianic attitude inherited from the Romantics, perhaps especially from Shelley; and Tennyson certainly did not need the reviewers to tell him about devolved responsibilities: they were a part of the abiding temper of the Apostles. (The circle was full of keen Shelleyans, even 'a sort of sect, in behalf of his character & genius' (*HL* 683): Hallam became for a time 'a furious Shelleyist';[25] and Tennyson recalled later in life, 'Nobody admires Shelley more than I once did' (*M.* ii. 70).) To be '*the* artist of modern times', as Tennyson's friend Venables told him he was bound to be (*M.* i. 123), meant sharing in the task of 'regenerating England', in the heroic phrase of John Kemble.[26] 'To become the most *purely*, the most *thoroughly*, the most *excitingly*, & the most *permanently* benevolent that endeavor can make us', was Hallam's account of the end of life (*HL* 302): the busy strenuousness of virtue sounds callow, and frankly tiresome, but there is no doubting the force of its impact upon Tennyson. 'A volume of poetry written in a proper spirit.... would be, at the present juncture, the greatest benefit the world could receive,' Blakesley, yet another Apostle, counselled the young poet, which was hardly setting sights low (*M.* i. 68); and Tennyson was evidently far from immune to the enobling prospect of 'the world's renewèd youth',

> when Poesy shall bind
> Falsehood beneath the altar of great Truth . . .
>
> (R. 'To Poesy' (i). 63, ll. 6, 7–8)

Progressiveness of mind and resolve were what the age most urgently required, as an upright Cambridge sonnet addressed to

Conrad, a (presumably) fictional acquaintance, makes determinedly clear: his indolent friend's boat is becalmed because 'The wave of Life hath no propelling tide', and the poet advises, 'We live but by *resistance*' – 'breast | This sloth-sprung weed with progress sensible' (R. (i). 129, ll. 8, 9, 13–14).

Keeping so clear a head and so firm a will about the duty to progress was also celebrated in 'To — [Clear-Headed Friend]' (R. (i). 74), another Cambridge poem, in which an Apostolic mental clarity 'cuts atwain | The knots that tangle human creeds' (ll. 2–3). But it was more often the tangle, and not the achievement of its extrication, that Tennyson found most truly compelling himself, even while remaining uneasily aware of a duty to get things straightened out. The tangles in question could be ostentatiously metaphysical: 'The "How" and the "Why"' (R. (i). 72) tries to make light of such ultimate mysteries, and the consequence is a cumbersome frivolity ('How you are you? Why I am I? | Who will riddle me the *how* and the *why*?' (ll. 19–20)). The heartily untroubled is one of the few notes in Tennyson which sounds untrue whenever it emerges; but as 'a piece of perplexity' (Leigh Hunt's not unadmiring description (R. (i). 72, headnote)) the poem importantly anticipates better Tennyson poems.

The protracted title of 'Supposed Confessions of a Second-Rate Sensitive Mind' (R. (i). 78) hedges round its irresolution, over-anxious to distance the poet from the suicidal perplexities of his speaker: the ghost of a plot is sketched in (the speaker's mother is dead (ll. 85–6)), which tilts the dejection in a mawkish direction (ll. 40–4); but the dramatization is pretty exiguous, and the desire to fix the unhappy spirit seems squarely Tennyson's own. An edge of Byronic self-congratulation in the flashes of linguistic display ('Unpiloted i' the echoing dance | Of reboant whirlwinds' (ll. 96–7)) implies anything but distracted misery: in his review, Fox shrewdly remarked 'a timid sceptic . . . who has not lost his pride in the prowess of his youthful infidelity' (*CH* 26). Of the 'doubt and fear' (l. 138) that animates the speaker, it is the fear that emerges most strikingly, in the lurid Jacobean swerve of the closing prayer:

> Oh teach me yet
> Somewhat before the heavy clod
> Weighs on me, and the busy fret

> Of that sharp-headed worm begins
> In the gross blackness underneath.

(ll. 183–7)

('Somewhat' before – as almost to say, 'in your own time' – poignantly strikes a note of would-be nonchalance amid the increasingly frantic urgency.) The speaker had earlier challenged himself,

> Why not believe then? Why not yet
> Anchor thy frailty there, where man
> Hath moored and rested?

(ll. 123–5)

But the poem manages no such anchor, and its prayer breaks off in a forlorn, Hamlet-style apostrophe: 'O damnèd vacillating state!' (l. 190).

That the poem fails to resolve its spiritual predicament is presumably what makes its mind 'second-rate'. In his review, Hallam claimed the title misjudged, as the poem portrayed 'rather the clouded season of a strong mind, than the habitual condition of one feeble'; and he disputed too the implication that a mind might only be first rate once it had reached 'such trustful reliance on a principle of repose, which lies beyond the war of conflicting opinions, that the grand ideas . . . cease to affect him with bewildering impulses of hope and fear' (CH 46, 47). Tennyson returned to that state of bewilderment in 'The Two Voices' (R. (i). 209), which was associated by his son with 'overwhelming sorrow after the death of Arthur Hallam' (but which was actually already begun when Hallam died). The poem is a soliloquy, taking place within its protagonist's troubled spirit; the main literary antecedent for its self-entangling death-wish is Hamlet again: 'Were it not better not to be?' (l. 3). A voice of doubt speaks, at length, and then disappears, replaced by a voice of faith; and the poem's ostensible business is to make a decision between them, which Leigh Hunt thought it did most satisfactorily: 'a summary of the argument, *pro* and *con*, about suicide, capitally well put on both sides, and ending, as they ought to do, in the victory of a cheerful wisdom befitting the beauty of the universe and the goodness of its Creator' (CH 134). Kemble thought the poem 'a mighty stride in intellect since the *Second-Rate Sensitive Mind*' (R.,

68

headnote), and the poem does indeed appear to stride with greater purpose towards its cheerful conclusion, rather as a Wordsworth poem like 'Resolution and Independence' firmly sets its spirits on a course from dejection to renewal. The two voices of the title may indeed come from Wordsworth: his sonnet 'Two Voices are There' has nothing to do with suicide, but it does move towards a precarious sort of hope, as Tennyson's poem means to. Spedding reasonably thought the consolatory ambition of the poem might draw on book IV ('Despondency Corrected') of Wordsworth's *The Excursion* (*CH* 149–50); and the thought of so distinguished a precursor in hope makes Tennyson's conspicuous failure quite to arrive at any equivalent resolve all the more impressive.[27]

The first of the voices, bleak and unyielding, dismisses all the reasons to be cheerful that the poem's protagonist manages to think up, including the plucky faith in progress: that

> '. . . men, through novel spheres of thought
> Still moving after truth long sought,
> Will learn new things when I am not.'

(ll. 61–3)

The voice is especially scornful of the protagonist's prospective quest for 'Truth', which he mimics: 'I will go forward, sayest thou, | I shall not fail to find her now' (ll. 190–1). The last defence against the dismal voice is a turning of scepticism upon scepticism, something which Tennyson's early philosophical songs had already played with:[28] ' "If all be dark, vague voice," I said, | "These things are wrapt in doubt and dread, | Nor canst thou show the dead are dead.["]' (ll. 265–7). But the protest stumbles against the manifest tautology – 'the dead are dead' – which it struggles to dispute: a later, better poem will triumphantly claim a paradox, 'the dead are not dead but alive' ('Vastness', R. (iii). 413, l. 36). The poem's protagonist asks the doubting voice:

> 'Who forged that other influence,
> That heat of inward evidence,
> By which he doubts against the sense?[']

(ll. 283–5)

The question means to be confident, but expresses a genuine perplexity ('sense' here meaning the evidence of the senses,

which do not lead one to a belief in immortality).[29] The attempt
to enlist 'doubt' on the side of hope is deft enough; but, as Ricks
happily observes, the choice of 'forged', especially so close to
'evidence', is ingenuously, ingeniously, maladroit;[30] and the
connotations of 'heat' are hardly those of calm-headed refuta-
tion: this kind of double utterance, as though the poem's
protagonist were being more honest than he knew, strikes a
characteristically Tennysonian split note. Belatedly, the second
of the 'two voices' enters the poem to address the speaker, this
time a hopeful and intently uplifting voice; but quiet sorts of
constraint similarly work to qualify anything too single-mind-
edly consolatory. To place trust in 'A hidden hope' (l. 441), for
instance, or to find that 'Nature's living motion lent | The pulse
of hope to discontent' (ll. 449–50), is to inhabit a spiritual state in
which the reasons to celebrate (there is hope) are inextricably
entwined with the reasons not to (hope is hidden; we are
discontent). 'There seemed no room for sense of wrong' (l. 456)
sounds a ringing victory for the hopeful voice; but then
'seemed' has a wary scrupulousness. (It is a nice detail that a
poem entitled 'The Two Voices' should so prominently feature
three, as though instinctively denying any two-sided *'pro* and
con' clarity to the case by including a perplexed voice that speaks
in between: Lewis Carroll's striking parody 'The Three Voices'
saw an opening there.)

For some time, according to his brother-in-law Lushington,
Tennyson had not 'fully made up his mind to what conclusion
he should bring it'; [31] and, while the closing lines that he finally
decided upon appear to have settled upon resolving hope, they
quietly maintain an inconclusive hesitancy that stays true to the
poem's initial bewilderment:

> I marvelled how the mind was brought
> To anchor by one gloomy thought;
>
> And wherefore rather I made choice
> To commune with that barren voice,
> Than him that said, 'Rejoice! Rejoice!'

> (ll. 458–62)

There is something curiously impressed about 'marvelled' for
one thing: the mind ought by now to be frankly incredulous
about at its spell in the dark; and it is, perhaps, a sign of the

70

secret proximity of despair and faith that (as Ricks points out) gloomy thoughts should have brought the mind to a welcome-sounding *anchor* – the 'Supposed Confessions' had looked to *faith* and asked, 'Why not yet | Anchor thy frailty there ?' [32] The poem ends on a *non sequitur*: 'The meditated suicide . . . is arrested, not by an effort of reason or an act of faith, but by the sound of the church bells, and the sight of happy people going to church' (*CH* 188). There is a closing note of rejoicing; but it is an injunction borrowed (in inverted commas) from the second voice, rather than a report of first-person experience; and there is a slightly bluff feel, too, about the ending's sadder-and-wiser puzzlement, as though jumping to an aftermath that has not really been attained: 'choice' hardly seems to have been the point at issue at any stage. (The triplet verse throughout has contributed to the finally irresolved effect, as though awakening local thoughts of purposeful triadic, syllogistic progress – from proposition and counter-proposition to deduction – that are thwarted by the poem at large.) Tennyson's friend Spedding, who saw the work in progress, passed the most acute judgement on the poem's embarrassed spiritual progress, capturing its undecided life in a sharp-eyed parenthesis: 'the design is so grand, and the moral, if there is one, so important that I trust you will not spare any elaboration of execution' (*M.* i. 139). A fine thing to say about so double voiced a poem: 'the moral, if there is one'; and something that might be said as well about many of Tennyson's irresolute poems about willing yourself to come to a decision.

One solution to Arthur Hallam's 'war of conflicting opinions' was *action*, the moral primacy of which was a large part of Apostolic seriousness. Hallam forlornly wrote to Gladstone: 'one day the conflicting elements of my mind may settle into a calm, & I may fulfil the aim of my being in a clear harmony of action' (*HL* 371); Trench, about to throw himself behind the Spanish uprising, wrote hectically to a friend, 'anything seems to me preferable to rotting in England, one's energies turning inward and corrupting: it is action, action, action that we want'.[33] For several members of the group, as for W. H. Auden's generation a hundred years later, Spain was a place where allegiances were defined with a simpler clarity than the domestic scene could supply: where, as Auden would say in 'Spain 1937', 'Our fever's menacing shapes are precise and alive'. Tennyson's equivalent poem, 'Written during the Convulsions in Spain' (R. (i). 53), gratefully resolved the dilemmas of action into simple-hearted apostrophe: 'Rouse thee, Valladolid; | Where are thine heroes hid? | Arm them for combat and shout, *"To the fight!"'* (ll. 31–3). Tennyson was certainly not unmoved by the thought that value is in activity. Hallam Tennyson reports his advice, that a young man 'should embark on his career in the spirit of selfless and adventurous heroism', a lesson glossed in the *Memoir* with lines from 'Œnone', italicized to confirm the point at issue: 'to live by *law*, | *Acting* the law we live by without fear' (*M*. i. 317, 317-18). Tennyson told a friend, squarely: 'to move on is better than to stand still' (*M*. i. 141); but more characteristically in his poetry, and more memorably, voices sure about their progress meet other, complicating kinds of voice, and a compulsion to move on is ever contested by 'energies turning inward' (in Trench's phrase).

The Apostle Kemble wrote in a letter: 'There never was a more hateful sentence written than that "Suave mari magno" of Lucretius.' The tag comes from the opening of book II of *De rerum natura*: in Dryden's translation,

> 'Tis pleasant, safely to behold from shore
> The rowling Ship; and hear the Tempest roar:
> Not that anothers pain is our delight;
> But pains unfelt produce the pleasing sight . . .

and opposition to such Lucretian ease was, Peter Allen suggests, 'an Apostolic commonplace'.[34] Tennyson set about the theme in 'The Lotos-Eaters' (Spedding recognized its Lucretian credentials (*CH* 144)), a poem that at once sets the imperative to act against the desire to suspend action:

> 'Courage!' he said, and pointed toward the land,
> 'This mounting wave will roll us shoreward soon.'
> In the afternoon they came unto a land
> In which it seemèd always afternoon.
> All round the coast the languid air did swoon,
> Breathing like one that hath a weary dream.
> Full-faced above the valley stood the moon;
> And like a downward smoke, the slender stream
> Along the cliff to fall and pause and fall did seem.
>
> (R. (i). 170, ll. 1–9)

(Storm-driven at sea for days, Odysseus lands his men on the Lotos-eaters' island, where his crew promptly becomes addicted to the opiate-like lotos.) Tennyson's abrupt opening establishes a voice of exploit, which the verse then consummately lures into idleness: 'land', at first the object of a determination, makes an unadventurous reappearance in a perfect rhyme (Tennyson originally had 'strand', but thought 'the no rhyme of "land" and "land" was lazier'); while the forward motion described in the opening two lines (riding the wave) lapses into the unprogressive circling of the third and fourth ('In the afternoon . . . always afternoon') – lines that 'touch the key-note of the poem', said Mill (*CH* 91), a happy remark to make of a poem so full of music. The prologue poem is written in the stanza which Spenser used, as William Empson described it, to enact 'the prolonged and diffused energies of his mind';[35] and prolongation and diffuseness characterize Tennyson's lines too: the vigorous bisyllabic bark, 'Courage!', dwindles to the drawling over-extended bisyllable of 'seemèd' – as, a little later, 'tired' will stretch itself lethargically across two syllables (in 'Than tired eyelids upon tired eyes'), 'neither monosyllabic nor disyllabic', as Tennyson said, 'but a dreamy child of the two'. Dreamy recurrences and drawings-out of sound occur throughout the poem, 'dewy echoes calling | From cave to cave' (ll. 139–40): in, for example, 'Lo! in the middle of the wood, | The folded leaf is wooed from out the bud' (ll. 70–1), how lullingly 'wood' extends into 'wooed'; and how unhurried the unfolding of 'wings' into 'wanderings' in 'Nor ever fold our wings, | And cease from wanderings' (ll. 64–5). Armstrong writes well about the island's 'repetition without progression and disjunction without change'.[36]

The druggily reiterative life of the island, 'deep-asleep . . . yet all awake' (l. 35), evokes a familiar Tennysonian fantasy of changelessness ('A land where all things always seemed the same!' (l. 24)), at once monotonous and marvellous: what Sterling found in 'Recollections of the Arabian Nights', 'little progress in imagery, and none in thought . . . undeniable splendour, but somewhat wearying monotony' (*CH* 116). The men are naturally keen to avoid the evidence of change that Tennysonian returns normally provide:

> Then some one said, 'We will return no more;'
> And all at once they sang, 'Our island home
> Is far beyond the wave; we will no longer roam.'

(ll. 43–5)

'Let us alone', they repeatedly sing (ll. 88, 90, 93), preferring, in the Lucretian spirit that Kemble deplored, 'Only to hear and see the far-off sparkling brine' (l. 143). But of course we know from Homer that they are soon to return to that brine, forced back on board by Odysseus, whose undeflected courage, evoked in the first line, hangs tacitly over Tennyson's poem. 'How they got home you must read in Homer,' Croker acidly noted in his review, facetiously adopting the reiterative manners of the island: 'Mr Tennyson – himself, we presume, a dreamy lotos-eater, a delicious lotos-eater, leaves them in full song' (CH 78). It is quite true that Tennyson abandons the narrative with which he began as though he himself were going native;[37] but the thought of a reversion to the life of action does not quite elude the poem. It features in the original ending to the poem within the cordon of a Tennysonian 'no more' ('Oh! islanders of Ithaca, we will return no more' (viii. [40])); and just before that, the first version had the crew protest, 'Surely, surely, slumber is more sweet than toil, the shore | Than labour in the ocean, and rowing with the oar' (viii. [38–9]). How well 'surely' insists on certitude ('Certainly, assuredly') while acknowledging room for doubt ('surely' as 'may not one be sure that . . . ?'(OED)), an equivocation in the word that the echo in 'shore' quietly returns to dwell upon.

For, of course, this poem is anything but sure of the virtues of having 'had enough of action' (l. 150): the condition of mind is deplorable; but nor can the poem quite bring itself to endorse renewed action either. Paul Turner is firm that the doped crew 'in no way represent an ideal: they are merely backsliders from the heroic ideal, whom Odysseus punishes by forcing them back to the boats, shoving them under the benches, and tying them up';[38] and Tennyson's revisions to the poem for its 1842 publication sought to make some such moral clearer by likening the Lotos-eaters' to the 'Epicurean and therefore hard-hearted repose' enjoyed by the Lucretian gods (M. i. 504). But even the later poem still ends in a remarkably irresolved way: you can imagine a Browning monologue on the subject dissecting with acerbic glee the discrepancy between the protracted casuistry of the crew's self-defence and the inebriate self-indulgence of their unheroic appetites; but Tennyson's poem, to its advantage, is altogether less firm-minded. (J. M. Robertson, for one, thought the poem great for quite a different reason, declaring it 'his masterpiece in sheer form and the loveliness of repose' (*CH* 437).) The poem has recently come in for a good deal of intently political rereading, and some critics have discerned in it a fantastical expression of enthusiasm for life in the expanding colonies; but this kind of reading seems to miss the formative ambiguity about action that I have been talking about. The charmed Lotos-eaters lead lives of suspended animation, savingly remote from the enterprise required, say, to sustain an empire; and if, on the other hand, their slothfulness is the point and we are to regard them as shamefully unmanly (an Apostolic finger wags in 'What pleasure can we have | To war with evil?' (ll. 93–4)), then the poem's support for the imperial project is scarcely more straightforward. You could (with Isobel Armstrong) see their doped mindlessness as but another expression of the soul-destroying system that they are forced normally to endure.[39] In a wholly Tennysonian way, their still life on the island is at once luxurious and deadly: no wonder the expats drink so much in the club-house (as much as the workers back home). Anyway, it seems right to concur with Matthew Reynolds that the poem 'offers little encouragement to prospective colonialists'.[40]

'The Lotos-Eaters' lightly dramatizes a division between two voices, between the alluring call of inaction and the heroic claims of decisiveness. The Odyssean virtues reappear in 'Ulysses' (R. (i). 217), written shortly after the death of Hallam, 'under the sense of loss and that all had gone by', but with conviction that 'still life must be fought out to the end' (*IR* 96): Hallam Tennyson records his father saying that the poem 'gave my feeling about the need of going forward, and braving the struggle of life' (*M*. i. 196). A genuinely noble sentiment; but the poem's greatness lies in the complicating feeling with which it dramatizes such a need: that going forward may be driven less by fortitude than by contemptuous world-weariness, and that such tireless pushing-on may be accompanied by an unforgivingly clear-eyed sense of the futility of action. The speaker is

Ulysses (Odysseus), now old, who, long back from his Homeric adventures, summons his men to embark on one last voyage. He has long endured the alienation of a Tennysonian homecoming: a good deal of the distaste with which he regards life evidently stems from the exemplary behaviour of his son Telemachus (Hutton heard him take a 'contemptuous satisfaction in the capacity of Telemachus to fill his place' (*CH* 365)). Ulysses himself, by contrast, is 'idle', the hearth is 'still', and his people are 'a savage race, | That hoard, and sleep, and feed, and know not me' (ll. 1, 2, 4–5). That string of four phrases establishes a rhetorical form which will recur in the poem (ll. 14, 22–3, 70): the three-part phrases normally utilized by the accomplished orator have grown distended, drawn out in a style of fatigued egotism ('and know not *me*'). A kindred lassitude marks the drifting syntactical direction of the opening lines, in which what looks like a regal use of the third person – 'It little profits that an idle king' – only belatedly resolves itself into the grammar of a subordinate clause – 'It little profits that, an idle king . . . I mete and dole'.

The heroizing lines that follow convey a mixture of self-congratulation and weary diminishment, Ulysses' overpowering sense of himself at once a triumph to be gloried in and an unshifting burden to be borne: 'I cannot rest from travel . . . I am become a name . . . I am a part of all that I have met.' Suffering is retrospectively conjured into accomplishment by sheer obduracy of will; but a desolating sense of the emptiness of activity is never far away: in 'For always roaming with a hungry heart | Much have I seen and known', the boast of 'Much' is subtly diminished in the company of 'always' (only 'much'?), and it feels diminished further when we learn that all this boasted experience amounts to nothing much more than an unending preamble.

> Yet all experience is an arch wherethrough
> Gleams that untravelled world, whose margin fades
> For ever and for ever when I move.
> How dull it is to pause, to make an end,
> To rust unburnished, not to shine in use!

(ll. 19–23)

Arnold wittily thought the first three lines 'by themselves take up nearly as much time as a whole book of the *Iliad*'[41] –

extending clauses arise as soon as you feel a sentence has completed itself ('wherethrough . . . whose . . . when'), creating the sense of an end ever receding as you approach it. But is taking up time here really a way of putting off decision – the decision to embark ('Push off' (l. 58)) that Ulysses' speech purports to espouse? W. W. Robson shrewdly notes 'a radical discrepancy between the strenuousness aspired to, and the medium in which the aspiration is expressed'[42] – enterprise competes with lassitude, as happened in 'The Lotos-Eaters', but now both voices resound within Ulysses himself. A sense of defeat quietly swells in the poem's speculative futures and faltering negatives and double negatives:

> but something ere the end,
> Some work of noble note, may yet be done,
> Not unbecoming men that strove with Gods.
>
> (ll. 51–3)

(How deftly the prevailing negative spirit of the lines draws a 'no' each from 'noble' and 'note'.) ''Tis not too late to seek a newer world' (l. 57) beautifully tempers a public call to press on valiantly with a private sense of declining (not a 'new' world, but a 'newer'); and, when Ulysses claims

> my purpose holds
> To sail beyond the sunset, and the baths
> Of all the western stars, until I die . . .
>
> (ll. 59–61)

purpose and aimlessness seem inextricable.

'We say he roams aimlessly,' wrote Goldwin Smith; 'we should rather say, he intends to roam, but stands for ever a listless and melancholy figure on the shore' (CH 188). At the end of the poem, Ulysses is still on land, still speaking, as though immobilized by the conflicting impulses of heroism and defeatism that his closing words intricately entwine; a rousing rhetorical triplet yields at the last minute, moved to deny a counteracting thought of failure:

> One equal temper of heroic hearts,
> Made weak by time and fate, but strong in will
> To strive, to seek, to find, and not to yield.
>
> (ll. 68–70)

77

The verbs offer themselves as grammatical equivalents, intransitively describing actions that are their own end; but the ambition to 'find' might normally be felt to require an object (finding *something*), and the absence of one here emphasizes an uncertainty of goal that Ulysses has already let slip: 'It may be that the gulfs will wash us down, | It may be we shall touch the Happy Isles' (ll. 62–3). Ricks suggests that the last line is accompanied by a shadow line, one that catches the more dejected feelings moving in the poem: 'To strive, to seek, to yield, and not to find.'[43] This is, I think, an effect not seldom associated with Tennyson's willed refusals to mourn. Edward Lear told a story about meeting a man who presumed the poet a reluctant traveller, on the basis of his lines, 'And I will *die* before I see | The palms and temples of the South' (*M*. ii. 45). The lines, from 'You ask me, why, though ill at ease' (R. (i). 195), are really:

> And I will see before I die
> The palms and temples of the South.
>
> (ll. 27–8)

But, after all, Lear's acquaintance had not wholly mistaken the spirit: the hope of any such sight is more deferred ('before I die') than depended upon, and there seems precious little inclination to get moving right now. Tennyson rather yearns to be swept out of himself, reduced to a wonderful passivity, as Shelley in the 'Ode to the West Wind' ('Be thou, Spirit fierce, | My spirit! be thou me, impetuous one!'): 'Yet waft me from the harbour-mouth, | Wild wind! I seek a warmer sky' (ll. 25–6).

Goldwin Smith said sceptically of Tennyson: 'Everywhere we feel the force of circumstances, nowhere the energy of free will' (*CH* 188); and where free will does exercise itself energetically, the results are usually (as Ulysses expects of his own journey) catastrophic. The Lady of Shalott (R. (i). 159) lives a life of enisled immobility until, by an impetuous decision, she breaks the charm that has suspended her being, and springs suddenly into emphatic and purposive action:

> She left the web, she left the loom,
> She made three paces through the room,
> She saw the water-lily bloom,

> She saw the helmet and the plume,
> She looked down to Camelot.

(ll. 109–13)

The stiff price to be paid for this abrupt flash of volition is death: as though under the mysterious compulsion of a dream, laid in her boat and floating down to Camelot, 'Singing in her song she died' (l. 152). When Tennyson returned to a version of the story in *Idylls of the King*, he went out of his way to emphasize that the narrative turns upon the Lady's being momently 'so very wilful':

> Her father's latest word hummed in her ear,
> 'Being so very wilful you must go,'
> And changed itself and echoed in her heart,
> 'Being so very wilful you must die.'

('Lancelot and Elaine', R. (iii). 470, ll. 775–8)

The first version of 'The Lady of Shalott' ends with the Lady's own words, and strikingly announces the individuation which is at once her ruin and the making of her: a parchment upon her breast reads,

> *The charm is broken utterly,*
> *Draw near and fear not – this is I,*
> *The Lady of Shalott.*

(ll. 169–71 n.)

That sounds a note of strange triumph, as though the Lady has achieved a state of belated self-realization – even if, by the darkly comical rules of the Tennysonian universe, it can only be a posthumous achievement. The later, revised version ends, also remarkably but quite differently, with the moved inconsequence of Lancelot not knowing what to make of it all:

> 'She has a lovely face;
> God in his mercy lend her grace,
> The Lady of Shalott.'

(ll. 169–71)

The aftermath of action is often a space of distracted, morbid wonderment in Tennyson: doing and dying prove as nearly synonymous as homophonous for the Lady of Shalott as they do for the foredoomed Light Brigade (R. (ii). 315), at whose 'wild charge', Tennyson twice says, 'All the world wondered' (ll. 31, 52). Action and death are also one and the same in 'Tiresias' (R. (i). 219), in which the sage seeks to persuade Menœceus to save Thebes, something he can do only by killing himself: 'Nobly to do, nobly to die' (l. 119).

The disastrousness of decision appears as classical myth in 'Œnone' (R. (i). 164). Paris, a shepherd but also a Prince of Troy, must choose between three goddesses, Aphroditè, Pallas, and Herè; and he chooses Aphroditè, who laughingly promises him 'The fairest and most loving wife in Greece' (l. 183). This turns out to be Helen, wife of Menelaus: Paris's successful seduction of her is destined to cause a terrible war and ultimately the fall of Troy, the burning catastrophe glimpsed in the last lines. In the meantime, the atmosphere is savagely still:

> For now the noonday quiet holds the hill:
> The grasshopper is silent in the grass:
> The lizard, with his shadow on the stone,
> Rests like a shadow, and the winds are dead.

(ll. 24–7)

The judgement scene, as Œnone recalls witnessing it, might promise a clear logic: Herè offers Paris power, which she conceives in a literal-minded sort of way ('homage, tax and toll, | From many an inland town and haven large' (ll. 114–15)); while Pallas appeals to a life of upright Kantian rectitude ('Self-reverence, self-knowledge, self-control' (l. 142)). Œnone's view, expressed unheard at the time, is that Paris should choose Pallas, which feels like an Apostolic stance, and Tennyson quoted the lines himself in later years as a memo of the good life (M. i. 317–18): Paris opting for Aphroditè seems squarely like the victory of sensuality over conscience.[44] But the poem is actually less simply didactic than that; Tennyson muddies the clarity of the decision by complicating what is on offer.[45] Herè's power seems curiously otherworldly, given the worldliness of its finances ('men, in power | Only, are likest gods, who have attained | Rest in a happy place and quiet seats | Above the thunder' (ll. 127–30)); while Pallas appears quickly to recognize that her pitch ('to live by law, | Acting the law we live by without fear' (ll. 145–6)) sounds too selfless to be terribly winning, and anxiously insists on the benefits, not so very far from 'self-profit', that her personal devotion would bring him: 'rest thee sure | That I shall love thee well and cleave to thee' (ll. 156–7). No wonder that Paris is left wondering what to do (l. 165); the choice is imponderable. At least Aphroditè's alternative seems uncomplicated, and Paris promptly goes for it, a decision made while Œnone has her eyes shut (ll. 184–5); but even Aphroditè's offer is tangled. To promise 'the fairest wife', without mentioning that the wife in question is someone else's, is a piece of divine dissembling, as Richard Cronin says: 'it is the domestic disguise rather than the adulterous substance that tempts'.[46]

What looks like a dramatic scenario of parabolic intelligibility turns out to be, instead, a tale about the treacherously ambiguous gifts that gods give – like the immortality that Aurora grants to Tithonus, while omitting to grant him eternal youth: no wonder Aphroditè was laughing. Paris's story, in Tennyson's hands, is not really a myth of decision, in which the hero chooses virtue over pleasure (as in the noble choice of Hercules) or fails to (which would be simply wrong-headed); it is a myth of indecision: the poem dramatizes the extreme difficulty of choosing at all in so fickle a universe, where outcomes prove so wholly unknowable. (Culler says that Paris's error is 'in choosing any one of the goddesses over another', which he takes to be 'the traditional Renaissance interpretation of the myth'.[47]) In the aftermath of Paris's decision, Œnone, like Mariana and many other Tennysonian characters, longs to die; but (also like Mariana) her wish is premature, and she does not die yet: the reiterations of her speech enact a kind of suspended animation, biding time before decision. (W. David Shaw: 'her circling syntax is necessary as a psychological defense, a stay against confusion.'[48]) Fearful intimations of the future begin to gather in the poem's last verses; Œnone, all at once quite unlike Mariana, is filled with a sense of 'far-off doubtful purpose' and sudden, apocalyptic determination ('I will rise and go' (ll. 247, 257)): like the Lady of Shalott's, this abrupt decisiveness will inevitably lead to catastrophe, and the sense of 'fiery thoughts' (l. 242) is pressing (Œnone is eventually to perish on a flaming pyre).

Paris is only one of many Tennysonians who find it impossibly hard to make up his mind: the Lady of Shalott acts

81

precipitously, but even she had grown only 'half sick of shadows' (l. 71). Half-mindedness of one sort or another crops up all the time, as a quick look in the *Concordance* will confirm: the impressive poet portrayed in 'The Ante-Chamber' (R. (i). 207), originally an introductory poem to 'The Gardener's Daughter', enjoys but 'some half-consciousness of inward power' (l. 8); in 'The Death of the Old Year', Tennyson glumly confides, 'I've half a mind to die with you, | Old year, if you must die' (R. (i). 182, ll. 26–7). Being neither one thing nor another is a recurrent Tennysonian state, sometimes a pleasure: the liberation of the mermaid world (R. (i). 76, 77) derived chiefly, as Leigh Hunt suggested, from its 'half-human, half-fishy sympathy' (*CH* 131), neither wholly familiar nor quite alien. The Lotos-eaters are looking forward to their own version of semi-existence:

> How sweet it were, hearing the downward stream,
> With half-shut eyes ever to seem
> Falling asleep in a half-dream!
>
> (ll. 99–101)

But such half-minded pleasures are dubious too: being neither one thing nor another is hardly an Odyssean virtue. The testing first voice in 'The Two Voices' scorns the protagonist for possessing 'a divided will' (l. 106); and the striking little poem 'Will' sets out with programmatic purpose to celebrate the inner strength that comes of single-mindedness:

> O well for him whose will is strong!
> He suffers, but he will not suffer long;
> He suffers, but he cannot suffer wrong . . .
>
> (R. (ii). 310, ll. 1–3)

Well, Pallas might have said so too; even bibulous Will Waterproof, moved by Dutch courage, protests himself set on a resolute singleness of mind: 'I will not cramp my heart, nor take | Half-views of men and things' (R. (ii). 267, ll. 51–2).

Admirably wilful men of such resolution occasionally feature in Tennyson, the Duke of Wellington most remarkably, 'Whose life was work' and who relentlessly pursued 'The path of duty' ('Ode on the Death of the Duke of Wellington', R. (ii). 309, ll. 183, 210):

> Let his great example stand
> Colossal, seen of every land,
> And keep the soldier firm, the statesman pure . . .

(ll. 220–2)

At one stage, probably, Tennyson thought about incorporating the poem 'Will' into the Wellington 'Ode' (R. (ii). 310, headnote); and the Duke certainly exemplifies the virtues nominated by the shorter poem: unchanging ('In praise and in dispraise the same, | A man of well-attempered frame' (ll. 73–4)), an 'ever-loyal iron leader' (l. 229); firm enough, like a rock, to build upon: 'On God and Godlike men we build our trust' (l. 266). But it is not finicky to find this undeviatingly godlike giant of an example, 'Whole in himself' (l. 26), monstrously alien: the poem nicely glimpses the stiff gaucherie of the great man's common touch in 'No more in soldier fashion will be greet | With lifted hand the gazer in the street' (ll. 21–2). The completion of the poem's protracted act of laying to rest is accompanied by something not unlike relief: 'that relief of a nation', as Peter Conrad spryly observes, 'which can now relax, with no exorbitant victor to rouse it'.[49] The duke's superhuman indomitability of purpose identifies him with his actions (so his afterlife must be more work (ll. 255–8)) – rather as Tennyson thought Thomas Becket single-mindedly 'lost himself in the idea'. (Tennyson thought well of Becket, whose will was certainly strong, while regarding his 'enthusiasm' with some disquiet (*M.* ii. 195).) In the poem 'Will', the man of singular will is said to stand, dukelike, a rock against the blast, while the weak-willed, 'bettering not with time', unprogressively wanders about a desert of irresolution: the moral could not seem clearer, until the poem successfully confuses the issue at the last minute.

> He seems as one whose footsteps halt,
> Toiling in immeasurable sand,
> And o'er a weary sultry land,
> Far beneath a blazing vault,
> Sown in a wrinkle of the monstrous hill,
> The city sparkles like a grain of salt.

(ll. 15–20)

The unachievable city's salty sterility comes as a surprise, almost like a joke, were the line not so splendid: has the object of the

83

strenuous will's long toiling really been so barren? (The spectacle looks much grander from down here.) The joke is bleak enough, in implication not so unlike the character in Samuel Beckett who bitterly reproaches 'this bitch of an earth'; but Tennyson's lines carry it off with a self-delighting pleasure in the fantasy landscape and its quiet surrealism ('wrinkle'). 'Will' quite inverts the sequence that a more obviously doctrinaire poem would have assumed (in which error is superceded by virtue), and so clouds its forthright moral: the poem ends dwelling wonderingly in the imaginative life of weak-willedness, finally released into the homeground of a Tennysonian landscape.[50]

Several of Tennyson's poems treat strong-willed decisiveness with rather more than such *sotto voce* reservation: as a subject of psycho-pathological fascination, even fascinated repulsion. The anti-heroic speaker of 'St Simeon Stylites' (R. (i). 210), written about the same time as 'The Two Voices' (to which it is a kind of complement), has a single-minded and lofty sense of rectitude that is comically appalling. (Tennyson read the poem with 'grotesque Grimness', FitzGerald records, 'especially at such passages as "Coughs, Aches, Stitches, etc.", laughing aloud at times' (R., headnote).) The moribund Simeon has lived agonizingly on a pillar for years, seeking to prove his suitability for sainthood by a life of ostentatiously cruel self-punishment: Leigh Hunt much admired its portrait of 'the sordid and the aspiring – the selfish and the self-sacrificing – the wretched, weak body and mind and resolute soul' (*CH* 133). The implicit joke running through the poem is nice: that one who protests his baseness and lowliness should choose to live at a great height above everyone else, as though his subconscious were inadvertently betraying his fantasies of spiritual superiority; but Tennyson can work more delicately with the confusions of genuine humility and self-deception too. The poem's hauntingly great line is 'And lower voices saint me from above' (l. 152), which, like the poem at large, teeters between a superb conviction and a dreadful lack of final sureness: the heavenly voices from on high concur with the crowd's acclaim, but sound worryingly 'lower' – softer and fainter, as befits an angelic calm, but also perhaps (for the voices might be but in his head) baser, more self-interested.

The poem defers a final judgement on Simeon's holiness: it makes a satirical twist on Tennysonian suspendedness, for everyone is waiting for the end, and for Simeon to fall. (Tennyson arranges a line ending to play teasingly with the idea ('and oft I fall, | Maybe for months, in such blind lethargies' (ll. 100–1)), momentarily co-opting us into the crowd of bystanders waiting ghoulishly for the end.) Attempting to prove to God (and to himself) the severity of his dedication, Simeon constructs pentameter-stretching lists of woes undergone ('Rain, wind, frost, heat, hail, damp, and sleet, and snow' (l. 16)) and lunatic pedantries of arithmetical suffering :

> Then, that I might be more alone with thee,
> Three years I lived upon a pillar, high
> Six cubits, and three years on one of twelve;
> And twice three years I crouched on one that rose
> Twenty by measure; last of all, I grew
> Twice ten long weary weary years to this,
> That numbers forty cubits from the soil.
>
> (ll. 84–90)

The crazy extremism ('more alone' picks up 'More slowly-painful', 'More than this' (ll. 56, 68)) is at once boastful and reproachful ('while thou and all the saints | Enjoy themselves in heaven' (ll. 103-4)): Tennyson does not come closer to the unwittingly self-betraying verbosity of Browning's monologuists than this. Keen to become a name (like Ulysses), he names himself ('I, Simeon') obsessively (ll. 157–61): his need for reassurance, darkly entwined with his desire for death, is a monstrous version of the predicament of mind portrayed in 'The Two Voices' and elsewhere; and, as in that poem, the possibility of reassurance is not exactly gratified (we are not certain of his sanctification), and not quite ungratified either (we do not know for sure he is a self-deluding fraud), but left hanging.

Vehemence of opinion also goes along with instability of mind in 'Locksley Hall' (R. (ii). 271), which Kingsley thought the poem of Tennyson's with 'most influence on the minds of the young men of our day' (CH 178). The poem has the skeleton of a plot: child of an Indian army family, orphaned and brought up by a selfish uncle (ll. 155–6), the narrator has lost his shallow-hearted cousin Amy to an unworthy but richer rival. The thought of it has turned the speaker's head: 'He will hold thee, when his passion shall have spent its novel force, | Something better than his dog, a little dearer than his horse' (ll. 49–50) – how cleverly the phrase 'He will hold thee' (really meaning 'He will judge thee') separates itself out for a space, voicing the dark sexual jealousy that accompanies his ostensibly sympathetic concern. Mind-occupying action – 'I myself must mix with action' (l. 98) – is the only possible solution to the self-destroying thought, 'Can I but relive in sadness?' (l. 107): a marvellous verb, *relive*, for what protagonists of Tennysonian paralysis do instead of *living*. Despite a utopian glimpse of a new dispensation, 'In the Parliament of man, the Federation of the world' (l. 128), the speaker lapses back into an ugly contempt, fantasizing about migration to a exotically distant island: 'There the passions cramped no longer shall have scope and breathing space; | I will take some savage woman, she shall rear my dusky race' (ll. 167–8). The lines are full of spiteful sexual disgust and have received their share of deploring commentary; but, as Gabriel Pearson once said well of some flashes of lurid malice in a poem by T. S. Eliot, 'It is pointless merely to execrate because execration is precisely what the poem seeks to provoke.'[51] Tennyson is portraying a poisonous combination of sexual aggression, imperialist race-hatred, and deep self-loathing – though whether the lightly sketched dramatic context provides quite enough sanction is another question, as is whether the portrayal of the obnoxious emotions gains much from the speaker's anxious protestations of his infirmity ('I *know* my words are wild' (l. 173)). 'We have the impression of something left unsaid or imperfectly rendered', B. C. Southam says of the poem, 'of effect without cause'.[52] The dark genius of *Maud* will embrace that perplexity of cause and effect as its central subject.

For all its impelling stridency, 'Locksley Hall' remains quite as irresolved as 'St Simeon Stylites': notwithstanding the speaker's clamorous investment in the idea of action, his is another poem of matters pending. To say one must *mix* oneself with action feels subtly odd, says Ricks, as though an attempt to evade the balder thought of simply *acting*; and, despite some sort of enterprise seeming his best hope of salvation, the speaker shows all the Tennysonian disinclination to move on that we have seen in 'Ulysses' and elsewhere: the 'long farewell' (l. 189) he bids to Locksley Hall is lengthy not only in the amount of time likely to elapse before he sees it again. And this is the sporadically unhinged voice to which Tennyson entrusts his most resonant proclamation of progress: 'Not in vain the distance beacons. Forward, forward let us range, | Let the great world spin for ever down the ringing grooves of change' (ll. 181–2); and yet, how quietly undermining is the verb the speaker has chosen ('range': 'to rove, roam, wander, stray' (*OED*)), as though quietly embracing a fundamental aimlessness at the very moment he is cheering for a purposive march forward.

3

████████████████████████████████

The Story and the Songs

> Between the motion
> And the act
> Falls the Shadow . . .
>
> (T. S. Eliot)

A story is normally obliged to make progress of a kind too: to have things happen with purpose, so as to satisfy that 'desire for orderly narration' that George Eliot once strikingly identified as a mark of growing up.[1] Tennyson read novels voraciously, and much admired *Vanity Fair* (*IR* 148, 113); and he was, by all reports, a marvellous teller of stories in the flesh, 'told with such lifelike reality, that they convulsed his hearers with laughter' (*M.* ii. 461).[2] But in his poetry, says T. S. Eliot, 'Tennyson could not tell a story at all';[3] at least, his storytelling in verse (of which there is a good deal) is customarily odd, marked by a kind of imaginative vacillation, analogous to those I have been describing in the previous chapter: a wavering between the purposeful business of narrative and curiously regressive counter-currents of feeling and idiom that embarrass the proper ambitions of plot. (A progress, W. David Shaw reminds us, is a kind of poem as well as a sort of movement, like Gray's 'Progress of Poesy', in which a history gradually unfolds along a learning curve: a Tennysonian example would be 'The Palace of Art', the relationship of which to the traditional sequentiality of the 'progress' genre is almost parodically evasive.[4]) With admiring good humour, Henry James said of Tennyson's language, 'When he wishes to represent movement, the phrase always seems to me to pause and slowly pivot upon itself, or at most to move backward.'[5] It was an unprogressive gift, which (as James thought) necessitated the failure of any attempt Tennyson might make to dramatize action. Certainly, gathering events to a denoument promises to be uphill work for a poet who finds his instinctive subject matter in things that are still to occur: picturesquely, like Galahad, questing for the grail, but not reaching it yet; or mundanely, like a walk to meet the mail, which, by the poem's end, is still only just about to arrive (R. (ii). 234, 273); or with alarming jollity, as in 'The Voyage', an upbeat *Ancient Mariner*, which describes a trip that never ends ('We know the merry world is round, | And we may sail for evermore' (R. (ii). 257, ll. 95–6)).

Simply getting things to happen can prove mysteriously difficult: 'The irony of all Tennyson's most haunting poems, including the *Idylls'*, as John Bayley once put it, 'is that if anything happens it happens outside them';[6] and the irony underwrites Tennyson's long career as a writer of narrative verse, sometimes, as in 'The Lover's Tale' and 'The Gardener's Daughter', producing an unadmitted sort of comedy, like the dislocations of a dream. ('The Captain' (R. (ii). 230) is a winning example of Tennyson's narrative interest in inactivity: the story turns on the crew refusing to act at all.) When the Southern Mariana dreamed of her lover, 'She felt he was and was not there' (R.(i). 160, l. 50): she was asleep, but a similar haziness about what is afoot often permeates Tennyson's supposedly wakeful narratives too. Perhaps the most telling case here is *The Princess*, a boldly conceived (though, increasingly, a timidly executed) attempt to tackle a current *issue*; and the poem nicely shows how, for Tennyson, the attempt to work out a progressive position on politics quickly interweaves itself with more private dilemmas of poetic voice – another instance of Eliot's law, then, that the accomplishment of Tennyson's technique is intimate with his depths. For the attempt to imagine the trajectory of a political experiment and to enact debate about it obliges *The Princess* to be a narrative poem, and so throws down the challenge of imagining progress in an obvious and quite normal way: the directed movement of a story, with its necessary stage-management of motive and consequence and outcome. As I shall be saying, *The Princess* is an absorbing failure idiomatically (and a less respectable failure ideologically); and similar obstacles present themselves before *Idylls of the King*, the episodic Arthurian cycle that occupied most of Tennyson's later years. In principle, the *Idylls* possess all the raw ingredients of compelling ethical drama; but in practice the task of imagining its human density is repeatedly waylaid; really, the poem's real protagonist is its own preoccupying style, something that both enchants and disconcerts its author. Perhaps uncoincidentally, by that stage in his career, Tennyson's fatalism (which was always strong) had grown, and his investment in the global idea of progress, normally troubled anyway, had dwindled.[7] The curiously impeding texture of the verse embodies the poem's deepest instincts, that decision and activity are already incorporate in implacable and impersonal patterns of determination and undoing. A normal story can work its progress through this viscous idiom only with ostentatious difficulty, so giving rise to one of the most characteristic qualities of Tennyson's narrative verse: what Hutton saw, most brilliantly, as 'the air of moving through a resisting medium' (CH 365). Of the longer poems, only *Maud* discovers a kind of solution, by embracing resistance: the poem ingeniously accepts the imponderable status of action in the Tennysonian universe and conjures Bayley's 'irony' into a new dramatic principle. Where the *Idylls* tries to imagine, in the third person, the historical trajectory of an entire society, *Maud* is firmly cast as a monologue, so what might elsewhere have appeared narrative shortcomings can, deftly handled, justify themselves as evidence of a psychological pathology; and I end this chapter by saying something about that peculiar achievement.

'Locksley Hall' ends with one of Tennyson's best departure lines: 'For the mighty wind arises, roaring seaward, and I go' (l. 194), after which the poem must leave its speaker to an uncertain future (does he go?). Still, for all its infirmity of purpose, that takes a step nearer action than, say, Mariana managed: 'and a step, too, in the right direction', praised Kingsley, admiring the way 'Locksley Hall' resisted the brooding incapacity of dark romanticism, 'just because it *is* a step forward . . . forward on the road on which God has been leading him' (CH 179). 'If Alfred Tennyson could only make that long wail, like the winter wind, about Mariana in the Moated Grange', said Carlyle, 'and could not get her to throw herself into the ditch, or could not bring her another man to help her ennui, he had much better have left her alone altogether'.[8] The

90

point is inimitably Carlyle's: 'not in turning back, not in resisting, but only in resolutely struggling forward, does our life consist';[9] but the sentiment also participates, in its idiosyncratic way, in a more general spirit of the age. Matthew Campbell plausibly suggests that Arnold had 'Mariana' in mind when he protested, not so dissimilarly to Carlyle, about poetry 'in which the suffering finds no vent in action; in which a continuous state of mental distress is prolonged, unrelieved by incident, hope, or resistance; in which there is everything to be endured, nothing to be done'.[10]

For Carlyle and Arnold, a type of ethics implies a manner of writing: a moral commitment to the life of action naturally goes along with the artistic duty to *represent* action – getting Mariana to *do* something, relieving a stasis of distress by some redeeming *incident*. Aubrey de Vere presumably had some such point in mind when he colourfully complained about the poet: 'Why will not Tennyson give up absurdities of every kind – the errors of his morbid, Germanized, and smoke-sodden temperament; and set about writing like a man?'[11] Such awkward feelings about poetry's close alliance with passivity and Hamlet-like incapacity form a principal part of the Victorian poets' Romantic inheritance, a counterpoint to the Messianic sense of poetic vocation. Keats had fretted exemplarily in *The Fall of Hyperion* about the precise difference between a healthful poet ('A humanist, physician to all men') and a vexingly idle dreamer; and the same restless self-consciousness persists through to the twentieth century – as witnessed in Yeats's tendentious dismissal of Wilfred Owen from his *Oxford Book of Modern Verse* ('passive suffering is not a theme for poetry'). Carlyle proposed to Tennyson a robust solution to such scrupulous problems: FitzGerald recalled Carlyle 'assiduous in exhorting him to leave Verse and Rhyme, and to apply his genius to Prose' – he was 'a life-guardsman spoilt by making poetry' (*M*. i. 188). But for Tennyson, as for Keats and Yeats, the problems of art were themselves raw material for art: objections against poetry did not curtail it, but found themselves incorporated into it.

A gruff Carlylean voice is heard in 'The Golden Year', for instance. 'Doubt of any sort cannot be removed except by Action,' Carlyle pronounced in *Sartor Resartus*: 'Produce! Produce! . . . Work while it is called Today.'[12] 'What stuff is

91

this!' cries old James in Tennyson's poem, 'old, but full | Of force and choler' (R. (ii). 276, ll. 64, 60–1), dismissing poetical talk of some great era to come, and advocating instead the solving immediacy of activity:

> ' . . . well I know
> That unto him who works, and feels he works,
> This same grand year is ever at the doors.'

(ll. 71–3)

That is doughty and almost wholly unconvincing, and the grand imperative it announces is immediately placed, by an inspired *non sequitur*, within the context of actual work, which has been going on throughout the poem but so far unnoticed:

> He spoke; and, high above, I heard them blast
> The steep slate-quarry, and the great echo flap
> And buffet round the hills, from bluff to bluff.

(ll. 74–6)

Ricks rightly praises the choice of 'them' as just the right pronoun for *those* anonymous workers, taken for granted while their dignity is loftily philosophized;[13] and the lines nicely imply, without overpointing, a contrast between Old James's verbal explosion ('He spoke') and the real thing (what *they* did), the explosion going on over his head ('o'erhead' was a manuscript reading for 'high above'). This work might be intended to stand for something exemplarily wholesome, as though to confirm the abstractions of Old James's moralism in the valour of real labour; but then again it might as well sound a much less comforting note of sudden destruction, threateningly close, undermining the pretensions of all such talk: the suspension of judgement is finely caught in the irresolved Tennysonian cadence of the last lines.

But in one way, of course, the closing lines of 'The Golden Year' indicate that a very clear decision has indeed been made, an idiomatic one: the poem leaves behind the contentious voices and assumed positions that have constituted its purposeful and timely debate, and loses itself in a self-sufficing release of Tennysonian noise. You quickly come to recognize a highly idiosyncratic transition in register that punctuates the poetry's progress:

> Then said the fat-faced curate, Edward Bull:
> 'God made the woman for the use of man,
> And for the good and increase of the world.'
> And I and Edwin laughed; and now we paused
> About the windings of the marge to hear
> The soft wind blowing over meadowy holms
> And alders, garden-isles; and now we left
> The clerk behind us, I and he, and ran
> By ripply shallows of the lisping lake,
> Delighted with the freshness and the sound.
>
> ('Edwin Morris or, The Lake', R. (ii). 275, ll. 90–9)

The verse leaves the dreary cleric behind too, finding a momentary release from its proficiency in telling a tale, and delights instead in sound ('By ripply shallows of the lisping lake, | Delighted with the freshness and the sound'). Tennysonian narrative repeatedly slips away from incident and anecdote, just like that, to find sonic pleasures or the musical splendour of Tennyson lightscapes, like the lingering last line of 'Edwin Morris' ('and overhead | The light cloud smoulders on the summer crag' (ll. 146–7)), or the resonant close of 'Audley Court':

> So sang we each to either, Francis Hale,
> The farmer's son, who lived across the bay,
> My friend; and I, that having wherewithal,
> And in the fallow leisure of my life
> A rolling stone of here and everywhere,
> Did what I would; but ere the night we rose
> And sauntered home beneath a moon, that, just
> In crescent, dimly rained about the leaf
> Twilights of airy silver, till we reached
> The limit of the hills; and as we sank
> From rock to rock upon the glooming quay,
> The town was hushed beneath us: lower down
> The bay was oily calm; the harbour-buoy,
> Sole star of phosphorescence in the calm,
> With one green sparkle ever and anon
> Dipt by itself, and we were glad at heart.
>
> ('Audley Court', R. (ii). 274, ll. 73–88)

The verse frankly admits the antithetical nature of its poetic voices with a 'but', scarcely bothering to negotiate the poetry from a conversational register – 'The farmer's son, who lived across the bay' and the slangy drollery of 'wherewithal' – to the rapt, deepening, suspended night-piece of the last lines, which gently sparkle with a life as autonomous as that of the dipping buoy ('by itself'). The last phrase is really little more than a decent piece of tidying-up, a gesture at a conclusion; something had to be said.

The charm of 'Audley Court', like many of the poems Tennyson grouped as 'English Idyls', lies in that kind of studied emptiness or waywardness. In 'Audley Court' the protagonists have a picnic (we learn the contents in some detail (ll. 21–6)); Francis sings a song (with the burden, 'let me live my life' (l. 42)), to which the narrator replies with a lullaby he remembers from a book he picked up at an auction (l. 57); and then come the closing lines I have just quoted. Song enters the narrative and quickly overpowers it: getting things to happen is a challenge not only for the Carlylean moralist, it turns out, but for the lyricist too – as some of Tennyson's earlier attempts at tales show with unwitting comedy. 'The Lover's Tale', a heavily passionate account of love lost, obscures the incidents of its notional tale in thick mists of fantastic verbalism, and it is often hard to know quite what is going on:

> We turned: our eyes met: hers were bright, and mine
> Were dim with floating tears, that shot the sunset
> In lightnings round me; and my name was borne
> Upon her breath. Henceforth my name has been
> A hallowed memory like the names of old,
> A centered, glory-circled memory,
> And a peculiar treasure, brooking not
> Exchange or currency: and in that hour
> A hope flowed round me, like a golden mist
> Charmed amid eddies of melodious airs,
> A moment, ere the onward whirlwind shatter it,
> Wavered and floated . . .

> (R. (i). 153, i. 431–2)

Verse could hardly go about the task of a tale with less direction; agency disappears in grammatical constructions of hallucinatory passiveness: 'my name was borne | Upon her breath' (not, 'She spoke my name'); 'A hope flowed round me' (not, 'I entertained a hope'). The poem evokes experience so intensely subjective that it has become practically solipsistic ('Even then the stars |

Did tremble in their stations as I gazed' (ll. 570–1)); and even the
discovery of his rival's name is somehow found, exuded from an
engulfing state of feeling, rather than something he is simply
told:

> The written secrets of her inmost soul
> Lay like an open scroll before my view,
> And my eyes read, they read aright, her heart
> Was Lionel's . . .

(i. 577–83 n.)

So stood the strangely bathetic narrative climax in 1832, anyway;
the recalcitrantly objective detail of someone else's *name* was
eased out in the revised version (replaced not altogether
successfully by a melodramatic cry: '*Another!*' (l. 583)): for the
poem really lives wholly within its charmed 'magic cirque of
memory' (ii. 157), 'O day which did enwomb that happy hour'
(i. 475).

'The Gardener's Daughter' (R. (i). 208), one of the English
Idyls, veers with rather more command between a charmed
lyrical stasis and the narrative business of wooing. She is the
daughter of the garden, 'the garden that I love' (l. 34), more than
she is of the gardener; she is a kind of Eve in a kind of Eden (ll.
141–3 n., 187), into which she merges, 'a Rose | In roses, mingled
with her fragrant toil' (ll. 141–2):

> From the woods
> Came voices of the well-contented doves.
> The lark could scarce get out his notes for joy,
> But shook his song together as he neared
> His happy home, the ground. To left and right,
> The cuckoo told his name to all the hills;
> The mellow ouzel fluted in the elm;
> The redcap whistled; and the nightingale
> Sang loud, as though he were the bird of day.

(ll. 87–95)

This narrator is lucky in love, though luck is hardly the point,
since there seem no real obstacles to be overcome, and the story
has little narrative draw of any kind. More interested in evoking
the luxuriance of Tennysonian suspendedness than in creating
suspense, it offers an alluring fantasy of effortless fulfilment:

95

> my desire, like all strongest hopes,
> By its own energy fulfilled itself,
> Merged in completion . . .
>
> (ll. 232–4)

(Like *all* strongest hopes? A less charmed Tennyson would stay sharply aware of the possible non-fulfilment of even the strongest.) A manuscript version enquires:

> Would you rather learn
> Amplier detailed how these spring shoots of love
> Through circumstantial changes, prosperously
> Accomplishing all grades of increase, rose . . .
>
> (ll. 234–8 n.)

But no such circumstantial details are on offer here. Indeed, so innately counter-narrative are the poem's instincts, so absent any thought of a proper denoument, that the narrator does not know how to bring his poem to a stop: 'Shall I cease here?' he asks, but carries on; 'Here, then, my words have end,' he says, only to continue (ll. 231, 245). The delayed close restores us to the present, and makes a game attempt to psychologize the tale's dreamy exorbitance: the gardener's daughter has died, and the narrator is unveiling to a visitor her portrait as a young woman, 'the idol of my youth' (l. 271). 'Idol' is nice there: the word had appeared in 'Supposed Confessions' (R. (i). 78, ll. 179, 180), meaning 'false mental images', and its appearance in 'The Gardener's Daughter' similarly carries a sense of moral short-coming, as though belatedly acknowledging the element of delusion or fantasy in the tale (but rather too late for us to recast the poem as a dramatic exhibition of its idealizing speaker).[14] 'Idol' also crosses paths, in punning self-criticism, with Tennyson's generic label, the 'Idyl'.[15] (What Tennyson meant to imply by 'idyl' is difficult firmly to say, no doubt because he did not firmly mean anything by it; but, whatever else, a pictorial quality seems importantly involved, with a sense of highly self-conscious artfulness.[16]) That an idyllic turn of mind might be put to a more strenuous and worldly sort of purpose, ideological as well as narrative, was the ambition of *The Princess*, yet another story about wooing a young woman: its anxiously self-conscious imaginative incoherence records in a peculiarly exposed way the Tennysonian perplexities that poems like 'The

Gardener's Daughter' find themselves discovering more intuitively.

Aubrey de Vere, who urged upon Tennyson the duty of writing like a man, was doubtless pleased to hear the poet 'denouncing exotics, and saying that a poem should reflect the time and the place' (*L.* i. 238); but that was always likely to prove a stiff task for a poet who had felt since a boy 'the passion of the past' and confessed, 'it is the distance that charms me in the landscape, the picture and the past, and not the immediate today in which I move' (*IR* 92). *The Princess* was the immensely equivocal result: Tennyson's attempt to tackle firm-mindedly a contemporary question, and be 'more than ever the poet of the day' (*CH* 180); but a poem that is, as Elaine Jordan has well said, 'in more than one mind'.[17] (Writing like a man turns out to mean writing about women.) Some disabling obliquity in the realization of so timely a project is comically obvious at once, for most of the poem takes place, not in the time and the place at all, but in the charmed distance of a dimly chivalric past. A Prince (the narrator) finds his long-arranged marriage to Ida, a neighbouring Princess, scuppered by the intended's refusal to go along with the plan; and so, heavily in love with the idea of Ida, he travels to her country with some friends to plead his suit. They learn that she has founded an all-female academy that men must not enter, but on pain of death; and nothing daunted, they dress up as women and enrol. The friends in drag accompany the Princess on a field trip, where their true identities are revealed: she angrily rejects the Prince's suit and ejects them; but now his misogynistic father turns up in bellicose mood, and a violent jousting competition ensues for the Princess's hand (possibly: v. 395–6). The Prince ends up badly wounded and deep in a trance, at which point the women's academy promptly turns itself to a hospital to tend for the injured; Ida herself nurses the Prince back to health. Once better, he declares his love again, evinces an appropriately enlightened attitude towards marriage; and they end the poem betrothed (though we do not actually hear her agree).

A story that 'seems scarcely pro-feminist', as Paul Turner drily remarks;[18] but Tennyson means, at least, to be progressive. He was genuinely much concerned with the question of higher education for women, one of 'the two great social questions impending in England' (the other was care of the poor (*M*. i. 249)); he had written with some visionary force about the 'insult, shame, and wrong' endured by women in 'A Dream of Fair Women' (R. (i). 173, l. 19), and remained sympathetically interested in the question of women's rights.[19] The course of his story is supposed to be significant, as it should be in 'a parable', which is what he described it as (*M*. i. 249), in which 'all, as in some piece of art, | Is toil cöoperant to an end' (*IM* cxxviii. 23–4); and, in particular, the marital settlement, the end meant to be in view, bears an exemplary weight, representing a mutually concessive step forward for both parties, and a 'type' for the future relation of the sexes:

> [']either sex alone
> Is half itself, and in true marriage lies
> Nor equal, nor unequal: each fulfils
> Defect in each, and always thought in thought,
> Purpose in purpose, will in will, they grow,
> The single pure and perfect animal,
> The two-celled heart beating, with one full stroke,
> Life.'
>
> (vii. 283–9)

The rhythms there are managed with great poise, the interactive dualism-in-unity of marriage acted out by the well-paced movement of the pairings ('thought in thought, | Purpose in purpose, will in will') toward a 'single' organism, 'two-celled' but with 'one' stroke, and finally absorbed within the numinously encompassing monosyllable, 'Life'. The girlish prince (i. 1–3) is redeemed from the self-absorbed idealism of his youthful sentimentality, and Ida is restored from the 'theories' of both autonomy ('living wills, and sphered | Whole in ourselves and owed to none' (iv. 129–30)) and gender equivalence with which she has been indoctrinated, 'Maintaining that with equal husbandry | The woman were an equal to the man' (i. 128, 129–30): the pun in 'husbandry' is sprightly. ('Theory' is a bad word throughout the poem.)

But, if *The Princess* were meant to contain 'Tennyson's solution', as a critic put it, 'of the problem of the true position of woman in society – a profound and vital question',[20] several things conspire against. For one thing, there is a lot wrong with the antithetical positions that the poem offers for the middle way of enlightened marriage to resolve: the misogyny of the Prince's father is that of a caricature club-room bore ('Man is the hunter; woman is his game: | The sleek and shining creatures of the chase, | We hunt them for the beauty of their skins' (v. 147–9)); while the witching belligerence of the theorist Blanche ('the Lady stretched a vulture throat, | And shot from crooked lips a haggard smile' (iv. 344–5)) is no less ludicrously villainous – her malevolence appears tellingly confirmed at one point by her dyed hair ('all her autumn tresses falsely brown' (ii. 426)). The association between educating women and murdering men is daft; and partly thanks to the glare of that extremism, the question of women's education is wholly forgotten at the story's conclusion: there seems little chance of the college opening up again anyway.[21] Not that much has been adjudicated exactly: the incipient debate between principles in part four is pushed aside by the hot emotions of the tourney-*cum*-battlefield[22] – emotions that the Prince recognizes as a male preserve: 'the blind wildbeast of force, | Whose home is in the sinews of a man' (v. 256–7). That blind force, with its supposedly spontaneous female corollary ('the tender ministries | Of female hands and hospitality' (vi. 56–7)), pushes the story through to its close: any comedy of ideas is abruptly forgone.

The final emptiness of most of the intellectual positions that the poem sets up participates in a wider sense of irreality: none of the alleged dangers, death-threat included, ever comes close to materializing: 'I trust that there is no one hurt to death,' says Ida's father after the jousting is done (vi. 225), but he had no cause to worry here, for perils no sooner arise than the poem dissipates them. (When the Princess falls into the rushing river, she is promptly saved, and shortly appears only a little 'Damp from the river' (iv. 159–71, 258).) The murderous prohibition against men comes out of a fairy tale, with all the unquestioned arbitrariness that such injunctions enjoy in fairy tales: it is quite alien to the pondered world of a moral fable. (At one disarming moment, the Prince's friend Cyril promises Ida 'Some palace in our land, where you shall reign' (iii. 146): the funny bluff of 'Some palace' might be his own inept duplicity, but it sounds more like a telltale Tennysonian absence of mind.) 'There have not been wanting those who have deemed the varied characters and imagery of the poem wasted on something of a fairy tale without the fairies,' Hallam reported from his father's conversation (*M*.i.249); and Elizabeth Barrett Browning, for one, evidently found the whole thing immensely puzzling: 'I dont know what to think . . . isn't the world too old & fond of steam, for blank verse poems, in ever so many books, to be written on the fairies?' (R., headnote). In response to such reactions, presumably, Tennyson revised the 1851 text of the poem, adding to the character of the Prince a disposition to strange trances of cataleptic distraction. This was partly to suggest the weakling Prince's 'comparative want of power'; but also, Tennyson said, 'the words "dream-shadow," "were and were not" doubtless refer to the anachronisms and improbabilites of the story' (*M*. i. 251). The 'doubtless' there manages to sound wholly doubtful about his own creative decision – rather as, in this, the Prince's own account of his malaise, the intent sureness of 'truly', in such close company with the yielding vagueness of 'more or less', betrays Tennyson's uncertainties over the whole palaver:

> And, truly, waking dreams were, more or less,
> An old and strange affection of the house.
> Myself too had weird seizures, Heaven knows what . . .
>
> (i. 12–14)

Well, *Heaven* knows what. (If few of Tennyson's other poems are so oddly embarrassing to read as is, in parts, *The Princess*, this is because few are themselves so clearly embarrassed by their own proceedings.) The device of the seizures inspires some lumpen plotting, marked by the mirthless good humour that always signals something wrong in Tennysonian narratives: as Cyril,

> laughing 'what, if these weird seizures come
> Upon you in those lands, and no one near
> To point you out the shadow from the truth![']
>
> (i. 81–3)

(What if? – oh *come*.) When the seizures do, predictably, arise, they only confirm a sense of dreamlike insubstantiality that is more generally felt:

> The Princess Ida seemed a hollow show,
> Her gay-furred cats a painted fantasy,
> Her college and her maidens, empty masks,

> And I myself the shadow of a dream,
> For all things were and were not.
>
> (iii. 169–73)

The irreality effect is curiously marvellous, I do not deny; but it efficiently subverts any ambitions abroad to be making a contribution to social policy. The nearest the story comes to a turning point is the tournament, which is no sooner embarked upon than it dissolves, too, into the Prince's weird affection ('like a flash' (v. 466)): 'it seemed a dream, I dreamed | Of fighting' (v. 481–2). Wounded, he stays for a time in 'some mystic middle state' (vi. 2), in which the practical business of narrative becomes once more suspended:

> Seeing I saw not, hearing not I heard:
> Though, if I saw not, yet they told me all
> So often that I speak as having seen.
>
> (vi. 3–5)

The blank unassertiveness of that kind of statement-counter-statement might strike one as memorable psychological curiosity; but such grammatical hedging seems a little more troublesome when the poem is making its concluding positive noises about marriage:

> either sex alone
> Is half itself, and in true marriage lies
> Nor equal, nor unequal.

Unwilling to decide how seriously to credit its own fancifully archaic story, *The Princess* is also uneasy with its duty to be progressive. (Both these problems will trouble *Idylls of the King* too.) The contemporary relevance of the poem is chiefly asserted by the frame poem that surrounds it (a distancing device characteristic of ancient idyll, apparently).[23] A group of mostly young men and women are sitting in the ruins of an abbey, in the grounds of an estate that has been opened for the day for the use of a workers' educational institute. Lilia, the most vivacious of the party, has dressed the broken statue of a knight in a woman's scarf; and the men have begun to recollect tiresome pranks and scandals at college, which provokes Lilia to an outburst about the inadequacy of female education and the possibility of a woman's college; and when the group decide to improvise a story between them to pass the time, that becomes the subject. A device that, if anything, only exacerbates the irreality of the main narrative: Tennyson was pleased by the way that there was 'scarcely anything in the story which is not prophetically glanced at in the prologue' (M. i. 251), so that the relationship between the tale and the frame-poem becomes something like that between a dream and waking experience. (The way dreams build themselves up from elements of conscious life is the subject of the haunting 'Sea Dreams' (R. (ii). 319).)

In the 'Prologue', we learn that the Institute has brought along several gadgets to enlighten the workers; the equipment is regarded as something admirably up to date, but also as the source of a literary joke, a juxtaposition of modern and poetical: 'and here were telescopes | For azure views' (ll. 67–8), say, or

> round the lake
> A little clock-work steamer paddling plied
> And shook the lilies . . .
>
> (ll. 70–2)

The joke feels mock-heroic, a literary mode that can be conscripted to express the most strenuous moral judgements, of course, as in *The Rape of the Lock*: the genre's systematic confusion of classical nobility and contemporary triviality fits Pope's society so well because (as he thinks) values really have been corrupted and mistaken in Queen Anne's England; the ludicrousness is meant to be dreadful and true. In the Tennysonian case, the joke seems much cosier and more introvertedly literary, as though chiefly amused by the verse's ingenuity in incorporating so rum a thing: the lilies do not seem so badly shaken. In the main story, as well, nothing finally proves too awful, the 'Prologue' having loosed a strain of mollifying banter from which the poem at large never quite escapes. Of course, Tennyson means the poem to be comical, 'full of original incident, humour and fancy' (M. i. 247); but it is set on serious social commentary too: so, how funny is it, and what exactly is it that is meant to be funny? It is crucial to the economy of the poem, for example, that Ida's feminism is principled and justly motivated. Her staunch account of continuing injustices certainly has its power: 'I saw | That equal baseness lived in sleeker times | With smoother men' (v. 374–6); and you do not doubt that Tennyson himself thought the intellectual development of women a good thing. But Ida is a jokey Amazon too ('I tamed my leopards: shall I not tame these?' (v. 390))); her most 'educated' remarks make her sound spectacularly hard work ('There sinks the nebulous star we call the Sun, | If that hypothesis of theirs be sound' (iv. 1–2))); and the mock-heroic feelings set adrift in the poem occasionally gather around the thought that a women's college should have existed at all. In the 'Prologue', the idea strikes one of the men as 'Pretty' (l. 139), and the reality is not noticeably more dignified in the main tale (ii. 429–42; iii. 337–45): the older students would rather marry anyway, and Psyche's canny daughter Melissa is already being satirical about the set-up (ii. 441, 444–6). (There is a possible edge of disdain, too, when Psyche assures the men that wearing their academic hoods about their faces will not look amiss: 'They do so that affect abstraction here', she says (ii. 338).) Ida herself recognizes, in the last canto, that she has been made a figure of fun, seeing herself as 'a Queen of farce', 'A mockery to my own self' (vii. 228, 317): her dejection is recorded with sad conviction (ll. 14–28). Even the androgyny which the poem hesitantly advocates – 'The man be more of woman, she of man' (vii. 264) – is implicitly sent up, before it is expounded, in all the cross-dressing larks: 'woman-vested as I was' (iv. 163) and the rest of it.

This running uncertainty about the poem's seriousness or jokiness encounters another kind of self-division. The 'Prologue' tells us that the labour of improvising the story is divided between the sexes, the women responsible for lyrical interludes while the gentlemen catch their breath:

> we will say whatever comes.
> And let the ladies sing us, if they will,
> From time to time, some ballad or a song
> To give us breathing-space.'
>   So I began,
> And the rest followed: and the women sang
> Between the rougher voices of the men,
> Like linnets in the pauses of the wind:
> And here I give the story and the songs.
>
> ('Prologue', ll. 232–9)

The union of those voices in a single work is meant to emulate the virtues of marriage that the poem espouses at large, 'Like perfect music unto noble words' (vii. 270); but the poem candidly confesses itself merely a 'medley' (Prologue, l. 230; and the subtitle), as though the marriage of voices is not so easy to pull off. (Who calls the tune?) When Ida hears her maid recite 'Tears, Idle Tears', she takes a firmly Carlylean view, angrily rejecting as reactionary any such poetry which does not contribute to the progress of things:

> with some disdain
> Answered the Princess, 'If indeed there haunt
> About the mouldered lodges of the Past
> So sweet a voice and vague, fatal to men,
> Well needs it we should cram our ears with wool
> And so pace by: but thine are fancies hatched
> In silken-folded idleness; nor is it
> Wiser to weep a true occasion lost,
> But trim our sails, and let old bygones be,
> While down the streams that float us each and all
> To the issue, goes, like glittering bergs of ice,
> Throne after throne, and molten on the waste
> Becomes a cloud: for all things serve their time
> Toward that great year of equal mights and rights,
> Nor would I fight with iron laws, in the end
> Found golden . . .

> (iv. 43–58)

Lyricism is there cast as a Siren's voice, dispelling an Odyssean propensity to press on (Odysseus stopped the ears of his crew with wax to stop them hearing the Sirens' song); harping on the past (iv. 20) is not to the point. Ida scorns the lyric's idle tears as the self-indulgent product of 'silken-folded idleness', a lingering upon pastness and its 'idols' (iv. 62), which resists the movement of history towards an egalitarian future: better an *art engagé*, composed of what she shortly calls 'the hues | Of promise' (iv. 68–9). The perplexity of gender is very nice here: Ida (given voice by the men in the ruined abbey) is rejecting lyricism (for which the women are responsible); she wants the poets to write like a man. 'You hold the woman is the better man' (iv. 391), Ida is told by the Prince's old brute of a father; and, compared to his son anyway, she certainly is.[24] Her

104

resoundingly Apostolic injunction is 'up and act' (iii. 248): Cyril tells her she's 'Fixed in [her]self' (vi. 161), and both Psyche and the Prince recognize an 'iron will' (ii. 185; vi. 102), really not so unlike the great Duke himself. The Prince, by contrast, spends much of his time unsure how to proceed, if not wholly out of his depth: one of the poem's more winning strains of comedy is his hamstrung ineptitude before her fearsome magnificence (e.g. iii. 255–7). Tennyson was enough of an Apostle to concur with Ida's stand against idleness: 'Perpetual idleness', he told his son firmly, 'must be one of the punishments of Hell' (M. i. 123–4); and a determination not to be idling in poetry often meant not idylling. But when Ida calls for a song from the Prince (he is still in drag and so singing in falsetto, as though apeing a stereotype femininity), he responds with a song of archetypally lovely lingering, a poem uniting all the most passionately felt Tennysonian motifs – cyclical recurrences, lyrical immobility, yearning repetitiveness:

> 'O Swallow, Swallow, flying, flying South,
> Fly to her, and fall upon her gilded eaves,
> And tell her, tell her, what I tell to thee.[']
>
> (iv. 75–7)

No wonder Ida should sound so exasperated with such a slow student when he has done, reiterating her protest that 'great is song | Used to great ends' (iv. 119–20): we know from her trepidatious father that her own verses were 'rhymes | And dismal lyrics, prophesying change' (i. 140–1) – the progressive change 'With claim on claim from right to right' that she vigorously espouses before the tourney (v. 407).

Writing about Ida's response to 'Tears, Idle Tears', Griffiths shrewdly connects 'the conflict between Ida's progressivism and the lyric's harking-back' and 'the poise between reformism and restoration of old norms which *The Princess* seeks'[25] – it seeks a poise, but discovers a disagreement. To attribute such inconsistencies to the poem would sound more damaging, had the poem itself not spelt out so lucidly in sharp self-commentary how it had 'wrestle[d] with burlesque' ('Conclusion', l. 16) and so failed to progress in the straight line it had purposed. The boys had wanted mock-heroic and the women 'true-heroic', complains the narrator,

105

> And I, betwixt them both, to please them both,
> And yet to give the story as it rose,
> I moved as in a strange diagonal,
> And maybe neither pleased myself nor them.
>
> ('Conclusion', ll. 25–8)

(The story has no sooner finished than the frame narrative publishes the first of many sceptical critical responses: 'Walter said, | "I wish she had not yielded!" then to me, | "What, if you drest it up poetically?"' (ll. 4–6).) Recalcitrances of idiom and content find themselves overlapping in *The Princess*, a would-be progressive work that struggles stylistically, as it does ideologically, with the thought of progressing, as though Tennyson's imagination made a subterranean connection between the frustration of Ida's endeavour and his lyricism's embarrassment of narrative purpose. 'There is a hand that guides,' the narrator reassures his friends ('Conclusion', l. 79), with a confidence hardly justified by their own tale, which has wandered guidelessly, the production of toil notably *non*-coöperant. And not only between the story and the songs; within the story, Tennyson repeatedly stills narrative incident into an impertinent lyricism:

> His name was Gama, cracked and small his voice,
> But bland the smile that like a wrinkling wind
> On glassy water drove his cheek in lines . . .
>
> (i. 113–15)

> [']He has a solid base of temperament:
> But as the waterlily starts and slides
> Upon the level in little puffs of wind,
> Though anchored to the bottom, such is he.'
>
> (iv. 235–8)

> And she as one that climbs a peak to gaze
> O'er land and main, and sees a great black cloud
> Drag inward from the deeps, a wall of night,
> Blot out the slope of sea from verge to shore,
> And suck the blinding splendour from the sand,
> And quenching lake by lake and tarn by tarn
> Expunge the world: so fared she gazing there . . .
>
> (vii. 20–6)

106

Tennyson felt moved to defend 'what some have called the too poetical passages' (*M.* i. 253–4): such incidental beauties are his candidates for 'jewels five-words-long | That on the stretched forefinger of all Time | Sparkle for ever' (ii. 355–7), like the grand fragments of epics the women learn about in their lectures; but they live a naturally marginal life in a poem so suspiciously alert to the 'barren verbiage, current among men' (ii. 40).

The conflict between poetic voices is all the more striking as the interspersed lyrics include some of the finest that Tennyson ever wrote, his fine art of suspendedness at its most superb. Best (besides 'Tears, Idle Tears') are 'Now sleeps the crimson petal' and 'Come down, O maid, from yonder mountain height' (vii. 161–74, 177–207; the second is described as a 'small | Sweet Idyl' (vii. 175–6)), which are the lyrics that Ida reads while undergoing her final conversion to the poem's revivified idea of marriage. 'Now sleeps' conjures into a spell of breathless stillness a succession of immobilities ('Nor waves the cypress in the palace walk; | Nor winks the gold fin in the porphyry font'); the isolated stirrings of firefly, meteor and the folding lily are set against that background of dreamlike silence, each moving with a tranquillity of untroubled instinct that the beloved is invited to share ('waken thou with me'). The verse closes with a rallantando of bidding, at once erotic and mystical, 'So fold thyself, my dearest, thou, and slip | Into my bosom and be lost in me': after a poem constructed around tenderly emphatic verbs, the last is an unemphasized *be*, as though finally reaching an uninsistent ground of effortless existence, at once passive and impassioned. 'Come down, O maid' reissues an invitation to descend, but now from the strenuous mountain tops (Ida was the mountain in 'Œnone') to the valley, which is abundant with reiterative music: 'sweet is every sound, | Sweeter thy voice, but every sound is sweet'. But the poem does not deny the claims of mountain life too, 'height and cold, the splendour of the hills': especially telling given Ida's state of mind when she reads the 'Idyl' (and marvellous anyway) is the description of the mountain's 'thousand wreaths of dangling water-smoke, | That like a broken purpose waste in air'. The shepherd-lover continues, adeptly, 'So waste not thou; but come', with the rhetorical confidence of one clinching an argument ('Therefore, do not waste yourself'); but really he is amorously drawing an analogy ('Do not waste yourself, like the water-smoke, in broken purposes'). The poem leaves nicely undecided whether life down in the valley is the 'purpose' she should not break; or whether, her true mountain 'purpose' sadly broken, she might as well resign herself to coming down to his level; either way, she has not reached a decision by the Idyl's end.

Tennyson's Arthurian blank verse first stirred into life in 'Morte d'Arthur' (1833), a poem that appeared self-consciously within a frame, like *The Princess*, and shows a very similar embarrassment about meaning and action. The frame poem for 'Morte d'Arthur' is called 'The Epic' (R. (ii). 225), and features the fictive author of the lines to follow bashfully disowning his work (most of which, we learn, he has burnt). Seeking to excuse the incongruity of a modern poem 'telling an old-world [Fairy-]tale', as FitzGerald said (R., headnote), 'The Epic' chiefly succeeds in advertising the author's uncertainty about the wisdom of proceeding.

> 'Why take the style of those heroic times?
> For nature brings not back the Mastodon,
> Nor we those times; and why should any man
> Remodel models? . . . [']
>
> (ll. 35–8)

says the poet-within-the-poem: why spend time making art out of art, that is, rather than engaging with what the cancelled drafts of the poem had called squarely 'the life' (ll. 35–8 n.). His scruples were not idiosyncratic: John Sterling, in a review, had endorsed Tennyson's self-deprecations ('The miraculous legend of "Excalibur" does not come very near to us, and as reproduced by any modern writer must be a mere ingenious exercise of fancy' (*CH* 119)); and his review had put Tennyson off the subject for years (*L.* ii. 451). (Jowett came to think Arthur a bad idea too (*L.* ii. 271).) Tennyson did eventually return to the task of Arthur, but did not escape the uncertainty of purpose that marked its origins. He often announced ambitious schemes of meaning to friends and visitors, sometimes of hair-raising abstraction.[26] 'By King Arthur I always meant the soul, and by the Round Table the passions and capacities of a man' (*IR* 96); but 'always' there betrays the over-insistence that defending the

Idylls often provoked in him. 'He troubles himself that the Idylls do not form themselves into a whole in his mind', Emily Tennyson privately reported (*L.* ii. 148); Clough thought 'idylls' more or less a synonym for 'fragments' (*L.* ii. 166), taking as read Tennyson's failure to emulate the controlling teleology of classical epic, such as in the *Aeneid*. Hallam Tennyson was more modest in asserting that '[t]he general drift of the "Idylls" is clear enough', quoting his father: ' "The whole . . . is the dream of man coming into practical life and ruined by one sin [''']' (*M.* ii. 127) – the presiding theme of the *Idylls*, that is to say, is just that failure to respond to 'practical life' that Tennyson had been worrying about in 'The Epic', as though they were to be a kind of immense allegory of his artistic irresolution. To speak of a 'drift' at all, as Hallam does, nicely allows for a wandering purpose; while imagining the worldly business of practice within a 'dream', as Tennyson does, agreeably complicates at once any imaginative commitment to 'the life'.

It is perfectly possible to frame the kind of question that the Arthurian material might suggest: say, 'What is the spiritual authority by which we can regulate our society, and what are the grounds for giving it our allegiance?';[27] and it is not hard to offer an answer, though it feels very remote from the way the *Idylls* actually strike us. Arthur is an embodiment of the nation, or what the godly nation should be, so implying the political analogy I talked about in the previous chapter: that 'a well-governed State is like a person'.[28] In the *Idylls* this is conflated, really quite arbitrarily,[29] with the idea of marriage that brought *The Princess* to a close:

> ['] . . . were I joined with her,
> Then might we live together as one life,
> And reigning with one will in everything
> Have power on this dark land to lighten it,
> And power on this dead world to make it live.'
>
> ('The Coming of Arthur', ll. 89–93)

The Knights of England, like Arthur and Guinevere, are to be united into the virtue of 'one will'; and the decline and fall of England is the dissipation of that will into conflicting individualities. Guinevere's adultery breaks the unity of the marriage, which rupture serves as a type for the wider dissolution of the state into uncontained passions. Matthew Reynolds puts the point well, talking about Balin: 'he ceases to obey Arthur and gives himself up to his own agency, behaving in a manner which therefore cannot be understood in terms of the State personality, and ending up completely outside it, i.e. dead'.[30] (It is the conservative fretfulness about individual agency that I talked about in Chapter 2.)

Guinevere is officially to blame: Arthur reproaches her because 'the loathsome opposite | Of all my heart had destined did obtain | And all through thee!', a judgement she clearly accepts ('Guinevere', ll. 488–90, 650–6). But the mechanism by which her infidelity spreads its influence across an entire culture is perplexing: Arthur says it is her 'foul ensample' ('Guinevere', l. 487); but Tristram equivocates a little on the point – 'First mainly through that sullying of our Queen' ('The Last Tournament', l. 677). We see rumours about Guinevere turning Geraint's head about Enid's fidelity, though at that stage there is no evidence of the Queen's crime: the disease seems firmly established in Geraint already ('The Marriage of Geraint', ll. 29–32); and, generally, the Queen's exemplary taint seems to communicate itself to the wider world by mysterious diffusion. 'The sin of Lancelot and Guinevere begins to breed' was Hallam's gloss on 'Geraint and Enid' (R. (iii). 467, headnote), and the *Memoir* reports Tennyson himself describing how the sin 'spreads its poison through the whole community' (*M.* ii. 131), as though it were something done to the poems' personages, not something they did themselves. The comparison with Malory, in which the fall of Arthur is largely couched in stoutly unimaginative terms of political and military mistakes and contingencies, is very striking: Tennyson's Arthur, as everyone remarks, is characterized by his wholly uncharacterful passivity, and (as Coleridge once said of matter) acts chiefly by his inactivity. Swinburne was tart about this 'incongruous edifice of tradition and invention where even virtue is made to seem either imbecile or vile': such a man as this King is hardly 'man at all' (*CH* 319) – hardly manly, and also hardly human. And, by the same instinct of self-deploring ingenuousness that inspired 'The Epic' and the frame to *The Princess*, Tennyson himself warmly vocalises the objections, having Guinevere speak at some length about 'the faultless King, | That passionless

perfection' and (devastatingly) 'this fancy of his Table Round, |
And swearing men to vows impossible' (R. (iii). 470, ll. 121–2,
129–30).

Dwight Culler once identified as 'the basic problem for
Camelot . . . that there is nothing for the knights to do';[31] and the
inactivity is all-important. For Tennyson takes a characteristic
mood (in which there is nothing to be done) and casts it,
incongruously, as an allegorical story 'shadowing Sense at war
with Soul' ('To the Queen', l. 37). But he scarcely attempts to
imagine Arthur's kingdom whole and good.[32] The poem comes
into its proper life only once Camelot begins to decline, as
though by some implicit law – once the awareness has caught
hold that, in the haunting first words of 'Merlin and Vivien', 'A
storm was coming'. Elaine Jordan rightly identifies the poems'
'eerie pessimism'[33] – the attribution of blame to Guinevere (or to
Vivien and Modred) envisages a universe of individual agency
that is scarcely to the point. Does Arthur know about Guinevere
or not? He would not come out of it well either way; but the
poems hardly know what to do with such intrusive questions.
For they are really strikingly anti-individualistic (compare them
with Browning's *The Ring and the Book*) – not in the slightest
concerned to distinguish the characters, who all sound alike:
Bagehot noticed 'the remarkable similarity of the conversational
powers of all the various personages' (*CH* 231). The sameness of
the speeches is largely responsible for the curiously anti-
dramatic atmosphere; any conflict seems to be going on a
higher level of abstraction: the poems were 'defective in
dramatic power', thought Bagehot, 'admirable in monologue,
but quite incapable of dialogue' (*CH* 230).

Tennyson sturdily maintained, 'there is no single fact or
incident in the "Idylls", however seemingly mystical, which
cannot be explained as without any mystery or allegory
whatever' (*M*. ii. 127). But, considered apart from the require-
ments of the allegorical drift, behaviour in Camelot often
appears wholly bizarre (as in 'Gareth and Lynette' and 'Geraint
and Enid', say); and the *Idylls* struggle to make themselves
sound at home whenever they set out on unmysteriously
narrative business.

> Yet lo! my husband's brother had my son
> Thralled in his castle, and hath starved him dead;
> And standeth seized of that inheritance
> Which thou that slewest the sire hast left the son.
>
> ('Gareth and Lynette', ll. 349–52)

The sense of a resisting medium that Hutton described is engagingly obvious in such passages; sometimes fulfilling its expository duties makes the verse tangle its fingers:

> So Gareth past with joy; but as the cur
> Pluckt from the cur he fights with, ere his cause
> Be cooled by fighting, follows, being named,
> His owner, but remembers all, and growls
> Remembering, so Sir Kay beside the door
> Muttered in scorn of Gareth whom he used
> To harry and hustle.
>
> ('Gareth and Lynette', ll. 686–92)

The *Idylls* tend to greet all such activity with unease; they are more at ease imagining things done in a dreamlike abstraction of great charm: 'So leaving Arthur's court he gained the beach; | There found a little boat, and stept into it' ('Merlin and Vivien', ll. 195–6), or 'Then got Sir Lancelot suddenly to horse, | Wroth at himself' ('Lancelot and Elaine', ll. 158–9). Most readers have found the poems' best moments in their fleeting escapes from even such exiguous narrative burdens, especially in the landscaped evocations of mood (often a pervasive fatedness) that emerge within the long paragraphs of talk and exposition. Best of all is:

> he was mute:
> So dark a forethought rolled about his brain,
> As on a dull day in an Ocean cave
> The blind wave feeling round his long sea-hall
> In silence . . .
>
> ('Merlin and Vivien', ll. 227–31)

That comes in a moment of quiet amidst one of Vivien's trying passages of seduction, opening out a sudden glimpse of a parallel universe before returning to the ruinous tale again. Such glimpses are not always so doomy:

> Meanwhile the new companions past away
> Far o'er the long backs of the bushless downs,
> To where Sir Lancelot knew there lived a knight
> Not far from Camelot, now for forty years
> A hermit, who had prayed, laboured and prayed,
> And ever labouring had scooped himself
> In the white rock a chapel and a hall
> On massive columns, like a shorecliff cave,
> And cells and chambers: all were fair and dry;
> The green light from the meadows underneath
> Struck up and lived along the milky roofs;
> And in the meadows tremulous aspen-trees
> And poplars made a noise of falling showers.
> And thither wending there that night they bode.

('Lancelot and Elaine', ll. 397–410)

The framework of that has a sturdily narrative sequentiality: 'Meanwhile . . . Not far from . . . thither'; but Tennyson incorporates within it a charmed and fantastic existence ('*ever* labouring'?) in which the arduous business of carving out rock is conjured into the ease of a hand scooping: it is an alternative life, like that of the green light or the tremulous trees – and entirely preferable to the dull routine of 'And thither wending there that night they bode'. Poetry distracts narrative in a very obvious way: the stilling repetition of 'And . . . And . . . And', a favourite device in the *Idylls*, immobilizes the syntax, ambushing sequentiality and transforming it to pleasurable simultaneity.

Hopkins's shrewd and unforgiving verdict on the *Idylls* largely sticks: 'they are unreal in motive and incorrect, uncanonical so to say, in detail and keepings. He sh[oul]d have called them *Charades from the Middle Ages* (dedicated by permission to H.R.H. etc.)' (*CH* 334). To have realized 'motive' would have required a psychological kind of attention that the *Idylls* habitually prefer to eschew, in favour of vast legendary simplicities ('So large mirth lived and Gareth won the quest' ('Gareth and Lynette', l. 1391)) and picturesque unlikelihoods ('Gawain the while through all the region round | Rode with his diamond'('Lancelot and Elaine', ll. 611–12)); while avoiding the hollow sense of a 'charade' would presumably have needed the imagining of a densely lived social space, full of the sort of practicalities that the nineteenth-century novel found so compelling. As though in reaction to the prevailing irreality of its imagined world, Tennyson's cycle is full of extreme violence ('"Mark's way," said Mark, and clove him through the brain' ('The Last Tournament', l. 748)); 'smote' is a favourite word. But archaism manages to keep the violence incorrigibly literary (compared with the bloody reportage of Malory, anyway), more peculiar than unsettling:

> And at the midmost charging, Prince Geraint
> Drave the long spear a cubit through his breast
> And out beyond[.]

('Geraint and Enid', ll. 85–7)

Hopkins's remark picks up something important about Tennyson's own sense of his creativity and its uncertainties: he worried, says Emily, 'that the subject has not reality enough' (*L.* ii. 148). The justification for the cycle was the moral cogency of its allegory; but Tennyson grew evasive when critics' allegorical interpretations drew too tight: 'They are right, and they are not right . . . I hate to be tied down to say, "*This* means *that*"' (*M.* ii. 127). That is not far from the dreamy equivocation of *The Princess*: things 'were and were not'.

Hopkins's mention of 'H.R.H.' is sharp (the poems were dedicated to the memory of Prince Albert): many readers thought (and think) the parallel between the mythical king and the Prince Consort a risible piece of misproportion. 'Morte d'Albert as it might perhaps be more properly called,' suggested Swinburne (*CH* 318). But the mock-heroic or burlesque nature of such a parallel is not just a matter of Tennyson's heart-felt royalism; it really corresponds to something important stirring in the poems. As Elaine Jordan says, '"Style" is always a major presence in the *Idylls*';[34] but not always so welcome a presence as we might think, and here the presence in his thoughts of the Malory source may be important: he praised Malory's *Morte d'Arthur* for the 'very fine things in it, but all strung together without Art' (*M.* i. 194). Ruskin told Tennyson that he felt 'the art and finish in these poems a little more than I like to feel it' (*M.* i. 453); and Tennyson was not easy with the 'art' either: the self-consciousness announced by 'The Epic' about the respectability of such incorrigibly literary pursuits ('Remodel models') is never wholly quietened, and occasionally emerges as a kind of near-burlesque amusement about poetry and its relations with

normality. Violence cannot puncture the authority of Tennyso-
nian music, but mundanity can, and a mock-heroic possibility is
always ready to assert itself. The phenomenon can be wearily
arch, I agree: 'So Gareth all for glory underwent | The sooty
yoke of kitchen-vassalage' ('Gareth and Lynette', ll. 468–9); but it
is hard not to see a better, more inward joke in such audacious
lines as 'Doorm, whom his shaking vassals called the Bull'
('Geraint and Enid', l. 439), or in droll juxtapositions of the
ordinary and the fairy, like 'And Merlin locked his hand in hers
and said, | "I once was looking for a magic weed . . ." ' ('Merlin
and Vivien', ll. 468–9), or in the unresisting dottiness of lines like
'And ever and anon a knight would pass | Outward, or inward
to the hall' ('Gareth and Lynette', ll. 303–4). Empson might have
called such a line 'mouldy' (see above, p. 2); but the effect might
just be more witting than that allows: they are jokes about the
idioms of poetry and the idioms of 'the life', and, as 'The Epic'
implies, they were there almost from the start in the Arthurian
poetry.

Tennyson sometimes takes a showy fun in the business of
poeticism:

> He spoke in words part heard, in whispers part,
> Half-suffocated in the hoary fell
> And many-wintered fleece of throat and chin.

> ('Merlin and Vivien', ll. 837–9)

Which is to say, he mumbled in his white beard. Some dashes of
mundanity are extremely winning: 'It was the time when first
the question rose | About the founding of a Table Round'
('Merlin and Vivien', ll. 408–9), which makes it sound a gritty
piece of committee work, like putting on the Great Exhibition;
'But hire us some fair chamber for the night', says Geraint at one
point ('Geraint and Enid', l. 238), as though taking a decent
room in the Savoy. Gladstone was properly moved (*CH* 262) by a
half-chewed piece of food: 'He spoke: the brawny spearman let
his cheek | Bulge with the unswallowed piece, and turning
stared' ('Geraint and Enid', ll. 628–9). Tennyson long fought shy
of the Holy Grail as a subject on the grounds that it would seem
like 'playing with sacred things. The old writers *believed* in the
Sangraal' (*L.* ii. 244) – the implication being, I suppose, that a
kind of playfulness and an associated scepticism were an

unacknowledged ingredient in his own Arthurian habits. (When he finally did write 'The Holy Grail', it became a study in 'mass hysteria'.[35]) The *Idylls* are open enough to the incongruities of burlesque even to admit the thought that Camelot is actually a very tiresome place:

> All ears were pricked at once, all tongues were loosed:
> 'The maid of Astolat loves Sir Lancelot,
> Sir Lancelot loves the maid of Astolat.'

('Lancelot and Elaine', ll. 719–21)

And Arthur himself concedes, 'I know my knights fantastical', as though a man trying to forge an epic with slightly disappointing raw material ('Lancelot and Elaine', l. 591). Indeed, Arthur himself does not always seem quite up to the role in which he has been cast: Tennyson goes elaborately out of his way to cast doubts on his origins (in 'The Coming of Arthur'); and, at his atmospheric passing, he voices a sudden pang of uncertainty in the midst of properly resonant valediction:

> But now farewell. I am going a long way
> With these thou seëst – if indeed I go
> (For all my mind is clouded with a doubt) –
> To the island-valley of Avilion . . .

('The Passing of Arthur', ll. 424–7)

Bagehot offered a characterization of the ubiquitous Camelot ideolect: 'a peculiar kind of language, a sort of a dialect of sentimental chivalry' (*CH* 231). Tennyson was proud of his blank verse in *The Princess* (*M.* i. 251), and, besides the great inset-pieces, some of it is indeed remarkable for the supple flexibility of its movement:

> She remembered that:
> A pleasant game, she thought: she liked it more
> Than magic music, forfeits, all the rest.
> But these – what kind of tales did men tell men,
> She wondered, by themselves?'

('Prologue', ll. 190–4)

That has almost the fluidity of consciousness in a Woolf novel (in the less visionary stretches); the Arthurian idiom, by contrast, is stiffer and more ostentatiously formulaic, its exponents not speaking so much as making speeches. Here is Sir Bedivere, debating with himself whether to throw Excalibur into the lake as instructed by Arthur, lines from the early 'Morte d'Arthur' that later reappeared in 'The Passing of Arthur':

> were this kept,
> Stored in some treasure-house of mighty kings,
> Some one might show it at a joust of arms,
> Saying, 'King Arthur's sword, Excalibur,
> Wrought by the lonely maiden of the Lake.
> Nine years she wrought it, sitting in the deeps
> Upon the hidden bases of the hills.'

(R. (ii). 226, ll. 100–6)

Sir Bedivere's momentarily distracting fantasy of some future tour guide, showing the sword to interested parties, is not untypical of the best of the Arthurian poetry: sumptuous and verbose, dallying, an exercise in a resonant and idiosyncratic kind of art speech, conscious of its own untimely exhorbitance: 'Then loudly cried the bold Sir Bedivere' (l. 226). FitzGerald records Tennyson declaiming the lines about the Lady of the Lake's unlikely piece of smelting, and enquiring, 'Not bad that, Fitz, is it?' (M. i. 153).[36] It was the sort of remark he would apparently often make while repeating verses: 'Tennyson recited or intoned choice passages from his poetry, and . . . from time to time he would turn round to me with a childish satisfaction and say, "Isn't that grand?" '[37] But maybe childish satisfaction is not quite it: rather, a winning and quite unabashed pleasure in the art – 'I thought *that* . . . a bit of a *tour de force*' (of 'Alcaics' (*IR* 46)) – goes along with a rueful uncertainty about the art, 'his doubts about the style and subject of such a poem, and an audience's possible reactions to it' (as John Bayley puts it).[38] Leigh Hunt disapproved of the self-deprecatory gestures of 'The Epic', suspecting 'Morte d'Arthur' 'among those [poems] which Mr Tennyson thinks his best, and is most anxious that others should regard as he does . . . The reader's opinion is at once to be of great importance to him, and yet none at all' (*CH* 127–8). In 'Morte d'Arthur', that mixture of flamboyant performativeness and private insecurity appears as what John Bayley calls (in an essay to which I am gratefully indebted here) a 'large collusive amusement'.[39] Such intricately associated emotions would reappear in *In Memoriam* with a more inward and reticient voice.

* * *

'The general public will like this,' said Bagehot in a review, quoting some lines from the *Idylls*, 'but scarcely the youthful admirers of broken art and incomplete beauties who accepted *Maud* with great delight' (*CH* 220). One of Tennyson's favourite sayings was 'The artist is known by his self-limitation' (*M*. i. 118); and the brokenness and incompleteness of *Maud* (R. (ii). 316) is perhaps his own most successful response to the limitations of his narrative imagination: 'turning his limitations to good purpose', as Eliot said.[40] Tennyson referred to the work as 'a little *Hamlet*' (*M* i. 396; cf. *L*. ii. 127), an important clue to the way the poem works. Empson once imagined Shakespeare landing the commission for *Hamlet* and quickly realizing that only by making Hamlet's inactivity the central point of the play could he stop it proving a ludicrous impediment: the Prince would have to keep saying, 'the motivation of this play is just as blank to me as it is to you; but I can't help it'.[41] *Maud* evinces a mysteriousness of action not unlike that experienced by Shakespeare's hero: 'what it means to have sufficient identity to be capable of consistent and meaningful action,' in A. S. Byatt's words.[42] Where Tennyson's other stories often find themselves perplexed by their duty to enact incident, *Maud* conjures that perplexity into its theme, and Tennyson was evidently proud of its conception: 'It is a poem written in an *entirely new form*, as far as I know,' he told a correspondent (*L*. ii. 134–5). Song and story jostle with one another in Tennyson's other long narrative poems; story in *Maud* has been dissolved into songs: the poem is a sequence of dramatic lyrics, all uttered by the same speaker, diversely set in moments when action is imminent or its aftermath evident – a poetry of inflections and innuendos, then, on the edge of events or just after. We can more or less deduce a story, but the narrator does not reflect much upon incidents to produce a narrative for us; and the pivotal event of the story is left obscure: 'What is it, that has been done?' (ii. 7). The individual poems juxtapose without connection, 'not directly and connectedly' as Robert James Mann explained in *Maud Vindicated* (of which Tennyson approved (*M*. i. 394)), 'but, as it were, inferentially and interruptedly, through a series of distinct scenes' (*CH* 198): the abrupt discontinuity of its sections is dramatically justified by the audacious choice of the narrating persona, whose own sense

118

of continuity is thoroughly shaken, because of bad nerves, and near-madness, and then madness. So, *Maud* casts as a matter of pathological interest one of Tennyson's abiding concerns – the oneness and yet multiplicity of the self through time (see above, pp. 47–50): 'The peculiarity of this poem', he told his son, 'is that different phases of passion in one person take the place of different characters' (*M.* i. 396). (That might strike a proleptically modernist note, resembling the way all the characters are united into the single 'personage' of Tiresias in *The Waste Land*: Humbert Wolfe remarked long ago, 'when Mr T. S. Eliot wrote *The Waste Land* he was merely carrying the *Maud* scheme to an almost painfully logical conclusion'[43] – though I suppose 'merely' begs a question or two).

'I took a man constitutionally diseased and dipt him into the circumstances of the time and took him out on fire' (*L.* ii. 138). The voice at once seems unbalanced, distorting a Tennysonian responsiveness to landscape into agitated visceral disgust: 'I hate the dreadful hollow behind the little wood, | Its lips in the field above are dabbled with blood-red heath' (*Maud*, i. 1–2). The speaker is haunted by the death of his father (as Hamlet is): he was destroyed by the disappointment of a speculation (i. 9–12); the mother too is dead, worried away by the aftermath of ruin (i. 701–8), and the speaker has been left alone, Mariana-style, in the empty house,

> Where I hear the dead at midday moan,
> And the shrieking rush of the wainscot mouse,
> And my own sad name in corners cried,
> When the shiver of dancing leaves is thrown
> About its echoing chambers wide,
> Till a morbid hate and horror have grown
> Of a world in which I have hardly mixt,
> And a morbid eating lichen fixt
> On a heart half-turned to stone.

(i. 259–67)

Hatred and horror 'have grown' upon him, the grammar working to imply his own helpless passivity before his own emotions; the same (bleakly comforting) thought that one is the victim of forces beyond one's control appears early on in the poem's unhappy speculations: 'Do we move ourselves, or are moved by an unseen hand at a game . . .' (i. 127).

119

His first sighting of Maud – a childhood playmate returning to the big house, now an orphan in the charge of her brother – attributes to her a kindred stoniness, like a statue's. 'Faultily faultless, icily regular, splendidly null, | Dead perfection, no more', and his dreams are soon troubled by her 'Cold and clear-cut face' (i. 82–3, 88). His observation of details is vividly hallucinatory: 'Pale with the golden beam of an eyelash dead on the cheek'; 'Walked in a wintry wind by a ghastly glimmer, and found | The shining daffodil dead, and Orion low in his grave' (i. 91, 100–1). He begins to fall into a kind of love when he hears her sing a 'martial song', but his admiration is really reserved for a disembodied idea of the woman, an idea that he hopes to separate from the chilly recalcitrance of the real woman: 'Not her, who is neither courtly nor kind, | Not her, not her, but a voice' (i. 166, 188-9). No Tennyson poem uses repetition more resourcefully than *Maud*, to register language-defying exhilaration or mind-paralysing fixation; and repetitiousness quickly becomes the hallmark of his thoughts about Maud, obsessional and self-mystifying:

> Birds in the high Hall-garden
> When twilight was falling,
> Maud, Maud, Maud, Maud,
> They were crying and calling.

(i. 412–15)

The connection between such heightened experience and a real world outside the speaker's mind is genuine but diffracted: the birds are rooks cawing; Maud's feet makes the daisies 'rosy' (i. 434–5) because the petals are turned to their pinkish underside (*IR* 67–8). Even when mundane detail more nearly survives incorporation into his personal psychodrama, it picks up an odd, emphatic, estranging inconsequentiality: 'Maud is not seventeen, | But she is tall and stately' (i. 426–7). (Part of the 'outstanding four-line banality' to which, on second thoughts, J. B. Steane attributes 'a weird simplicity'.[44]) His tense moment of longing is interrupted by the sight of Maud's offensive and disapproving *nouveau riche* brother; the contumely is snobbish and engrossed: 'barbarous opulence jewel-thick | Sunned itself on his breast and his hands' (i. 455–6). The idea of Maud keeps growing in intensity and abstraction in the narrator's thoughts;

she becomes his 'Delight', then his 'Oread' (i. 507, 544); he watches for her 'hand, as white | As ocean-foam in the moon' (i. 505–6). They finally meet and speak, which occasions an outburst of madly reiterative excess (much abused by the critics):

> Rosy is the West,
> Rosy is the South,
> Roses are her cheeks,
> And a rose her mouth.

(i. 595–8)

'There is none like her, none', he repeats (i. 600, 605, 611), having just walked her home, and the awe (what Mann calls the 'exaggerative earnestness' (*CH* 201)) conceals a dismal plausibility: that there really *is* no one like his Maud, 'whose gentle will has changed my fate, | And made my life a perfumed altarflame' (i. 621–2). He declares himself ready to 'accept my madness'; and 'mad', 'Maud' and 'made' begin to interweave bewilderingly: 'Maud my bliss, | Maud made my Maud by that long loving kiss' (i. 642, 655–6).

Maud has a suitor ('Bound for the Hall, and I think for a bride' (i. 355)); but, as in *The Princess*, the narrator supposes his own suit preferred by long-standing parental agreement:

> Maud's dark father and mine
> Had bound us one to the other,
> Betrothed us over their wine,
> On the day when Maud was born . . .

(i. 720-4)

He has dimly recalled this before (i. 285–300). That does not sound more than a whiskery joke; and anyway this is a poem in which (*Hamlet*-like again) the legacy of fathers is blighting: 'Maud's dark father and mine' nicely allows them to share an epithet. The darkness seems hereditary too:

> Sealed her mine from her first sweet breath.
> Mine, mine by a right, from birth till death.
> Mine, mine – our fathers have sworn.

(i. 724-6)

('Sealed' looks ominous, as though insinuating a doom.) Those emphatic possessive pronouns ('Mine, mine') linger to infect the possessives in the famous, innocent-sounding section xxii, one of Tennyson's greatest lyrics of imminence ('Come into the garden, Maud') that crowns the poem's first part. The narrator is waiting in the Hall's rose garden, as he supposes by arrangement – '(If I read her sweet will right)' (i. 846) – a marvellously judged parenthesis, the verse barely registering the very real possibility that her wishes are quite different from his, and his lurking in the shadows something other than a lovers' tryst:

> She is coming, my own, my sweet;
>   Were it ever so airy a tread,
> My heart would hear her and beat,
>   Were it earth in an earthy bed;
> My dust would hear her and beat,
>   Had I lain for a century dead;
> Would start and tremble under her feet,
>   And blossom in purple and red.

(i. 916–23)

The fame of the poem obscures its highly disturbed oddity. It is one of several places in *Maud* where what Hallam had called Tennyson's 'graft of the lyric on the dramatic' makes the poetic conventions grow weirdly estranged. He has been talking to the flowers about Maud arriving, and they have excitedly answered back, just as they might in an anthology piece; but, as Griffiths says, 'there is an accumulation of crazed speech harboured behind the lines'[45] – and here, after all, is a man who not only talks to plants but hears them talk back. Kinds of unliterary ordinariness cross the path of the *Idylls* to effect a burlesque sort of self-consciousness; in *Maud*, a similarly acute self-awareness of verbalism and its limits works a much more darkly unsettling effect. An undeluded realism underlies the romantic magic of Maud's turning the daisies pink (rather as a rational explanation often accompanies supernatural events in Gothick novels); and the same sort of literal instinct turns the lyrical tropes into psychological phenomena. The amorous hyperbole of 'My heart would hear her and beat, | Were it earth in an earthy bed' betrays a fantastic eroticism possessed by death, and driven by graphic self-abasing need. Walking over his corpse, Maud would make his pulse start again ('beat' repeats as a dead rhyme, as though the speaker's good lyrical behaviour is beginning to slip under the strain); but the excited pulsation of desire seems inseparable from dreadful fear ('start and tremble'). (Tennyson loathed the famous musical setting, which reduced the dangerous violence implicit in the stanzas to the domestic rectitude of a waltz.)

The 'red' that does ensue (as we subsequently deduce) is bloodshed: Maud's brother turns up, and the narrator, provoked, fatally wounds him. The recollection is vague and hallucinatory, with flashes of self-distracting clarity:

> When he lay dying there,
> I noticed one of his many rings
> (For he had many, poor worm) and thought
> It is his mother's hair.
>
> (ii. 115–18)

Nothing is clear: 'What is it, that has been done?' (ii. 7); and, later, 'Who knows if he be dead? | Whether I need have fled?' (ii. 119–20). What does seem sure is that Maud herself soon dies, though it is a piece of information that a song takes for granted, rather than announces: 'She is but dead' (ii. 139); and the speaker descends into madness, though whether Maud's death is the precipitating cause is uncertain. The sexual stirring from deathly immobility that the narrator had ecstatically imagined in the rose garden is gruesomely transformed in the derangement of his asylum monologue: he becomes convinced that he really is dead, but cruelly unable to stop his body beating in time with the mechanical rhythms of overheard life, just as the verse beats, with lunatic insistence:

> And my heart is a handful of dust,
> And the wheels go over my head,
> And my bones are shaken with pain,
> For into a shallow grave they are thrust,
> Only a yard below the street,
> And the hoofs of the horses beat, beat,
> The hoofs of the horses beat,
> Beat into my scalp and my brain,
> With never an end to the stream of passing feet . . .
>
> (ii. 241–9)

His erratic dips into colloquialism have the spurious lucidity of a good mad scene: 'Is it kind to have made me a grave so rough, | Me, that was never a quiet sleeper?' (ii. 335–6). A final shot at redemption comes in the short third section: like the speaker of 'Locksley Hall' (and compare 'The Two Voices', ll. 124–56), the narrator opts for a saving recourse to *action*, in this case the timely patriotic gore of the Crimean campaign (just glimpsed in the poem already (i. 110)). The burden of individualism and agency that has proved so dreadful throughout the poem appears savingly resigned, absorbed into a greater determining life, now that 'the heart of a people beat with one desire' and the speaker can say, for the first time, 'I am one with my kind' (iii. 49, 58).

Many reviewers understandably objected to the casting of the Crimean War as an efficient means of achieving psychic health; and some modern readers still do.[46] The account that Hallam Tennyson attributes to his father certainly makes the poem's scheme look sure about its redemptive shape: the speaker is 'raised to a pure and holy love which elevates his whole nature, passing from the height of triumph to the lowest depth of misery, driven into madness by the loss of her whom he has loved, and, when he has at length passed through the fiery furnace, and has recovered his reason, giving himself up to work for the good of mankind through the unselfishness born of a great passion' (R., headnote). But (more or less) those words appear as Hallam's, not his father's, in the *Memoir* (i. 396); Tennyson himself responded to the contemporary criticism, on the contrary, by firmly distancing himself from his madman: 'The poem was a dramatic monologue. The sentiments were in the mouth of a madman' (*IR* 115). But that no doubt makes things appear simpler than they are too: as with 'Locksley Hall', Tennyson takes the opportunity of an unhinging mind to voice some of his most trenchant social criticism, attacking 'rotten hustings' (i. 243) and the 'poisoned gloom' of coal mines (i. 337) and so on, in a way of which Tennyson himself might seem highly likely to approve.

> And the vitriol madness flushes up in the ruffian's head,
> Till the filthy by-lane rings to the yell of the trampled wife,
> And chalk and alum and plaster are sold to the poor for bread,
> And the spirit of murder works in the very means of life . . .
>
> (i. 37–40)

Gladstone, for one, found himself unsure 'whether the poet intends to be in any and what degree sponsor to these sentiments' (*CH* 247); and Tennyson himself admitted that, like his madman, he 'used to rage against the social conditions that made marriage so difficult' (*IR* 58). 'How could you or anyone suppose that if I had had to speak in my own person my own opinion of this war or war generally I should have spoken with so little moderation,' he asked a correspondent; but then promptly added in a postscript, 'I do not mean that my madman does not speak truths too' (*L*. ii. 138).

The firm spiritual progress that the paraphrase in the *Memoir* describes is one that the speaker of *Maud* believes in, but that the poem refuses finally to endorse: indeed, it almost treats the thought of such moral progress as a bleak joke, a sense of growth and meaningful consequence that it will not deliver. The redemptive turn to action that had so attracted the Apostles appears in the poem couched in the same compulsive language (blood, red, blossom, heart) that had described the speaker's initial disgust and, modulated, his adoration for Maud: 'The blood-red blossom of war with a heart of fire' (iii. 53). The implication is that his mind has not been salved so much as reoccupied by the old terms, and that the embracing of war is, really, not a step towards health, but rather a renewed bout of the same old disease: a characteristic Tennysonian reflection, of a kind at once grim and droll, that there is no escape but to be ill in a different way (like Mariana when she moves south). The ending of *Maud* is, even by the emphatic speaker's own testimony, equivocal: 'myself have awaked, as it seems, to the better mind' (iii. 56). Tennyson certainly shared on occasion his speaker's militaristic desire

> for a man with heart, head, hand,
> Like some of the simple great ones gone
> For ever and ever by . . .

> (i. 389–91)

But the insight of *Maud* is that the desire for such attractive simplicity may not be a solution but rather itself the symptom of a more pervasive contagion. The boisterous outrage of the early stanzas is moved by a society that is, after all, in an obvious way deranged ('When a Mammonite mother kills her babe for a burial fee' (i. 45)): it is a national lunacy that you could see the speaker's mental instability as merely replicating, and the turn

125

to national war as crowning ('the apotheosis of subjectivity in delusion and not its transformation', says Armstrong[47]). War is one way of trying to prove that 'we have hearts' (iii. 55): Maud is another. Goldwin Smith wrote shrewdly about the life of the women in Tennyson with *Maud* particularly in mind: 'Women seem to have no function but that of casting out the demon of hypochondria from the breast of the solitary', creatures 'without active life or interests of their own' (*CH* 188). The narrator's obsession ('Maud, Maud, Maud, Maud') is secretly close kin to the Prince's dreamy idolization in *The Princess* ('With Ida, Ida, Ida, rang the woods'): the one seeks to save himself in militarism, the other in matrimony; and both kinds of salvation may be illusory. Ida can speak for herself ('*she* can talk', says her weary father (v. 201)); Maud, of course, can not, this being a 'monodrama'. Indeed Maud eludes *Maud* entirely: her irreality in it is a mark of her absorption into the speaker's fantasy, as though Tennyson's original title 'Maud or the Madness' (*M*. i. 402) really was nominating a pair of synonyms. She is a darkly brilliant parody of the idealized women who featured in some of his earlier poems ('Claribel', 'Lilian', 'Isabel'), 'evolved, like the camel, from my own consciousness', as he put it (R. (i). 68, headnote); and her destruction acts out in the most fiercesome way that denial of female individuality which such idealizations necessarily involve, a kind of perceptual or imaginative violence. 'How separate and unearthly love is,' as Philip Larkin put it, in lines at once romantic and undeluded about their own unrealizing romanticism,

> Or women are, or what they do,
> Or in our young unreal wishes
> Seem to be: synthetic, new,
> And natureless in ecstasies.

> ('The Large Cool Store')

It was Tennyson's own favourite among his poems, and he felt especially protective of 'poor little Maud' (*L*. ii. 127): it was his most ambitious and blackly witty response to the problem of storytelling, and a marvellously adroit expression of the scepticism about progressiveness that accompanied his deep belief in its necessity.

4

Grieving

What but tall tales, the luck of verbal playing,
Can trick his lying nature into saying
That love, or truth in any serious sense,
Like orthodoxy, is a reticence?

(W. H. Auden)

A memoirist records: 'I only once heard him talk much about
Arthur Hallam, and that was one evening over his port wine
when he dwelt on his intellectual power, on his geniality, on his
courtesy, and ended by saying, "How you would have loved
him!"' (*IR* 113). Arthur Hallam, the brightest star among the
Apostles (the society features in *IM* lxxxvii), the fiancé of
Tennyson's sister, and the subject of Tennyson's greatest poem,
In Memoriam A. H. H. Obiit MDCCCXXXIII, died, suddenly, from
a blood vessel burst in his brain, at the age of 22, in September
1833. The first sections of *In Memoriam* to be written date from
the month Tennyson learned of the death; it grew and grew
over the next seventeen years, haphazardly: 'I did not write
them with any view of weaving them into a whole, or for
publication, until I found that I had written so many,' Hallam
Tennyson, his son, reported the poet saying (*M*. i. 304); 'The
general way of its being written was so queer that if there were a
blank space I would put in a poem' (*IR* 96). Rearranged into a
fictive chronological order spanning nine years ('Epilogue', l.
10), it was finally published, with some important revisions
made on the eve of its appearance, in 1850.

The preoccupations I have been describing as Tennysonian –
change and recurrence, progress and the resistance to progress
– find a local habitation in the occasion of grief. Loss naturally
plunges the bereaved into a life largely composed of repeats: as
Alphonso Smith, one of our analysts of poetic repetition from

Chapter 1, puts it, 'the elegiac mood, in which the thought turns back so often upon itself, is best voiced by some form of repetition'.[1] But, as a genre, elegy must fulfil duties other than sad recollection: its purpose is to recall, but to be prospective too. For elegy properly acts out, in an exemplary way, what Freud called the 'work of mourning': the endpoint of any adequate response to loss is successfully persuading yourself (and perhaps others as well) that the diminished world is still worth enduring – such recuperation, says Freud, sets 'the ego . . . free and uninhibited again' as 'respect for reality gains the day'.[2] Elegy grows, that is to say, from the need to resolve a kind of double-heartedness: the desire to linger in the company of the dead, but also the obligation to move on. It is not merely a lament;[3] but rather a dealing with despair, spoken from the other side of grief; and the feeling that it moves toward is consolatory, but not simply consolatory. As Milton's 'Lycidas', which begins as lamentation and turns to solace: it commences in the numb repetition of devastation ('Lycidas is dead, dead ere his prime, | Young Lycidas, and hath not left his peer'), but modulates into serenity ('So Lycidas sunk low, but mounted high, | Through the dear might of him that walked the waves') and ends with a famous case of pressing on ('Tomorrow to fresh woods, and pastures new'). 'In an anomalous but real sense, the end of each elegy precedes its beginning,' W. David Shaw says;[4] and the 'Prologue' that Tennyson added to *In Memoriam* is meant to recognize just that: prayerfully stating the end before we begin ('I trust he lives in thee, and there | I find him worthier to be loved' (ll. 39–40)). And many readers have indeed been moved by the success of *In Memoriam* in achieving just that end: Bishop Westcott is reported in the *Memoir* saying, 'I rejoiced in the Introduction, which appeared to me to be the mature summing up after an interval of the many strains of thought in the "Elegies" ' (*M.* i. 300). Jerome Buckley tells us that 'Most of the reviewers . . . welcomed the poem as a quite adequate and deeply moving testimony of one man's triumphs over the doubts that beset their whole culture', a sense of the poem that he seems himself to share;[5] and he was (and is) not alone. E. D. H. Johnson sees the poem as a journey from 'Despair' to 'Faith';[6] Alan Sinfield finds it moving toward an 'eventual satisfaction with time and existence in general'.[7]

But, just as the lingering verbalism of the *Idylls* fails to fulfil the purposive destiny of true epic, so, as I shall be saying in this chapter, Tennyson's greatest elegies, and *In Memoriam* in particular, elude the expectations of classical elegy, while continually invoking their possibility. Sidgwick praised what he saw as 'the *forward* movement of the thought'; but added: 'And yet I have always felt that in a certain sense the effect of the introduction does not quite represent the effect of the poem. Faith, in the introduction, is too completely triumphant . . . Faith must give the last word: but the last word is not the whole utterance of the truth' (*M.* i. 302, 304). The determination to progress that Sidgwick admired evidently parallels the theme Tennyson ascribed to 'Ulysses' (also written in the aftermath of Hallam's death): 'the need of going forward, and braving the struggle of life' (*M.* i. 196). But 'Ulysses' articulates that need with magnificent equivocation, as we have seen, contemplating an enterprise that it cannot resolve itself finally to embark upon; and Tennyson's elegiac enterprise similarly envisages, without quite attaining, the happy ending of classical precedent.[8] Ulysses is making a speech (to his mariners) that is undermined by undisclosed feelings – an embarrassment of rhetoric by experience that *In Memoriam*, which is markedly reluctant to reach a last word, duplicates more profoundly. Hallam himself had written distrustfully of 'that return of the mind upon itself, and the habit of seeking relief in idiosyncracies rather than community of interest' that he saw as characteristic of modern poetry (*CH* 41); and much of the poignantly uneasy progress of *In Memoriam* (which repeatedly returns upon itself) is marked by the difficult transition between incommunicably private feeling and public accountability. The poem is 'anonymous but confessional', Ricks says, 'private but naked'.[9] Tennyson is said to have described *In Memoriam* as 'too hopeful . . . more than I am myself' (*IR* 96) – as though the generic duties mismatched with the raw material they had to work upon, or as though the outward and inward inflexions of the voice failed precisely to chime. And that, as I shall be arguing, is something that the poem's moving double life of wandering irresolution and wilfully advancing optimism surely communicates even to readers who have never come across Tennyson's (alleged) remark.[10]

*   *   *

129

In Memoriam contains some of Tennyson's greatest poetry of things returning: thoughts that return insistently to the dead one, anniversaries that unforgivingly recur. Eliot likened the poem to a diary, implying the sense of passing months and years that is so important a part of the poem's life;[11] there is an uninsistent but unmistakeable 'internal chronology' (as Bradley discerned);[12] and 'again' has its part to play.

> The seasons bring the flower again,
> And bring the firstling to the flock;
> And in the dusk of thee, the clock
> Beats out the little lives of men.
>
> (ii. 5–8)

The clock beats out a rhythm, like the mechanism of the heart; but also beats out lives, like beating out a fire: the vernal hopefulness of the first line is swiftly undone. 'Again' sounds like a knell when the poem records such seasonal changes ('The seasons bring the flower again, | And bring the firstling to the flock') and the passing regularities of the calendar ('Again at Christmas did we weave | The holly round the Christmas hearth' (lxxviii. 1–2)):

> I almost wished no more to wake,
> And that my hold on life would break
> Before I heard those bells again . . .
>
> (xxviii. 14–15)

(The epilogue attempts, with great tenderness, to redeem the word by involving it in the duplications of the marriage service: 'The ring is on, | The "wilt thou" answered, and again | The "wilt thou" asked, till out of twain | Her sweet "I will" has made you one' (ll. 53–6); but here we might find one evidence of a willed hope shaping the poem's structure that exceeds the emotional truthfulness of its component parts.)

The poem is full of verbal reiterations and recurrences, emulating in the verse's texture its dramatic scenes of revisiting: 'No poem so obsessively remembers itself as *In Memoriam* does,' says Armstrong;[13] and words, like 'again', that come again gain their special resonance because the poem is so broodingly preoccupied by something that will not come again – 'The words that are not heard again' (xviii. 20). As in other Tennyson poems, recurrence enjoys an intricate and paradoxical relationship with changefulness, which is true of much great elegy. In 'Lycidas', a poem that Tennyson thought 'a test of any reader's poetic instinct' (*M*. i. 152), the movement of spirit from despair to affirmation is voiced in the shifting inflections of the words, 'no more' – a quintessentially mournful phrase, it might seem, articulating pastness and prospect at once, and we know it stirred Tennyson deeply (see above, p. 51). The regretful, recollective 'no more' of Milton's opening lines ('The Willows, and the Hazle Copses green, | Shall now no more be seen, | Fanning their joyous Leaves to thy soft layes') shifts unostentatiously towards the progressive and resolute 'no more' of the poem's close ('Weep no more, woful Shepherds weep no more'): the reiteration beautifully insinuates a sameness within the change it announces. The demands of life oblige the poet to cease weeping, but his primal desolation lingers still in the poem's auditory consciousness: the reiteration of the phrase forges a continuity between the sense of loss and a turn to the rest of life – which is the business of mourning. (An analogous, and beautiful, example of the innate doubleness of elegiac feeling comes in the haunting first song of Schubert's *Winterreise*: the last verse repeats the same mournful tune as the previous three, but now shifted, in a nuance of unforgetful progress, from D minor to D major.[14])

In Memoriam is largely about imagining a relationship between the living and the dead, between Tennyson and Hallam of course, but also between Tennyson now and Tennyson then: the self that died when Hallam left it. ('We die with the dying', says Eliot in 'Little Gidding'. 'See, they depart, and we go with them.') Paying a visit to his old college, where he had first known Hallam, Tennyson tells us he

> caught once more the distant shout,
> The measured pulse of racing oars
> Among the willows; paced the shores
> And many a bridge, and all about

> The same gray flats again, and felt
> The same, but not the same; and last
> Up that long walk of limes I past
> To see the rooms in which he dwelt.

> Another name was on the door;
> I lingered . . .
>
> (lxxxvii. 9–18)

'The same, but not the same': a return ('again') occasions a repetition ('same . . . same') while admitting an unrepeatability ('not the same'); and, as in 'Tears, Idle Tears' and 'All along the valley' and others (see Chapter 1), the self is revealed to be at once a single thing and a gathering of many. A lovely poem late in the sequence wistfully attempts to resolve the paradox into a matter of nomenclature, as the Morning Star and the Evening Star are the same:

> Sweet Hesper-Phosphor, double name
> For what is one, the first, the last,
> Thou, like my present and my past,
> Thy place is changed; thou art the same.
>
> (cxxi. 17–20)

But the sense of the self's sad disjunctions is too fraught for so witty an answer.

Denying that death is death is what elegies normally do: it is what Milton does in 'Lycidas' ('Lycidas your sorrow is not dead') and Spenser does in his elegy for Sidney (the incredulous enquiry 'Ay me, can so diuine a thing be dead?' is answered, 'Ah no: it is not dead, ne can it die, | But liues for aie, in blisfull Paradise'). When *In Memoriam* turns to imagine Hallam's afterlife, it tries to envisage his death as a change like the changes of life that Tennyson himself has experienced, merely one that Tennyson has not been around to witness:

> But thou art turned to something strange,
> And I have lost the links that bound
> Thy changes; here upon the ground,
> No more partaker of thy change.
>
> (xli. 5–8)

That is the subject that Hallam himself wrote about in his essay on sympathy: 'that the soul exists as one subject in various successive states' (see above, p. 49); but here the idea is passionately invested with the need to believe Hallam is still somehow alive, in a 'second state sublime' (lxi. 1). 'His belief in personal immortality was passionate – I think almost the strongest passion that he had,' recalled Knowles of Tennyson; and his passion stirred in a way that, while certainly strong, was scarcely serene:

> I have heard him thunder out against an opponent of it, 'If there be a God that has made the earth and put this hope and passion into us, it must foreshow the truth. If it be not true, then no God, but a mocking fiend, created us, and' (growing crimson with excitement) 'I'd shake my fist in his almighty face, and tell him that I cursed him! I'd sink my head to-night in a chloroformed handkerchief and have done with it all.' (*IR* 91)

And to Allingham: 'I feel myself to be a centre – can't believe I shall die. Sometimes I have doubts, of a morning' (*IR* 56).

Doubts feature in *In Memoriam* as grounds for self-reproach:

> My own dim life should teach me this,
> That life shall live for evermore,
> Else earth is darkness at the core,
> And dust and ashes all that is . . .

(xxxiv. 1–4)

The lines are passionately insistent (life . . . life . . . live), but the reasoning is poignantly precarious. (Coleridge, who importantly shaped the Apostles' religious views, urges something similar in his poem 'Human Life: On the Denial of Immortality'.) At his more hopeful, Tennyson sings to himself about the dead: 'They do not die | Nor lose their mortal sympathy, | Nor change to us, although they change' (xxx. 22–4), which nicely sets the proper assertion of elegy ('They do not die') against a gently concessive euphemism ('although they change'). But the 'change' in question is really immensely troubling: the poem broods so insistently upon the bodily presence of Hallam, especially his 'hands so often clasped in mine' (x. 19) – 'Reach out dead hands to comfort me' (lxxx. 16) – that the bleakly unspeakable thought of physical dissolution unmistakably shadows these thoughts of 'change': 'from his ashes may be made | The violet of his native land' (xviii. 3–4). And yet the thought of Hallam's continuing existence, 'whate'er he be' (cvii. 23), while a comfort, is also a torment, since it implies the friends are still alive to grow apart. Tennyson worries that the dead man in his 'novel world' is forgetting him (lxii. 9); and he invents as an analogy for their separated lives a lovely story of two villagers, one of whom

133

progresses far in the state: each thinks of the other with whom he is no longer living. The countryman wonders: 'Does my old friend remember me?' (lxiv. 28). The domesticity of the story only emphasizes the unimaginability of the state into which Hallam has really progressed; and the question 'Does my old friend remember me?' masks a more dejected thought: sometimes I cannot remember him.

> I cannot see the features right,
> When on the gloom I strive to paint
> The face I know . . .
>
> (lxx. 1–3)

Elegy regards change in a dual aspect, terribly aware of the destructive power of 'tenfold-complicated change' (xciii. 12) – as Milton's shepherd sings, 'But O the heavy change, now thou art gone, | Now thou art gone, and never must return!' – but stirred too by its possible healthfulness:

> good shall fall
> At last—far off—at last, to all,
> And every winter change to spring
>
> (liv. 14–16)

In Memoriam, like 'Lycidas', is a poem of 'no more': 'A hand that can be clasped no more' (vii. 5). 'No more?' is the most terrible possibility it entertains (lvi. 21). The poem circles around the thought of 'The darkened heart that beat no more' (xix. 2): it is the surviving half of a sadly interrupted conversation ('in dear words of human speech | We two communicate no more' (lxxxv. 83–4)), and moves, or means to move, towards consolation: 'No more shall wayward grief abuse | The genial hour' (cv. 9). The elegist's progressive duty to believe 'That men may rise on stepping-stones | Of their dead selves to higher things' (i. 3–4) is announced in the poem's opening lines; but any such movement is impeded by a countering emotion which Tennyson at once confesses:

> sweeter to be drunk with loss,
> To dance with death, to beat the ground,
>
> Than that the victor Hours should scorn
> The long result of love . . .
>
> (i. 11–14)

One of the abiding themes of the poem is the dismal
proximity of time's power to heal with its inducement to forget
– the thought that any reduction in the immensity of loss would
be a disloyalty: 'O grief, can grief be changed to less?' (lxxviii.
16). (Tennyson glossed some of his lines: 'Yet it is better to bear
the wild misery of extreme grief than that Time should
obliterate the sense of loss and deaden the power of love' (ii.
9–16 n.).) 'I long to prove | No lapse of moons can canker Love'
(xxvi. 2–3); and the poem prolongs so to prove, barely moving
toward an end which it desires but deplores ('A grief, then
changed to something else' (lxxvii. 11)), disposed to bid loss
farewell but unwilling to leave it behind; like Ulysses on the
shore, the poem repeatedly announces its imminent purpose to
move on, but finds itself lingering:

> Come; let us go; your cheeks are pale;
>   But half my life I leave behind:
>   Methinks my friend is richly shrined;
> But I shall pass; my work will fail.

> (lvii. 5–8)

Two voices are inextricably intertwined there, turning about a
repeated ambiguity in 'But' ('merely' and also 'and yet'): with
brave sardonicism, 'I abandon only half my life by pressing on';
but also a protest, as though the second line responded to the
bracing suggestion of the first, 'But I am abandoning half my life
by pressing on'. The third line hopes to boost a sense of purpose,
which the fourth promptly undoes: the heroic contrast is
between the dead friend's perpetual magnificence and the
erring poet's transience ('I alone shall pass away, not him'); but
if what enshrines the friend is *this* 'work', *these* elegies (which is
what Tennyson once said[15]), then the last 'But' of the stanza
uncompromisingly asserts the sad precariousness of the friend's
immortality, and retrospectively draws out the fallibility lurking
within the unconcealed subjectivism of 'Methinks'.

The wavering life of the thing is partly communicated
through rhyme. The political poems that Tennyson wrote in
the early 1830s, like 'Hail Briton!' (R. (i). 194), had applauded
change while fearing it (see Chapter 2), a mixture of minds that
had prompted Tennyson to devise a stanza rhyming ABBA: the
earliest fragments of *In Memoriam* used an ABAB stanza (see R.,

135

headnote), but Tennyson soon came to adopt the ABBA verse for the task.[16] Culler makes a connection between the way the poem leads 'uncertainly, fitfully, gradually to a doubtful conclusion' and the 'political gradualism' of the public poems, and links it to the verse form they have in common;[17] but the stanza's life is perhaps less one of gradual progress than suspended immobility – 'especially suited to turning round rather than going forward'[18] – though not quite without thoughts of going forward too. It is a Petrarchan sonnet that never reaches the turn of the sestet, and the poem as a whole a sequence of disappointed sonnets: there is a ubiquitous feel of incompleteness, as though registering 'The quiet sense of something lost' (lxxviii. 8). Many critics have written most beautifully about the verse form – as Charles Kingsley:

> The poems seem often merely to be united by the identity of their metre, so exquisitely chosen, that while the major rhyme in the second and third lines of each stanza gives the solidity and self-restraint required by such deep themes, the mournful minor rhyme of each first and fourth line always leads the ear to expect something beyond . . . (CH 183)

The stanza is one of the great formal responses to the occasion of elegy, recognizing the obligation to move on, while honestly registering a compulsion to retrogress – a paradoxical matter of 'loiter[ing] on' (xxxviii. 1). 'Rhyme has been said to contain in itself a constant appeal to Memory and Hope,' Hallam wrote in an essay to which Christopher Ricks alerts us (HW 222).[19] If each In Memoriam stanza begins with hope, it soon relapses into sad memory – the verse is self-enfolding ('that large grief which these enfold' (v. 11)). As Kingsley says, the verse couples a gesture of confirmation (in its middle couplet) with a backward movement of the mind (in its outer rhyme), so that each stanza, no matter the sense of purpose with which it embarks, ends haunted acoustically by the thought with which it began. It is a stanza 'which can "circle moaning in the air"', returning to its setting out, and with fertile circularity staving off its deepest terror of arrival at desolation and indifference', says Ricks, 'the perfect embodiment of the true relationship of faith to faintness in the poem'.[20]

As was true of our other Tennysonian spokesmen, the poet in *In Memoriam* repeatedly finds his resolution to press on stayed by a desire to keep oneself unmoved:

> I turn to go: my feet are set
> > To leave the pleasant fields and farms;
> > They mix in one another's arms
> To one pure image of regret.

(cii. 21–4)

(The first line's adroit enjambement – 'my feet are set' – works the stop–go effect – 'are set | To leave' – that the stanza articulates at large.) The interplay of resolve and remembrance is finely enacted in a succession of settings-out and dyings-back:

> Ah yet, even yet, if this might be,
> > I, falling on his faithful heart,
> > Would breathing through his lips impart
> The life that almost dies in me;
>
> That dies not, but endures with pain,
> > And slowly forms the firmer mind,
> > Treasuring the look it cannot find,
> The words that are not heard again.

(xviii. 13–20)

The 'firmer mind' finds a confirming rhyme; but the stanza quickly loses its fleeting sense of affirmation and returns, instead, to the sound of 'pain' again. This verse does not enact Sidgwick's '*forward* movement of the thought', but rather what Tennyson himself calls 'backward fancy':

> Ah, backward fancy, wherefore wake
> > The old bitterness again, and break
> The low beginnings of content

(lxxxiv. 46–8)

Moving in this way between the therapeutic success of elegy's comic progressiveness and the backward yearnings of regret, *In Memoriam* invents itself *sui generis* as it goes along: 'Still onward winds the weary way; | I with it' (xxvi.1-2).[21] The rival titles that Tennyson contemplated nicely suggest the impulses between which his poem wandered.[22] At one point he was considering 'Fragments of an Elegy' (*M.* i. 293), which (like his description of the work in section xlviii as 'Short swallow-flights

137

of song' that evade 'a larger lay') frankly concedes a kind of incompleteness; at other times, he called it *The Way of the Soul*, which implies a greater sense of an ending – at his most positive on the matter, he compared the progress of *In Memoriam* to that of 'a kind of *Divina Commedia*, ending with happiness' (*M.* i. 304). Well, the story certainly begins with grief ('He is not here' (vii. 9)) and ends with an auspicious marriage (Tennyson's sister's), and the 'Prologue' confirms the poem's present tense faithfully beyond the moment of devastation. Tennyson evidently worked to bring his poem within the expectations of elegy; and FitzGerald, for one, gruffly testifies to his outward success: 'it is about three years before the Poetic Soul walks itself out of darkness and Despair into Common Sense.'[23] But FitzGerald exaggerates the final victory: when Bradley scrutinized the poem for a structure like that of 'Lycidas' – what he called 'the transition from gloom to glory' – the poem proved itself stubbornly unwilling to oblige.[24] The poem is acutely mindful of such transitional expectations, but it is much less simply progressive: its recurrent pattern of feeling, as J. C. C. Mays describes it in one of the best accounts, 'is of movement forward, yet also retraction, and a going on again from there'.[25] A series of repeated returns from which to go on again sounds like something unfinished: Aubrey de Vere thought the task of a *Divina Commedia* incomplete, anyway, and with some tactlessness 'suggested that perhaps he might at some later time give to the whole work its third part, or Paradise. The poet's answer was this: "I have written what I have felt and known; and I will never write anything else"' (*M.* i. 294).

Critics were once much drawn by this question of the work's achieved unity: that is what drew Eliot to his comparison with a diary (the unity of which is real but uninsistent). I suppose the issue seems less pressing now, but it is not irrelevant: for it responds to a real anxiety already alive in the poem. Tennyson's own sense of the work, declared within the work, is as a directionless, recurrently retrodden path: the 'Prologue' apologizes before we begin for the 'wild and wandering cries' to follow (l. 41). Chesterton once said that 'rhyme does go with reason, since the aim of both is to bring things to an end'.[26] But rhyme in *In Memoriam* works with all the insistence of unmitigated grief to a quite opposite effect, insinuating not the achievement of an end but the atmosphere of unfinished business I have been describing (leading the ear 'to expect something beyond'); and what is true of the movements of the individual stanzas is true too of the poem as a whole:

> I wander, often falling lame,
> And looking back to whence I came,
> Or on to where the pathway leads . . .
>
> (xxiii. 6–8)

'To wander on a darkened earth' (lxxxv. 31) is not the proper business of elegy, however; and nor of life, as the poem seeks to make quite clear: 'My heart, though widowed, may not rest | Quite in the love of what is gone' (lxxxv. 113–14). (Everything there depends on the diverse inflexions of 'Quite', more surprising than the 'Quiet' we might have expected; the word is marvellously placed to qualify 'rest': 'may not rest complete in such love', but yet 'may *almost* rest in such love'.) And the highly self-conscious formal perplexities of the poem coincide with its doctrinal indecisiveness: Tennyson invokes with such disquiet the idea of 'some wild Poet, when he works | Without a conscience or an aim' (xxxiv. 7–8) because he is unable quite to exclude the possibility that such a poet might actually be holding true to the nature of things, emulating a wider purposelessness:

> Oh yet we trust that somehow good
> Will be the final goal of ill,
> To pangs of nature, sins of will,
> Defects of doubt, and taints of blood;
>
> That nothing walks with aimless feet . . .
>
> (liv. 1–5)

The scrupulous imprecision of 'somehow' takes 'trust' down a notch; and 'final' makes a nice appearance, as though to imply a sequence of intermediate goals that may be no good at all. For while (as we have seen) the thought of a final goal often preoccupied Tennyson, his poems rarely arrive at the ends they imagine (as we have also seen): *In Memoriam* entertains the thought of 'some settled end' (lxxxv. 97), but the uncertainty of an ending proves more fruitful:

saying; 'Comes he thus, my friend?
Is this the end of all my care?'
And circle moaning in the air:
'Is this the end? Is this the end?'

(xii. 13–16)

'*In Memoriam* never resolves anything,' says Armstrong.[27] Its inimitable greatness lies in its honest incapacity, as though registering in the disappointment of genre the spirit of an unpropitious age. The poem is secretly party to those whom it hopes to correct, 'those that eddy round and round' (liii. 12). Tennyson gathers his resources from time to time to announce an appropriate close – 'Yet Hope had never lost her youth; | She did but look through dimmer eyes' (cxxv. 5–6) – but hardly plausibly when Hallam is pictured beaming over the universe like a Cheshire cat, 'knowing all is well' (cxxvii. 18–20). The same message is delivered at one point by a 'sentinel', though hardly with a clarion trumpet: 'And whispers to the worlds of space, | In the deep night, that all is well' (cxxvi. 11–12). The poem attempts to imagine a permanent goodbye on several occasions, bidding ' "Adieu, adieu" for evermore' (lvii. 16) – but only to carry on at once ('In those sad words I took farewell' (lviii. 1)). In section xlvii, Tennyson imagines with gentle scepticism the possibility of re-encountering the dead ('And I shall know him when we meet' (l. 8)): 'to clasp and say, | "Farewell! We lose ourselves in light" ' (ll. 15–16). But even this would only be another point at which to begin again; he told Knowles: 'but at least one last parting! and always would want it again – of course' (l. 14 n.). Approaching the close of the sequence, Tennyson offers what might serve as motto for the whole: 'though my lips may breathe adieu, | I cannot think the thing farewell' (cxxiii. 11–12). That asserts a necessary hope – 'I cannot conceive that this is really a parting forever, that he is *really* dead' – but it quietly sounds a more disconsolate note too – 'I go through the motions of getting on, but I am simply unable to shift myself beyond this thing': the tenacity of bereavement is appalling. The reference in the hopeful line 'Ring out, wild bells, and let him die' (cvi. 4) is to the old year, not the dead friend; but in a poem that has used 'him' so insistently for Hallam ('And I shall know him when we meet' (xlvii. 8)) the line comes nevertheless with a sharp surprise, as though hinting at something compelling but scarcely admissible, a principle of self-preservation desperate to let grief go.

The poem comes nearest to the *peripeteia* of classical elegy in section xcv, which describes a numinous communion while Tennyson is reading Hallam's letters.[28]

> And strangely on the silence broke
>> The silent-speaking words, and strange
>> Was love's dumb cry defying change
> To test his worth; and strangely spoke
>
> The faith, the vigour, bold to dwell
>> On doubts that drive the coward back,
>> And keen through wordy snares to track
> Suggestion to her inmost cell.
>
> So word by word, and line by line,
>> The dead man touched me from the past,
>> And all at once it seemed at last
> The living soul was flashed on mine,
>
> And mine in this was wound, and whirled
>> About empyreal heights of thought,
>> And came on that which is, and caught
> The deep pulsations of the world,
>
> Æonian music measuring out
>> The steps of Time – the shocks of Chance –
>> The blows of Death. At length my trance
> Was cancelled, stricken through with doubt.
>
>> (xcv. 25–44)

Reading letters written by a dead loved one might well touch you; but Tennyson's lines invest the dead metaphor with the intensity of yearning to be *really* touched that has marked the whole poem: 'Descend, and touch, and enter; hear | The wish too strong for words to name' (xciii. 13–14). 'And all at once it seemed at last | The living soul was flashed on mine': both 'at once' and 'at last', the line confuses time, and a vertiginous movement of epiphany (a revelation of 'that which is') emerges in the space between 'whirled' and 'world'. Alan Sinfield finds in the lines 'a mystical apprehension of absolute reality';[29] but the whole event is held within the tentative rule of a 'seemed', and it is described in immediate retrospect as a 'trance': the poem's characteristic oscillation of spirit from assurance to doubt moves within four lines from the assertive grandeur of 'Æonian music' to 'doubt'. (The word 'flash' has been associated so far in the poem with the most fleeting and tenuous glimpses of hope: xli. 12; xliv. 8; lxxxviii. 12.) Most tellingly, as Kennedy has said well, the verses invert the typical turn of elegy: for they insist, not on Hallam's continuing survival, but on his implacable *removal* from Tennyson's world and life ('The dead man'). [30] Tennyson, glossing the line 'The living soul' (in earlier printings it was 'His living soul'), offered an exemplarily hesitant paraphrase: 'The Deity, maybe'.

Maybe. Tennyson's genius for irresolution – 'undulations to and fro' (cxiii. 20) – ensures that the more firm-hearted moments of hope in the poem seem painfully unfirm: the essayist's 'we' rarely rings true ('And yet we trust it comes from thee, | A beam in darkness: let it grow ('Prologue', ll. 23–4)), while the personal 'we' is often devastating ('We cannot hear each other speak' (lxxxii. 16)). Iris Murdoch once put the elegist's dilemma with memorable stringency: 'The temptation of art, a temptation to which every work of art yields except the greatest ones, is to console.'[31] *In Memoriam*, at its frequent best, scrupulously avoids indulging in consolations that it cannot honestly sustain. 'And like a man in wrath the heart | Stood up and answered "I have felt"' (cxxiv. 15–16): the absoluteness of that comes with a Wordsworth sanction (from 'Tintern Abbey': 'And I have felt | A presence that disturbs me with the joy | Of elevated thoughts'); but (as is true too of its Wordsworthian precursor) the certitude of the claim is not unaccompanied by a reserve. It is thrillingly emphatic to announce in that way, 'I have *felt*', a claim with an unanswerable spiritual obduracy, something like Luther's 'Here I stand'; yes, but is this *feeling* a bolstering of the normal business of, say, merely *knowing* or *understanding*, or is it a vulnerably emotive alternative? (Vulnerable because of the room for hesitancy that opens up in the sense of *feel*, 'to apprehend or recognize the truth of (something) on grounds not distinctly perceived' (*OED*).) As Sidgwick shrewdly noted, no sooner does Tennyson utter his heartfelt assurance than it is withdrawn ('No, like a child in doubt and fear' (cxxiv. 17)): 'he gives the turn to humility', says Sidgwick finely (*M*. i. 303). When, finally, Hallam's afterlife is imagined, fondly but unsentimentally, as a kind of Wordsworthian dispersal amidst nature (rolled round in earth's diurnal course), it is a continuity as close to a dissolution as might be:

> But though I seem in star and flower
> To feel thee some diffusive power,
> I do not therefore love thee less . . .

(cxxx. 6–8)

The poem's belated close maintains the poise of its 'doubtful gleam of solace' (xxxviii. 8):

> That friend of mine who lives in God,
>
> That God, which ever lives and loves,
> One God, one law, one element,
> And one far-off divine event,
> To which the whole creation moves.

('Epilogue', ll. 140–4)

All moves to the divine event, yet it remains 'far-off'; and the rhyme, an off-rhyme if not far-off (loves | moves), quietly insinuates something less than resounding harmony, as it has done before in the poem when moving to close confidently upon a hope: 'The truths that never can be proved | Until we close with all we loved' (cxxxi. 10–11). (Cf. xxvi. 2–3; xlviii. 5, 8; 'Epilogue', ll. 6–7.) The last section before the final 'Epilogue' deflects the sense of an ending with disabused wit, gathering up 'end' into the alternative, stoical destiny of 'endure': 'O living will that shalt endure' (cxxxi. 1). A little before that, what it is of Hallam that has endured is described with great tenderness, and recognized as a memory:

> Known and unknown; human, divine;
> Sweet human hand and lips and eye;
> Dear heavenly friend that canst not die,
> Mine, mine, for ever, ever mine;
>
> Strange friend, past, present, and to be;
> Loved deeplier, darklier understood;
> Behold, I dream a dream of good,
> And mingle all the world with thee.

(cxxix. 5–12)

A discreet triumph of *In Memoriam*, at once poetic and moral, is the way it concedes to Hallam – for all the idealization he

143

obviously enjoys[32] – a kind of independent reality, even when death has transformed him purely into an object of the poet's consciousness. 'Mine, mine, for ever, ever mine': in a way that is true of any memory; but the verses go on, most beautifully, to suggest that Tennyson's imaginative possession is very different from the self-serving appropriation of the bereft sentimentalist: 'Strange friend, past, present, and to be; | Loved deeplier, darklier understood'. The Tennysonian preoccupations of change and the unchanging seldom meet with more effect: 'Strange friend' lucidly admits a change as well as a continuing familiarity; 'darklier understood' gently concedes an obscurity as well as a lasting intimacy. 'I have thee still' (cxxx. 14).

Elegy's denial of death obviously finds an important precedent in Christ, who was dead but did not die, and in His healing of Jairus's daughter: 'the damosell is not dead, but sleepeth' (Mark v: 39). But the elegiac turn need not be Christian: in his elegy for Keats, the intently atheistical Shelley finds Platonic reasons to be cheerful: 'Peace, peace! he is not dead, he doth not sleep – | He hath awakened from the dream of life.' Shelley thinks of Keats's death as implicated within a persisting natural order (Keats is 'made one with Nature'), a primitive and profound elegiac instinct that is not irreconcilable with Christianity but not synonymous with it either: a sense of meaningful relationship with nature is what matters. ('To accept death is to catch a glimpse of the transcendent,' writes a contemporary, 'to see how nature furthers human purpose even when it most seems to frustrate it'.[33]) Classical elegies were often written as pastoral, placed in the mouths of artlessly grieving shepherds to emphasize the profound and beautiful connection between unsullied nature and the heart's vicissitudes. (Milton is following in an ancient tradition when he has nature mourn for Lycidas: 'Bid Amaranthus all his beauty shed, | And Daffadillies fill their cups with tears.') Ruskin's undeluded label for such comforting natural sympathy is 'pathetic fallacy': for it is an illusion to think the material world is somehow in tune with what we are feeling, even if, as Eric Smith says, ' "Fallacy" of this sort springs out of basic human needs'.[34]

The undeluded heart of *In Memoriam* certainly recognizes the old fallacies, and the egotistic distortion of nature's heedlessness that grief may incite: 'The wild unrest that lives in woe | Would dote and pore on yonder cloud' (xv. 15–16). In 'Lycidas', the attentive permanence of pastoral nature merges with the eternity of heaven; but in *In Memoriam*, nature exemplifies a frightening universal principle of flux and impermanence.[35] The Tennysonian obsession that the only constant thing is change grows here to a universal magnitude: 'O earth, what changes hast thou seen! . . . The hills are shadows, and they flow | From form to form, and nothing stands' (cxxiii. 2, 5–6). (It is an incidental pleasure that, in verses so moved by the thought of fluent mutability, we should be able to watch 'From' mutate into 'form'.) Sorrow tells him, early on, that 'The stars . . . blindly run' (iii. 5); and the seasons' unaffected succession, occurring in the background of the poem, is tacit testimony to nature's unstartled indifference.

Such indifference is often an important ingredient in Tennysonian elegy, coupled with an awareness of the 'basic human needs' that wish things were otherwise:

> Break, break, break,
>   On thy cold gray stones, O Sea!
> And I would that my tongue could utter
>   The thoughts that arise in me.
>
> O well for the fisherman's boy,
>   That he shouts with his sister at play!
> O well for the sailor lad,
>   That he sings in his boat on the bay!
>
> And the stately ships go on
>   To their haven under the hill;
> But O for the touch of a vanished hand,
>   And the sound of a voice that is still!
>
> Break, break, break,
>   At the foot of thy crags, O Sea!
> But the tender grace of a day that is dead
>   Will never come back to me.

(R. (ii). 228)

The lines couple the dark inconsequence that shapes 'Mariana' with all the fruitful incapacity of 'Tears, Idle Tears': the poem appears to base itself on an analogy between the breaking of the sea and the poet's unutterable loss, and ranges through a visible scene as though to confirm it, but discovers instead a series of imponderable gaps. 'Thus does Lord Tennyson turn an ordinary sea-shore landscape into a means of finding a voice indescribably sweet for the dumb spirit of human loss', said the excellent Hutton; but, movingly, the secret of the voice really lies in the *failure* of what Hutton goes on to praise: 'Lord Tennyson's power of compelling the external world' (*CH* 360). For the external world declines to be so compelled: the logic of the transitions from outer to inner – 'And I would that my tongue' and 'But O for the touch' – is sadly obscure; the conjunctions might as well be swapped, as though the normal meaningfulness of syntax were spent, or language itself had become pointless. The poem exhibits a wholly unostentatious heroism in striving to make sense, setting itself about rhetorical manoeuvres that imply an ordered connectedness to thought; but its attempts are undone, and instead of moving forward with its analogy, as the consequentiality of its grammar promises, the poem circles forlornly back to its initial perplexity: 'Break, break, break'. As with *In Memoriam*, the recurrences that do occur unforgivingly accentuate what 'will never come back': the effect is as far from histrionics as it might be, evoking a broken world, one that does not quite manage to make sense, as though something were missing. Which it is, of course; but the loss is made known in the most discreet of ways, as though too momentous to be brought nakedly to mind: 'the tender grace of a day that is dead | Will never come back to me'. ('[A] *day* that is dead' gently invokes poetry to evade the thought of a less figurative death.)

The best sections of *In Memoriam* similarly turn about a broken inability to articulate.

> Dark house, by which once more I stand
>   Here in the long unlovely street,
>   Doors, where my heart was used to beat
> So quickly, waiting for a hand,
>
> A hand that can be clasped no more –
>   Behold me, for I cannot sleep,
>   And like a guilty thing I creep
> At earliest morning to the door.
>
> He is not here; but far away
>   The noise of life begins again,

> And ghastly through the drizzling rain
> On the bald street breaks the blank day.

(vii)

It is one of the saddest returns in the poem, set in that melancholy time after a friend's death that Coleridge once described, 'when the dizziness, heat, & drunkenness of Grief is gone | and the pang of hollowness is first felt'.[36] The poignancy of Tennyson's poem, as with 'Break, break, break', is largely the work of its precarious sequentiality, as though it were driven by subterranean movements of feeling that disrupt the brave accomplishment of the surface. The vocative address to the 'Dark house' and to the 'Doors' appears the accomplished deployment of an ancient literary tactic; but the passing mention of 'a hand' stops the poetry in its tracks ('a hand, | | A hand') – things stunned still by the thought 'A hand that can be clasped no more – '. The dash there implies a train of thought abandoned, almost like one of Sterne's dashes from *Tristram Shandy*, as though enacting a real-time authorial interruption to the performance. The tone is quite different of course, as the poem's air of literary self-possession is punctured with a terrible plea for witness: 'Behold me' – which, especially following so hard upon the lost palpability of 'clasped', cannot wholly conceal a yet more naked cry, 'hold me'. The logic of 'Behold me, for I cannot sleep' is marvellously tenuous, as though the thought of sleeplessness had arisen with such insistence that the sentence was helpless to repress it: 'like a guilty thing I creep | At earliest morning to the door', a broken-spirited compulsion to return which the rhyme's familiar circling back sadly emulates. The idea that has lain unexpressed so far finally breaks into voice: 'He is not here'; and within it hope and despair commingle. 'He is not here; but far away': the line ending fleetingly allows the ghost of an optimism, 'He is not here, he is far away'; but also, and mostly, 'He is not here, where he would normally have been, because he is not, anywhere.' ('The intimation of a possible immortality plays over the line before the line drops into the blank space of the page, to re-emerge from it as something quite alien to hope,' is how Griffiths puts it.[37]) The sentence unfolds through the last stanza to describe another kind of unwelcome coming again: not life, but the noise of it; another day, 'blank' with *ennui*, not with the possibility of a

147

clean sheet. The blank day breaks, as a heart, or a chain of thought, might. (The marvellous fragmented narratives set into *In Memoriam* that report back from Tennyson's dreams strike a local note of hurt and haunted inconsequentiality, as though gathering into the unembarrassed clarity of dream logic the obscurer perplexities of the poem's waking life. In one, an angel rescues him from a reproachful crowd and speaks encouragingly, but the poem ends: 'The words were hard to understand' (lxix. 20). Another, telling the story of a boat journey, ends with a similarly evocative refusal to conclude, as if the episode were interrupted by an unannounced awakening: 'We steered her toward a crimson cloud | That landlike slept along the deep' (ciii. 55–6).)

Despite the prevailing, disabused anti-pastoral temper, Tennyson occasionally casts himself as a mourning shepherd, especially in some of the earlier sections ('I take the grasses of the grave, | And make them pipes whereon to blow' (xxi. 3–4)); and he sometimes imagines pastoral styles of responsiveness.[38] With needy tenderness, he enjoins the elements to bear the beloved's body across the sea, as though addressing a heedful universe ('Sleep, gentle heavens, before the prow; | Sleep, gentle winds, as he sleeps now' (ix. 14–15)); and he momentarily feels the hushed Wye to be in tune with his 'deepest grief' (xix. 10); the death of Hallam is said in one section to have 'sickened every living bloom, | And blurred the splendour of the sun' (lxxii. 7–8). Such lingering pastoralism has made some readers uneasy about its conventional feel; but the sense of the formulaic is really the point.[39] The pastoral gesticulations are a part of the 'sad mechanic exercise' (v. 7): the sort of thing elegies properly involve (as Hallam himself would have doubtless appreciated), even if they have now grown fallacious – an archaic sort of pursuit like writing epically in an age of steam about the fairies or King Arthur. 'Don't you think the world wants other notes than elegiac now?' FitzGerald asked, when he learnt of plans to publish the poem, 'Lycidas is the utmost length an elegiac should reach' (R., headnote). In his unimpressed but characteristically shrewd way FitzGerald puts his finger on the poem's moving experiment with tradition – how its forlorn genius lies just in the way that it alludes to a pastoral consolation that it cannot manage to bring off, nor for which it can abandon all hope – always aspiring (as does 'Break, break, break' on its smaller scale) to a purposeful 'way' but guiltily troubled by the thought of 'aimless feet' (liv. 5). The poem's pastoral elements are one way of keeping going: another of FitzGerald's sharp but insightful remarks about the poem noted its air of emerging from 'a Poetical Machine of the highest order'[40] – which tartly revises a self-deprecating thought that Tennyson himself entertains about the mechanic exercise that distracts him from despair.

The poem repeatedly professes itself merely a sort of sketch or ghost of the thing it should be ('given in outline and no more' (v. 12)), incapable of doing justice to the task in hand. Tennyson often himself imagines, within the poem, FitzGerald-style objections:

> 'Is this an hour
> For private sorrow's barren song,
> When more and more the people throng
> The chairs and thrones of civil power?[']
>
> (xxi. 13–16)

Doubt characterizes more than the poem's religious opinions: it dismisses itself as the work of 'an earthly Muse . . . | And owning but a little art' (xxxvii. 13–14). Words are here no certain good: again and again the poem doubts its own competence ('I cannot all command the strings' (lxxxviii. 10)), bemoans its inadequacy ('I leave thy praises unexpressed' (lxxv. 1)), and hopes anxiously to abandon its limits and 'ring the fuller minstrel in' (cvi. 20). These remarks revoice, in more sombre circumstances, that edgy self-deprecation with which (as we have seen) Tennyson often couched about his poems; and FitzGerald, who assumed a brusque line on the necessity of pushing on, picked up on their apologetic uncertainty acerbically, sounding like Carlyle on 'Mariana': 'if Tennyson had got on a horse and ridden twenty miles, instead of moaning over his pipe, he would have been cured of his sorrows in half the time.'[41] Instead, mournful and piping, the poem dwells in a state of anxious self-consciousness: a poem about the kind of poem it should be trying to be, about the kind it finds itself being instead.

149

In the *Memoir* his son repeats Tennyson's words: 'had it not been for the intervention of his friends, he declared it not unlikely that after the death of Hallam he would not have continued to write' (*M. i.* 97); and *In Memoriam* is, in a way, as much the record of his disinclination to write as the evidence of its overcoming, insistently questioning its own competence and appropriateness:

> I sometimes hold it half a sin
> To put in words the grief I feel;
> For words, like Nature, half reveal
> And half conceal the Soul within.

(v. 1–4)

It returns to the idea that verbal expertise might necessarily be at odds with emotional veracity ('My words are only words, and moved | Upon the topmost froth of thought' (lii. 3–4)), summonable only when the deepest reaches of desolation have been wordlessly navigated ('My deeper anguish also falls, | And I can speak a little then' (xix. 15–16)). Haunted by such thoughts, the poem keeps almost giving up: 'What hope is here for modern rhyme' (lxxvii. 1). It self-checkingly quotes itself ('"So careful of the type?" but no' (lvi. 1)), and mulls its purposes and procedures ('I count it crime | To mourn for any overmuch' (lxxxv. 61-2)) and its progress or lack of progress ('in my sorrow shut, | Or breaking into song by fits' (xxiii. 1–2)). All of which might sound tiresomely self-knowing; but such self-awareness here is a mark of diffidence, not aggrandisement, and anyhow possesses an important kind of psychological truth, for self-consciousness is not the least burdensome part of grief: 'I not only live each endless day in grief,' as C. S. Lewis wrote in his self-portrait of bereavement, *A Grief Observed*, 'but live each day thinking about living each day in grief'.[42]

A style of diffidence is one of the poem's greatest resources: few works bear out so well Marianne Moore's axiom 'that the deepest feeling manifests itself in restraint'.[43] (Eric Griffiths writes with special discrimination about Tennyson's uses of reticence in *The Printed Voice of Victorian Poetry*.[44]) Reticence was in order precisely because the obligations to speak out seemed so pressing: private dismay at Hallam's death within the

Apostolic circle was intensified by a sense of a nation bereft: statesman, scholar, poet he; and a sense of a public responsibility was evidently not lost on Tennyson as the sections of the poem gathered in manuscript. He was sharply aware of the relevance and universality of his theme and its religious predicaments: ' "I" is not always the author speaking of himself', he said, 'but the voice of the human race speaking thro' him' (*M.* i. 305); and, towards the end of the poem especially, there is a growing awareness that private lament must give over to a wider duty ('I will not shut me from my kind' (cviii. 1)).

But the sense of such public responsibilities is checked by a counter-sense, of the incommunicably personal nature of the poem's truest feeling:

> That loss is common would not make
> My own less bitter, rather more:
> Too common!

(vi. 5–7)

Reticence is all – as when a thought slips into view, giving the sense of something that had been all along in mind, but which the poetry could not bring itself publicly to acknowledge. (Section cviii is a good example of that: the poem's bracing and general rhetorical questions maintain a brave face; but, in a last turn of the verse, the final word – 'thee' – brings abruptly to light an always present but unmentionable thing.) The necessary reticence of Tennysonian elegy is beautifully exemplified in a poem that he wrote, also in the *In Memoriam* stanza, after the death of his son Lionel. It is addressed to the Marquis of Dufferin and Ava, with whom Lionel had been staying in India:

> But ere he left your fatal shore,
> And lay on that funereal boat,
> Dying, 'Unspeakable' he wrote
> 'Their kindness', and he wrote no more.

('To the Marquis of Dufferin and Ava', R. (iii). 427, ll. 33–6)

John Bayley writes finely about the way 'Unspeakable' there 'hovers between the colloquial exaggeration of social use . . . and a word that can mean exactly what it says'[45] – that the word comes from the private space of a letter home, brought into the publicity of a poetic epistle, is additionally appropriate, affording a glimpse of an unspeakable emotional life that the

151

poetry may register but cannot wholly comprehend. Unspeak-ability of one sort or another is always involved with the most characteristic Tennysonian acts of eloquence: 'What hope of answer, or redress? | Behind the veil, behind the veil' (lvi. 27–8). To say so implies that the poetry effects a kind of inwardness. Bayley writes elsewhere: 'To possess an "inside" a work of literature must display as a part of its achievement some kind of reticence, and the tensions of reticence; and these are a sure indication of powers unresolved below the surface.'[46] What remains productively unresolved in *In Memoriam* are the powers we have witnessed at odds throughout Tennyson's writing life: an assurance about the capacities of verbal expression, and a doubt about them; an intense emotional investment in the proper forwardness of thought, and a disinclination to trust in the reality of any such progress. Mays finds in the poem 'a sense of movement which d[oes] not move anywhere', a work equipped 'to travel rather than to arrive';[47] and it is in the relationship between the reality of the individual lyrics and the total grandeur that should be their end that Tennyson's genius for irresolution finds its most comprehensive expression. James Russell Lowell called *Maud* 'the antiphonal voice to "In Memoriam"' (*M.* i. 393), as though the two works were exploring the same territory from different angles. We have seen how the fragmentary nature of *Maud* breaks a coherent narrating voice into the changeful being of disjunctive lyrics, with 'different phases of passion' like 'different characters'. Less sensationally but really not so unlike, *In Memoriam* presents 'different moods of sorrow as in a drama' (*M.* i. 304). Tennyson writes, 'I see in part | That all, as in some piece of art, | Is toil cöoperant to an end' (cxxviii. 22–4): it is a nice qualification to a vision of parts-within-a-whole to say that you see it only 'in part'. The work's improvised form embraces its lyrical disarticulation: it does not really toil towards an 'end' convincingly achieved, 'A labour working to an end' ('The Two Voices', l. 297), but exists instead in the more characteristic Tennysonian state of waiting for an end – 'What end is here to my complaint?' (lxxxi. 6). Both *Maud* and *In Memoriam* dwell upon the discontinuities of the self: *Maud* is a poem about someone breaking apart, and *In Memoriam* a broken poem about trying to pull yourself together. 'Generally when he was asked to read the poem he would refuse, saying: "It breaks me down, I cannot"' (*M.* i. 436).

Coda
'Modern Rhyme'

> It is both the glory and the shame of poetry that its medium
> is not its private property.
>
> (W. H. Auden)

'What hope is here for modern rhyme . . . ?' The doubts that *In Memoriam* entertains about its own progress and procedures echo other kinds of self-consciousness that we have heard in Tennyson – the way that a rueful disquiet about his art's habitual distance from the ordinary marks the Arthurian poetry, say; or the way that a dramatic interest in extreme states of mind is invoked to license the lyrical inventiveness of *Maud*; or the way that, elsewhere, a tenacious Apostolic concern to address issues of 'the life' distracts a voice disposed to melodious self-delight. Such creative concerns all turn upon the relationship that poetry should properly strike up with the non-poetic: when Tennyson sought to defend in *The Princess* 'what some have called the too poetical passages' (*M.* i. 253–4) he voiced a telltale uneasiness. I began to suggest (in Chapter 1) that a way of understanding the intricately conflicted life of Tennysonian lyricism would be to place it in the aftermath of the great Romantic poets; and not least among the wide and contradictory legacy that Romanticism bequeathed to its successors was a fruitful vacillation about the ends of poetry: between the absolute allure of the poetical and the resolute refusal to succumb to any such charm.

Not only the poets inherit that predicament, of course: the critics do too. For F. R. Leavis – as for the contemporary critics I quoted in the Introduction – the central critical question is what sort of rapport poetry enjoys with the actual world outside it:

the poets of whom Leavis disapproved (like Shelley) were those with a 'weak grasp upon the actual'; and he held Tennyson largely responsible for perpetuating the attenuated sort of Romanticism that regarded 'the actual world' as 'alien, recalcitrant and unpoetical'.[1] That kind of remark gives Tennyson a practically proto-*symboliste* air, a connection that Marshall McLuhan once suggestively pursued: McLuhan found in Hallam's great essay on *Poems, Chiefly Lyrical* an implicit statement of 'Symbolist and Imagist doctrine' and an insistent case (anticipating Mallarmé, Eliot, and Valéry) for the creative self-sufficiency of 'pure poetry'.[2] His reading is tendentious, but not so out of line with what many good critics have made of Tennyson's instincts: Elaine Jordan, for instance, says, 'Tennyson's style itself can have the fetishistic quality of symbolist poetry, when it lets go of the questioning indeterminacy of *In Memoriam* to become a thing in itself, at odds with his Protestant suspicion of forms.'[3]

That does, indeed, make an important point about a part of the Tennysonian effect. 'Behind the veil, behind the veil': with each repetition a word or phrase grows strange, increasingly free from its original duty to signify. Such hollowness may be terrible in life;[4] but, in the contexts of art, it might equally allow a word or phrase to become an object of pleasure in its own right – the poet 'mouthing out his hollow oes and aes'. Take Whitman's example of Tennyson's artistry, 'And hollow, hollow, hollow, all delight': no line could look set about sterner moral business; yet sense increasingly drains away with reiteration, and the line discovers instead delight as its true end. That sounds rather like aestheticism; and McLuhan is obviously not wrong to see seeds of the aesthetic position in Hallam's review, and particularly in its injunction that poets be not 'led astray by any suggestions of an unpoetical mood' (*CH* 35). This is the Hallam whom Yeats adopted as a spokesman for 'the Aesthetic School', and to whom he attributed the view 'that vice does not destroy genius but that the heterogeneous does'.[5] It is in this ideal of aesthetic homogeneity, we might think, that we should find Coleridge's pure condition of 'Poetry . . . as *Poetry* independent of any other Passion'. As though true to Hallam's word, as Angela Leighton has persuasively argued, 'Tennyson, consciously or unconsciously, offers the nineteenth century one of its most memorable, sensuous, aestheticist voices', a voice marked by (among other things) the luxuriance of repetition: 'refrains and returns like audible embodiments of the tautology of art for art's sake'.[6]

And yet Tennyson's suspicions (Protestant or otherwise) are hardly ever allayed enough for his style to become self-contentedly 'a thing in itself', not in the way that Mallarmé's or even Hopkins's can seem to be. On the contrary, Tennyson's poetry frequently goes out of its way to experience the 'heterogeneous' that Yeats lamented – to incorporate just the 'unpoetical mood[s]' that Hallam had warned him off and Leavis thought out of his bounds. In doing so he was effectively following a paradoxical axiom of Coleridge's, that 'a poem of any length neither can be, or ought to be, all poetry'.[7] (So then: poems *chiefly* lyrical.) Looming behind Coleridge's riddling remark is the towering figure of Wordsworth – 'the poet of unpoetical natures', as J. S. Mill called him – whose provocative reaction against the 'literary' and the 'poetical' stands, in one way or another, over all nineteenth-century poetry. Like everyone else, Tennyson enjoyed making fun of Wordsworth's more nakedly prosaic lapses – he once held a little competition with FitzGerald to invent the 'weakest Wordsworthian line imaginable', and both claimed authorship of the winning entry, 'A Mr Wilkinson, a clergyman' (M. i. 153). But his admiration for Wordsworth, 'the greatest English poet since Milton' (M. ii. 288), was evidently profound too, and the example of Wordsworth's 'unpoetical' poetry was clearly too compelling to be resisted, a counter-current to the pure good of verbalism. (According to one of Hallam's correspondents, Tennyson received high praise for one of his unadorned efforts: 'Wordsworth said to him: "Mr Tennyson, I have been endeavouring all my life to write a pastoral like your 'Dora' and have not succeeded"' (M. i. 265). A wholly improbable anecdote, but it does at least imply the lineage of Tennyson's poem.)

I began this book by quoting Arnold, who preferred Homer's 'natural thoughts in natural words' to Tennyson's 'heightened and elaborate' manner: Arnold was an eminent and profound Wordsworthian and he expresses a Wordsworthian sort of partiality, and it was one to which Tennyson himself was far from immune. J. M. Robertson, writing towards the end of the nineteenth century, looked back and saw in Tennyson 'a reaching towards modern naturalness of speech, a preference for simple constructions, similar to that shown and argued for by Wordsworth' (CH 421); and if that claims a little too much, as no doubt it does, still, some such Wordsworthian counter-aesthetic was certainly moving in a lot of Tennyson's verse. The 'English Idyls', for instance, are deliberated exercises in what Coleridge called 'the language of ordinary life';[8] and Tennyson's Lincolnshire dialect poems are manifestly an attempt to follow a Wordsworthian path and use 'the very language of men'. So too, in their rather more urbane idiolect, are poems like 'To the Rev. F. D. Maurice' (R. (ii). 312) – a choice of idiom that laid him open to a familiar sort of criticism: '"*Belle comme la prose*", he said, "is the French expression for that kind of poetry, and a very good one . . . When I felt that I had done this in the dedication of 'Tiresias', the fools in the *Edinburgh Review* condemned it as 'prose in rhyme"' (IR 102–3). The engaging prosey preambles and frame poems and preludes of disparagement that introduce some of his more self-consciously literary or picturesque productions – '*I waited for the train at Coventry*' ('Godiva', R. (ii). 280, l. 1) – are only the most obvious expressions of this reach for the 'unpoetical', though I do not deny that his reach may sometimes exceed his grasp.[9] 'He dares, in every page, to make use of modern words and notions,' Charles Kingsley went so far as to say, 'from which the mingled clumsiness and archaism of his compeers shrinks, as unpoetical' (CH 180).

As the parodic lines about Mr Wilkinson winningly imply, the play between the poetical and the unpoetical is always predisposed to become comic: a joke about the idioms of art and their relationship with ordinarily unaesthetic sense. Another way of describing such a line as 'And hollow, hollow, hollow, all delight' would be to say it found that it discovered its vocation in nonsense; and it is perhaps no surprise that Edward Lear should have so often grown his own nonsensicality in Tennysonian ground – in the implacable indifference of the universe to human desire of course ('Two Owls and a Hen, four Larks and a Wren, | Have all built their nests in my beard!'), but also in the marvellous resources of Tennysonian noise:

> When awful darkness and silence reign
> Over the great Gromboolian plain . . .

That practically *is* Tennyson. In Lear's nonsense verse, Eliot said, 'we enjoy the music, which is of a high order, and we enjoy the feeling of irresponsibility towards the sense' – an irresponsibility towards sense that was not unconnected with what he found in the music of Tennyson's verse.[10] Critics have sometimes seen English nonsense verse as a sort of untheorized parallel to the autonomous, self-referential language experiments of symbolism; but really nothing could be less aesthetically 'pure' in the way it gets to work than the nonsense of Lear. Its 'music' may forsake any responsible interest in 'sense'; but its *humour* is entirely the product of the bizarre alliances it momentarily strikes up with the natural tongue:

> There was an Old Man in a tree,
> Who was horribly bored by a Bee;
> When they said, 'Does it buzz?' he replied, 'Yes it does!
> It's a regular brute of a Bee!'[11]

(What matters in that is the disarming yet unsettling mixture of the deadpan fantastical – 'There was an Old Man in a tree' – and colloquial mundanity – '*horribly* bored'.) When Tennyson wrote a verse letter to Lear, *belle comme la prose*, he showed himself, not the butt of Lear's joke about being poetical, but his partner in it. Tennyson's lines, 'returning the compliment' (as Hugh Kenner says[12]), enjoy the same comedy of mellifluous verbalism:

> Illyrian woodlands, echoing falls
> Of water, sheets of summer glass,
> The long divine Peneïan pass,
> The vast Akrokeraunian walls . . .

> ('To E.L., on his Travels in Greece', R. (ii). 301, ll. 1–4)

That is delightful, a fraternal drollery at his own expense about the *Tennysonian* and the performative excess of its marvellous noise. His epistolary lines enfold such aesthetically autonomous pleasures within the ambit of a social idiom (a letter): it makes for a kind of formalist wit, a joke about the verse's flamboyant divergence from speaking normally, outside poetry.

'Tennyson was not Tennysonian,' said a puzzled Henry James after meeting him, an observation of heterogeneity that might have its relevance to the poetry too.[13] If the 'Tennysonian' is the work of 'finest verbalism', then the poetry of Tennyson often thrives when that self-delighting verbalism encounters a sense of its limits. For example: 'Will Waterproof's Lyrical Monologue' is a poem that sends up the drunkenness of its own 'lyricism'. It is an inebriate would-be poet's address to the serving-man at the Cock tavern: wholly appropriate, as you might think, that the heroic subject of address should be engaged in the exemplarily Tennysonian business of repetitious waiting ('To come and go, and come again').

> We fret, we fume, would shift our skins
>   Would quarrel with our lot;
> Thy care is, under polished tins,
>   To serve the hot-and-hot;
> To come and go, and come again,
>   Returning like the pewit,
> And watched by silent gentlemen,
>   That trifle with the cruet.

('Will Waterproof's Lyrical Monologue', R. (ii). 267, ll. 225–32)

The poetry plays with the heterogeneity of burlesque, but without formalizing its sense of discrepancy into full-blown mock-heroic. The idiom we might regard as the private property of John Betjeman – a knowingly belated 'Tennysonianism' – is practically here already: Betjeman's peculiar genius was a matter of hearing it, when everyone else heard only the moan of doves in immemorial elms. Like a Betjeman poem, Will Waterproof's monologue hints, in the most amused and least melodramatic of ways, at what Thoreau once called (with much melodrama) 'lives of quiet desperation':

> I pledge her in non-alcoholic wine
> And give the H.P. Sauce another shake.

('Lake District')

The relish contained in Betjeman's lines – the pleasure they take in their incongruous alliance of the heroically artistic ('I pledge her') and the unembarrassedly ordinary ('H. P. Sauce') – is a wholly Tennysonian sort of pleasure. It was the same kind of amused sensitivity to the virtues of hetereogeneity that lay behind Betjeman's admiration for the ending of 'Enoch Arden', the 'unpoetical' wrapping-up of which had roused such complaints from its first reviewers: 'And when they buried him the little port | Had seldom seen a costlier funeral' (R. (ii). 332, ll. 910–11).[14]

Allingham reports: 'Tennyson quoted a passage from Shelley and said, "What can you do with a man who has such command of language?"' (*IR* 136); and Tennyson, too, often provokes the thought that an abundant verbal gift is something requiring constraint as much as opportunity. In fact, he not only provokes such a thought, he entertains it: it is the disquiet that lies behind 'The Palace of Art' (R. (i). 167) – a poem that is, in the words of the first line of its prologue, 'a sort of allegory' of his creative dilemmas. 'Trench said to me, when we were at Trinity together, "Tennyson, we cannot live in art"', a wisdom that long stayed with him (*M*. i. 118; ii. 91–2): the only time he came close to quarrelling with Carlyle, according to his son, was 'when Carlyle asserted that my father talked of poetry as "high art", which he flatly contradicted, "I never in my whole life spoke of 'high art'"' (*M*. i. 267). But when, in 'The Palace of Art', Tennyson's Soul, grown sick from her sumptuous incarceration, finally escapes to the homely and non-aesthetic Wordsworthian destiny of 'a cottage in the vale', she turns out not to be at all as absolute as a Trench might like:

> 'Yet pull not down my palace towers, that are
>   So lightly, beautifully built:
> Perchance I may return with others there
>   When I have purged my guilt.'

(ll. 293–6)

On the very point of pressing forward to a future of plain speaking virtue – and with everything in the poem working to confirm the dignity and rightness of her decision, the Soul is suddenly moved by the high artistry of the well-made towers, 'So lightly, beautifully built', and begins to think of going back to the separate existence of art once again. Apostolic single-mindedness is conjured at the last minute to Tennysonian vacillation, in one of the most telling and unexpected instances of his poetry of returning.

Notes

INTRODUCTION: 'FINEST VERBALISM'

1. From a draft passage intended at one stage to follow l. 68 of 'Edwin Morris': see R. (ii). 275.
2. Matthew Arnold, *On the Classical Tradition*, ed. R. H. Super (Ann Arbor, MI, 1960), 204, 205.
3. William Empson, *Seven Types of Ambiguity* (3rd edn.; 1953; repr. 1973), 11.
4. William Empson, 'Empson on Tennyson', *Tennyson Research Bulletin*, 4/3 (Nov. 1984), 107–9, at 109.
5. Christopher Ricks, *Tennyson* (2nd edn.; Basingstoke, 1989), 12.
6. See John Hollander, *Vision and Resonance: Two Senses of Poetic Form* (2nd edn.; New Haven, CT, 1985), 59–60, 68–70.
7. And see the requirements for blank verse he repeated to his son (*M*. ii. 14).
8. Recorded by James Knowles, 'Aspects of Tennyson', *Nineteenth Century*, 33 (1893), 164–88, at 182.
9. A. Dwight Culler, *The Poetry of Tennyson* (New Haven, CT, 1977), 6.
10. W. B. Yeats, *Essays and Introductions* (1961; repr. 1980), 163.
11. Ricks, *Tennyson*, 293.
12. W. H. Auden, *Forewords and Afterwords*, selected by Edward Mendelson (1973), 222.
13. G. K. Chesterton, *The Victorian Age in Literature* (1913; repr. 1947), 101.
14. With reference to 'Tithonus': Aldous Huxley, *Texts and Pretexts: An Anthology with Commentaries* (1935), 226. I owe the reference to J. B. Steane, *Tennyson* (1966), 52.
15. Kate Millett, *Sexual Politics* (1969; repr. 1972), 76, 79.
16. Alan Sinfield, *Alfred Tennyson* (Oxford, 1986), 51–2. Sinfield, 'Tennyson and the Cultural Politics of Prophecy', in Rebecca Stott (ed.), *Tennyson* (Harlow, 1996), 33–53, at 37; Sinfield, *Tennyson*, 86, 104, 91.

17. A. C. Bradley, *The Reaction against Tennyson* (Oxford, 1917), 14. Paul F. Baum wrote a testily vigorous book mostly out of irritation at Tennyson's tendency to be ' "poetic" at all costs': 'The *poetry* seems like a garment to put on or take off wherewith plain mundane things are made beautiful' (*Tennyson Sixty Years after* (Chapel Hill, NC, 1948), 305, 283).
18. Sinfield, 'Tennyson and the Cultural Politics of Prophecy', 45.
19. Harold Nicolson, *Tennyson: Aspects of his Life, Character and Poetry* (1923).
20. Eve Kosofsky Sedgwick, 'Tennyson's *Princess*: One Bride for Seven Brothers'; in Stott (ed.), *Tennyson*, 181–96.
21. Isobel Armstrong, *Victorian Poetry: Poetry, Poetics and Politics* (1993), 10.
22. *The Poems of Matthew Arnold*, ed. Miriam Allott (2nd edn.; 1979), 654.
23. Richard Holt Hutton, *Aspects of Religious and Scientific Thought: Selected from* The Spectator, ed. Elizabeth M. Roscoe (1901), 375. I owe the reference to Eric Griffiths, *The Printed Voice of Victorian Poetry* (Oxford, 1989), 123.
24. T. S. Eliot, *Selected Essays* (3rd edn.; 1951; repr. 1980), 328. Martin Dodsworth, 'Patterns of Morbidity: Repetition in Tennyson's Poetry', in Isobel Armstrong, (ed.), *The Major Victorian Poets: Reconsiderations* (1969), 7–34, at 14. Eliot, *Selected Essays*, 337.
25. T. S. Eliot, *The Sacred Wood* (3rd edn.; 1932), p. ix.
26. Griffiths, *Printed Voice*, 107.
27. Cf. 'His opinions too are not original, often not independent even, and they sink into vulgarity' (*The Correspondence of Gerard Manley Hopkins and Richard Watson Dixon*, ed. C. C. Abbott (1935), 24).
28. A. C. Swinburne, 'The Higher Pantheism in a Nutshell', in Dwight Macdonald (ed.), *Parodies: An Anthology from Chaucer to Beerbohm and Beyond* (1961), 117.
29. The duty to 'incorporate thought' into poetry seems to have been felt as part of the spirit of the age, perhaps: Leigh Hunt, a grand old man of letters, lamented of Tennyson's generation of poets that 'They *think* they must *think*' (*CH* 135).
30. The contrast with Browning is suggestively dwelt upon by Northrop Frye, 'Introduction: Lexis and Melos', in *Sound and Poetry: English Institute Essays 1956* (New York, NY, 1957), p. xi.
31. Eliot, *Selected Essays*, 336.
32. Philip Larkin, *Required Writing: Miscellaneous Pieces 1955–1982* (1983), 185.
33. Samuel Taylor Coleridge, *Biographia Literaria*, ed. James Engell and Walter Jackson Bate (2 vols.; Princeton, NJ, 1983), ii. 21.
34. Tennyson was, perhaps, exemplifying peculiarly well an exemplarily 'Apostles' attitude. The prevailing spirit of the society, as

formulated by Henry Sidgwick, was 'a belief that we *can* learn, and a determination that we *will* learn, from people of the most opposite opinions', a cast of mind that left him a thinker (or so a contemporary remarked) 'who so clearly saw all sides that he found it difficult to take any' (Peter Allen, *The Cambridge Apostles: The Early Years* (Cambridge, 1978), 4, 9).

35. Quoted by Ricks, *Tennyson*, 48.
36. Eliot, *Selected Essays*, 328.
37. Armstrong, *Victorian Poetry*, 11.
38. From a letter quoted in Richard Ellmann, *Eminent Domain: Yeats among Wilde, Joyce, Pound, Eliot and Auden* (1967; repr. 1970), 67.
39. Sinfield, 'Tennyson and the Cultural Politics of Prophesy', 45.
40. E. F. Benson, *The Way We Were: A Victorian Peep Show* (1930), 104.
41. Hopkins, *Correspondence of Hopkins and Dixon*, 24.
42. Ricks, *Tennyson*, 293.
43. W. David Shaw, *Alfred Lord Tennyson: The Poet in an Age of Theory* (New York, NY, 1996), 105.
44. Letter of 22 Sept. 1819. Leigh Hunt, who had known Keats well, thought Tennyson 'a kind of philosophical Keats' (*CH* 136). Hallam recommended Tennyson to Hunt as Keats's heir in 1831 (*HL* 396).
45. 'In some ways Tennyson is a poet of deep inarticulateness, but he is an *emotional* intelligence of the highest order', says James Richardson (*Vanishing Lives: Style and Self in Tennyson, D. G. Rossetti, Swinburne, and Yeats* (Charlottesville, VA, 1988), 90).
46. Griffiths, *Printed Voice*, 155.
47. Chesterton, *Victorian Age*, 100.
48. The sceptical might consult the essay on 'Tennyson as a Humourist' in Sir Charles Tennyson, *Six Tennyson Essays* (1954), 1–38.
49. Derek Attridge, 'The Movement of Meaning: Phrasing and Repetition in English Poetry', in Andreas Fischer (ed.), *Repetition* (Tübingen, 1994), 61–83, at 70. Kathleen Lea, 'The Poetic Powers of Repetition', *Proceedings of the British Academy*, 55 (1969), 51–76, at 52.
50. Eliot, *Selected Essays*, 336.
51. Ibid. 331.

CHAPTER 1. RETURNS

1. From a song from *Measure for Measure* quoted by A. E. Housman in 'The Name and Nature of Poetry', adduced as evidence that pure poetry is positively *non*-semantic, 'saying nothing' – 'That is nonsense; but it is ravishing poetry' (*Collected Poems and Selected Prose*, ed. Christopher Ricks (1988), 366).

2. Herbert F. Tucker, *Tennyson and the Doom of Romanticism* (Cambridge, MA, 1988), 13, 19.
3. Christopher Ricks, *Tennyson* (2nd edn.; Basingstoke, 1989), 45.
4. *The Journals and Papers of Gerard Manley Hopkins*, ed. Humphry House and Graham Storey (1959), 289; quoted, in part, by Jeffrey Wills, *Repetition in Latin Poetry: Figures of Allusion* (Oxford, 1996), 1.
5. George Puttenham, *The Arte of English Poesie*, ed. Gladys Doidge Willcock and Alice Walker (Cambridge, 1936), 198, 200–2.
6. Roman Jakobson, 'Closing Statement: Linguistics and Poetics', in Thomas A. Sebeok (ed.), *Style in Language* (New York, NY, 1960), 350–77, at 368.
7. F. W. Bateson, *The Scholar-Critic* (1972), 89–90 – drawing on J. W. Mackail, as quoted in *OED* (*poetry* §3).
8. Stamos Metzidakis, 'Formal Repetition and the Perception of Literature', *L'Esprit créateur*, 24 (1984), 49–61. For reflections on the subject, see Bruce F. Kawin, *Telling it Again and Again: Repetition in Literature and Film* (Ithaca, NY, 1972); and Laury Magnus, *The Track of the Repetend: Syntactic and Lexical Repetition in Modern Poetry* (New York, NY, 1989).
9. As noted in W. David Shaw, *Tennyson's Style* (Ithaca, NY, 1976), 275–7.
10. C. Alphonso Smith, *Repetition and Parallelism in English Verse: A Study in the Technique of Poetry* (New York, NY,/New Orleans, LA, 1894).
11. Émile Lauvrière, *Repetition and Parallelism in Tennyson* (1910).
12. Martin Dodsworth, 'Patterns of Morbidity: Repetition in Tennyson's Poetry', in Isobel Armstrong (ed.), *The Major Victorian Poets: Reconsiderations* (1969), 7–34, at 7.
13. The refrain from Dekker's 'The Happy Heart', included in *The Golden Treasury* on Tennyson's advice: *The Golden Treasury*, ed. Christopher Ricks (Harmondsworth, 1991), 68, 479.
14. *Collected Letters of Samuel Taylor Coleridge*, ed. E. L. Griggs (6 vols.; Oxford, 1956–71), ii. 812.
15. *Collected Letters of Samuel Taylor Coleridge*, ii. 812; and cf. Samuel Taylor Coleridge, *Biographia Literaria*, ed. James Engell and Walter Jackson Bate (2 vols.; Princeton, NJ, 1983), ii. 45.
16. John Hollander writes suggestively about the intricate relationship between convention and ('natural') expression in Romantic verse in *Vision and Resonance: Two Senses of Poetic Form* (2nd edn.; New Haven, CT, 1985), 187-211. The question is of ubiquitous concern: it is, for example, a nice point how *meaningful* the convention of repetition is in Anglo-Saxon poetry: Elizabeth M. Tyler, 'How Deliberate is Deliberate Verbal Repetition?', in M. J. Toswell and Elizabeth M. Tyler (eds.), *Studies in English Language and Literature:*

'*Doubt Wisely*' (1996), 508–30. My discussion of the rival justifications for post-Romantic poetic language owes much to Griffiths's discussion of the 'two voices' of Victorian printed verse.

17. 'Knowledge *and* power' looks tendentious, as though Hallam were offering an antithesis in parallel with 'dramatic' and 'lyric'. Perhaps he has De Quincey in mind – 'All that is literature seeks to communicate power; all that is not literature, to communicate knowledge' (*Collected Writing of Thomas De Quincey*, ed. David Masson (14 vols.; Edinburgh, 1889–90), x. 48). De Quincey's essay was first published in the *London Magazine* in 1823, and Hallam probably knew it: we know he thought fondly of 'the old times of the London – the golden age of Elia, De Quincy [*sic*], and a few more' (*HL* 437).

18. The recurrence of sounds in the line is nicely noted by Richardson, *Vanishing Lives: Style and Self in Tennyson, D. G. Rossetti, Swinburne, and Yeats* (Charlottesville, VA, 1988), 22: 'The end pauses, vaguely remembering the beginning; the beginning shoves wearily off what had seemed an end.'

19. Peter Conrad, *The Everyman History of English Literature* (1985), 522.

20. See A. Shewan, 'Repetition in Homer and Tennyson', *Classical Weekly*, 16/20 (2 Apr. 1923) and 21 (9 Apr. 1923), 153–8, 162–6.

21. Daniel Webb, *Observations on the Correspondence Between Poetry and Music* (1769); quoted in David Fairer, 'Creating a National Poetry: The Tradition of Spenser and Milton', in *The Cambridge Companion to Eighteenth Century Poetry*, ed. John Sitter (Cambridge, 2001), 177–201, at 188.

22. Puttenham, *Arte of English Poesie*, 198.

23. Robert Graves, *The Crowning Privilege* (1955), 110–11.

24. Ricks, *Tennyson*, 294. Repetition might even be recollected when it was not really there: 'I come on a poem out of "The Princess" which says "I hear the horns of Elfland blowing blowing",' wrote Thackeray to Tennyson, correcting at once to, 'no, it's "the horns of Elfland faintly blowing"' (*M*. i. 444–5).

25. As observed in Richardson, *Vanishing Lives*, 37.

26. Sir Charles Tennyson, in the introduction to Tennyson's *Unpublished Early Poems* (1931); Christopher Ricks, in his Chatterton Lecture, 'Tennyson's Methods of Composition', *Proceedings of the British Academy*, 52 (1966), 209–30 – partially repeated in Ricks, *Tennyson*, 281–94.

27. *Lady Tennyson's Journal*, ed. James O. Hoge (Charlottesville, VA, 1981), 44.

28. Ralph Wilson Rader, *Tennyson's Maud: The Biographical Genesis* (Berkeley and Los Angeles, CA, 1963), 1.

29. T. S. Eliot, *Selected Essays* (3rd edn.; 1951; repr. 1980), 331.

30. From Bram Stoker's reminiscences of Henry Irving: quoted in Harold Nicolson, *Tennyson: Aspects of his Life, Character and Poetry* (1923), 288.

31. For a most interesting account, see Ann D. Dowker, 'Modified Repetition in Poems Elicited from Young Children', *Journal of Child Language*, 18 (1991), 625–39.

32. John Bayley, *The Romantic Survival: A Study in Poetic Evolution* (1957), 139.

33. W. H. Auden, *Forewords and Afterwords*, selected by Edward Mendelson (1973), 228, 227.

34. Gerhard Joseph, *Tennyson and the Text: The Weaver's Shuttle* (Cambridge, 1992), 25.

35. *The Standard Edition of the Complete Psychological Works of Sigmund Freud*, ed. James Strachey et al. (24 vols.; 1953–66), xviii. 18. Tennyson and Freud keep company in Matthew Rowlinson, *Tennyson's Fixations: Psychoanalysis and the Topics of the Early Poetry* (Charlottesville, VA, 1994), 19, 22–3.

36. Auden, *Forewords and Afterwords*, 222.

37. Dodsworth, 'Patterns of Morbidity', 22.

38. Humphry House, *All in Due Time: Collected Essays and Broadcast Talks* (1955), 127.

39. Ricks, *Tennyson*, 43.

40. Kathleen Lea, 'The Poetic Powers of Repetition', *Proceedings of the British Academy*, 55 (1969), 51–76, at 70 – citing: 'O my son Absalom, my son, my son Absalom! would God I had died for thee, O Absalom, my son! my son!'

41. John Bayley, 'Tennyson and the Idea of Decadence', in Hallam Tennyson (ed.), *Studies in Tennyson* (1981), 186–205, at 189.

42. Tennyson converses with a tree in one longish poem, 'The Talking Oak' (R. (ii). 269), 'an experiment meant to test the degree in which it was in [his] power as a poet to humanise external nature'. The protagonist of 'Œnone' (R. (i).164) addresses a mountainous landscape throughout as 'mother'.

43. Denis Donoghue, *The Ordinary Universe: Soundings in Modern Literature* (1968), 99.

44. Isobel Armstrong, *Victorian Poetry: Poetry, Poetics and Politics* (1993), 51.

45. Edward Lear, *The Complete Verse and Nonsense*, ed. Vivien Noakes (2001), 342. Tennyson was fond of limericks himself (see E. F. Benson, *The Way We Were: A Victorian Peep Show* (1930), 103): Peter Levi prints one – as oral tradition records it anyway – though it does not repeat a line (*Tennyson* (1993), 251).

46. Cf. 'The description of the landscape uses the language of appearance so insistently that we feel the presence of a beholder'

(Carol Christ, 'The Feminine Subject in Victorian Poetry', *English Literary History*, 54 (1987), 385–401, at 390).

47. The point about the source is Culler's (A. Dwight Culler, *The Poetry of Tennyson* (New Haven, CT, 1977), 32).

48. Søren Kierkegaard, *Repetition: An Essay in Experimental Psychology*, trans. Walter Lowrie (New York, NY, 1941), 34.

49. *William Wordsworth*, ed. Stephen Gill (Oxford Authors; Oxford, 1984; repr., 2000), 594.

50. See James D. Wilson, 'Tennyson's Emendations to Wordsworth's "Tintern Abbey"', *Wordsworth Circle*, 5 (1974), 7–8.

51. As noted by Lea, 'Poetic Powers', 59–60.

52. As when he said: 'in "Tintern Abbey" the repetition of "that blessed mood, that serene and blessed mood" becomes ridiculous' (*M.* ii. 288).

53. A poem addressed (it seems) to his first Arthur, Hallam, found a peculiarly Tennysonian way of cherishing their friendship: it was as though it were happening *again*, happening for the second time, as though in that trance of 'mystical similitude' that provokes feelings of *déjà vu* – 'All this hath been before, | All this hath been, I know not when or where' ('To—— [As when with downcast eyes]', R. (i). 179, ll. 4, 6–7).

54. James Joyce, *Ulysses: The Corrected Text*, ed. Hans Walter Gabler (1986), 144.

55. Coleridge, *Biographia Literaria*, i. 72 n.

56. The Hallam essay is quoted and discussed by Eric Griffiths, 'Tennyson's Idle Tears', in Philip Collins (ed.), *Tennyson: Seven Essays* (Basingstoke, 1992), 36–60, at 51.

57. Coleridge's influence upon the Apostles is explored by John Beer, 'Tennyson, Coleridge, and the Cambridge Apostles', in Collins (ed.), *Tennyson: Seven Essays*, 1–35.

58. Jonathan Dollimore, *Sex, Literature and Censorship* (Oxford, 2001), 117.

59. The other Wordsworth passage lying behind 'Tears, Idle Tears' is the close of the 'Intimations' Ode: 'To me the meanest flower that blows can give | Thoughts that do often lie too deep for tears'. Wordsworth's thoughts are too deep for tears; Tennyson's tears too profound for thoughts.

60. As Cleanth Brooks says in 'The Motivation of Tennyson's Weeper', in John Killham (ed.), *Critical Essays on the Poetry of Tennyson* (1960), 177-85, at 180.

61. Quoted by F. W. Bateson, *English Poetry: A Critical Introduction* (1950), 15.

62. W. David Shaw, *Alfred Lord Tennyson: The Poet in an Age of Theory* (New York, NY, 1996), 122. Cf. 'you cannot employ the English

language to say "Nor winks the gold fin in the porphyry font" without our glimpsing – through the interstices of the negative – the winking fin' (Ricks, *Tennyson*, 192). Ricks draws a likeness with the absence of contradictoriness that Freud describes in dreams.

63. Richardson, *Vanishing Lives*, 32.
64. Brooks, 'Motivation', 180.
65. See Ricks, *Tennyson*, 262–3. My examples of the theme here – 'The Lotos-Eaters', *In Memoriam* section xc, and 'Enoch Arden' – are taken gratefully from Ricks's discussion.
66. Kierkegaard, *Repetition*, 35, 74, 74–5. For a succinct and lucid account, see Dianne Sadoff, 'The Poetics of Repetition and *The Defence of Guinevere*', in Carole G. Silver (ed.), *The Golden Chain: Essays on William Morris and Pre-Raphaelitism* (New York, NY, 1982), 97–113, at 98–100.
67. The point is made by Griffiths, 'Tennyson's Idle Tears', 56.
68. Shlomith Rimmon-Kenan, 'The Paradoxical Status of Repetition', *Poetics Today*, 1/4 (1980), 151–9, at 155.

CHAPTER 2. MAKING PROGRESS

1. See Jerome Hamilton Buckley, *The Triumph of Time: A Study of the Victorian Concepts of Time, History, Progress, and Decadence* (Cambridge, MA, 1967), 36. The entire chapter about 'the idea of progress' (pp. 34–52) is worth consulting.
2. William Makepeace Thackeray, 'The Speculators', in Geoffrey Grigson (ed.), *The Victorians* (1950), 33.
3. Recorded by James Knowles, 'Aspects of Tennyson', *Nineteenth Century*, 33 (1893), 164–88, at 186.
4. See Graham Hough, 'The Natural Theology of *In Memoriam*', *Review of English Studies*, 23 (1947), 244–56, at 251–2.
5. *Mill on Bentham and Coleridge*, introduced by F. R. Leavis (1950; repr. Cambridge, 1980), 96.
6. Herbert F. Tucker, *Tennyson and the Doom of Romanticism* (Cambridge, MA, 1988), 15.
7. See Christopher Ricks, *Tennyson* (2nd edn.; Basingstoke, 1989), 289.
8. See John Killham, *Tennyson and The Princess: Reflections of an Age* (1958), 22–4. For the Spanish adventure, see Peter Allen, *The Cambridge Apostles: The Early Years* (Cambridge, 1978), 103–18.
9. Richard Chenevix Trench, *Letters and Memorials*, ed. 'the author of *Charles Lowder*' [i.e. Maria Trench] (2 vols.; 1888), i. 72. Allen, *Cambridge Apostles*, 89.
10. Trench, *Letters*, i. 48.
11. Ibid. i. 103.

12. Ibid. i. 115. Cf. a letter from Spedding, describing Trench 'groaning over the prospects of mankind', quoted by A. Dwight Culler, The *Poetry of Tennyson* (New Haven, CT, 1977), 69.
13. Quoted by Robert Bernard Martin, *Tennyson: The Unquiet Heart* (Oxford/London, 1980), 125.
14. Trench, *Letters*, i. 97, 98.
15. Culler, *Poetry of Tennyson*, 59.
16. Quoted by Allen, *Cambridge Apostles*, 122.
17. Trench, *Letters*, i. 96.
18. So, for example, one critic can find Tennyson's politics 'rather vulgar, snobbish, and reactionary' (Robert Preyer, 'Tennyson's Conservative Vision', *Victorian Studies*, 9 (1965–6), 325-52, at 350), while another, and rather better, can describe his 'broad reformism' (Elaine Jordan, *Alfred Tennyson* (Cambridge, 1988), 88). Connections between the poetry and the politics are shrewdly established in Richard Cronin, *Romantic Victorians: English Literature, 1824–1840* (Basingstoke, 2001), 146–65 – to which I am much indebted.
19. Isobel Armstrong, *Victorian Poetry: Poetry, Poetics and Politics* (1993), 56.
20. Culler, *Poetry of Tennyson*, 81.
21. Quoted from *Nation and Athenaeum* (18 Dec. 1926) by Ricks, *Tennyson*, 289 n.
22. Roger Scruton, *The Meaning of Conservatism* (3rd edn.; Basingstoke, 2001), 34, 35. Scruton advocates 'the metaphor of society as person' which he sees corresponding 'to a clear and literal idea' (p. 14).
23. A wholly self-conscious conservative might live a life outwardly indistinguishable from the instinctive being of the unreflective; but his inner life would be wholly different – a matter of conscientiously imagining how he would be acting had he not thought about the question.
24. Quoted in Edgar Finley Shannon, *Tennyson and the Reviewers: A Study of his Literary Reputation and of the Influence of the Critics upon his Poetry 1827–1851* (1952; repr., New York, NY, 1967), 115.
25. From a letter from W.W. Farr to Gladstone, quoted in Allen, *Cambridge Apostles*, 46. For Hallam's Shelleyan proselytizing on the Glasgow steamboat, see *HL* 301.
26. Quoted by Allen, *Cambridge Apostles*, 100.
27. K. W. Gransden points the comparison, describing how Tennyson 'had genuinely hoped for a more positive enlightenment such as Wordsworth had experienced, and is genuinely surprised at his failure to get it' (*Tennyson: In Memoriam* (1964), 26). I owe the reference to Alan Sinfield, *The Language of Tennyson's* In Memoriam (Oxford, 1971), 121.
28. A footnote to 'Οἱ ῥέοντες' (R. (i). 122) reads: 'this very opinion is

only true relatively to the flowing philosophers.' See Armstrong, *Victorian Poetry*, 41–2.

29. When the Apostles debated, 'Is an intelligible First Cause deducible from the phenomena of the Universe?', Tennyson voted no (*M*. i. 44 n.); and his opinion on the question did not change (cf., e.g., *IR* 33).

30. Ricks, *Tennyson*, 99.

31. Quoted by Culler, *Poetry of Tennyson*, 152.

32. Cf. Ricks, *Tennyson*, 99.

33. Quoted by Allen, *Cambridge Apostles*, 104.

34. Ibid. 99.

35. William Empson, *Seven Types of Ambiguity* (3rd edn.; 1953; repr. 1973), 34.

36. Armstrong, *Victorian Poetry*, 88.

37. Cf. Ricks, *Tennyson*, 86.

38. Paul Turner, *Tennyson* (1976), 67.

39. Cf. Armstrong, *Victorian Poetry*, 87–94.

40. Matthew Reynolds, *The Realms of Verse 1830–1870: English Poetry in a Time of Nation-Building* (Oxford, 2001), 219.

41. Matthew Arnold, *On the Classical Tradition*, ed. R. H. Super (Ann Arbor, MI, 1960), 147.

42. W. W. Robson, 'The Dilemma of Tennyson', in John Killham (ed.), *Critical Essays on the Poetry of Tennyson* (1960), 155–63, at 158.

43. Ricks, *Tennyson*, 115.

44. Paul Turner says, 'Tennyson gave moral significance to this largely amoral subject-matter . . . by equating Paris's desertion of Oenone with his rejection of Here's true wisdom' (Turner, *Tennyson*, 60).

45. Cf. 'The longer one looks at Hera's offer and that of Pallas, the harder it is to tell them apart' (Tucker, *Doom*, 161).

46. Cronin, *Romantic Victorians*, 163.

47. Culler, *Poetry of Tennyson*, 78, 79.

48. W. David Shaw, *Tennyson's Style* (Ithaca, NY, 1976), 82.

49. Peter Conrad, 'The Victim of Inheritance', *Times Literary Supplement*, 15 May 1982, 529.

50. Cf. John Bayley, 'Tennyson and the Idea of Decadence', in Hallam Tennyson (ed.), *Studies in Tennyson* (1981), 186–205, at 205; and Matthew Campbell, *Rhythm and Will in Victorian Poetry* (Cambridge, 1999), 24–32.

51. Gabriel Pearson, 'Eliot: An American Use of Symbolism', in Graham Martin (ed.), *Eliot in Perspective: A Symposium* (1970), 83–101, at 90.

52. B. C. Southam, *Tennyson* (Writers and their Work; 1971), 34.

CHAPTER 3. THE STORY AND THE SONGS

1. George Eliot, *Essays and Leaves from a Note-Book* (Edinburgh, 1884), 369.
2. And he loved hearing a story too: Hallam Tennyson (ed.), *Tennyson and his Friends* (1911), 187.
3. T. S. Eliot, *Selected Essays* (3rd edn.; 1951; repr. 1980), 331.
4. Shaw says, 'though the poem is literally a "progress," a moving forward from panel to panel, any "progress," in the sense of development, is difficult to discern' (W. David Shaw, *Tennyson's Style* (Ithaca, NY, 1976), 57).
5. Henry James, *Views and Reviews*, ed. LeRoy Phillips (New York, NY, 1968), 171; quoted in Christopher Ricks, *Tennyson* (2nd edn.; Basingstoke, 1989), 216.
6. John Bayley, 'The Dynamics of the Static', *Times Literary Supplement*, 3 Mar. 1978, 247.
7. The fatalism could assume droll enough forms: 'as he was holding a candle to examine some book or picture (for he was very near-sighted), his wavy dark hair took fire; I was for putting it out: "Oh, never mind," he said, "it depends upon chance burnings"' (*M*. i. 511).
8. Carlyle's remark, made soon after publication of the poem and transcribed in a commonplace book of 1855–6; quoted in James Pope-Hennessy, *Monckton Milnes: The Flight of Youth 1851–1885* (1951), 59.
9. Thomas Carlyle, 'Signs of the Times', in *Scottish and Other Miscellanies* (Everyman, 1915; repr., 1967), 223–45, at 244.
10. Matthew Arnold, *On the Classical Tradition*, ed. R. H. Super (Ann Arbor, MI, 1960), 2–3. Matthew Campbell, *Rhythm and Will in Victorian Poetry* (Cambridge, 1999), 73.
11. Quoted in James Pope-Hennessy, *Monckton-Milnes: The Years of Promise 1809–1851* (1949), 16.
12. Thomas Carlyle, *Sartor Resartus and On Heroes and Hero Worship* (Everyman; 1908; repr. 1956), 147, 148, 149.
13. Ricks, *Tennyson*, 158.
14. See Paul Turner, *Tennyson* (1976), 53.
15. See Nelson Hilton, 'Tennyson's "Tears": Idle, Idol, Idyl', *Essays in Criticism*, 35 (1985), 223–37.
16. See Robert Pattison, *Tennyson and Tradition* (Cambridge, MA, 1979), 15–39.
17. Elaine Jordan, *Alfred Tennyson* (Cambridge, 1988), 83.
18. Turner, *Tennyson*, 104.
19. See Catherine Stevenson, 'Tennyson on Women's Rights', *Tennyson*

Research Bulletin, 3/1 (1977), 23–5. The best account of the ideological background to the poem remains John Killham, *Tennyson and* The Princess: *Reflections of an Age* (1958), 1–169.

20. Samuel Edward Dawson, *A Study of Alfred Tennyson's Poem* The Princess (1882); quoted in Killham, *Tennyson and* The Princess, 15.
21. A point made by Laurence Lerner, 'An Essay on *The Princess*', in Laurence Lerner (ed.), *The Victorians* (1978), 221.
22. The point is shrewdly made by Marion Shaw, *Alfred Lord Tennyson* (Hemel Hempstead, 1988), 46.
23. Pattison, *Tennyson and Tradition*, 19.
24. Cf. Marion Shaw, *Alfred Lord Tennyson*, 45.
25. Eric Griffiths, 'Tennyson's Idle Tears', in Philip Collins (ed.), *Tennyson: Seven Essays* (Basingstoke, 1992), 36–60, at 54.
26. See Ricks, *Tennyson*, 250-3.
27. A. Dwight Culler, *The Poetry of Tennyson* (New Haven, CT, 1977), 214.
28. Matthew Reynolds, *The Realms of Verse 1830–1870: English Poetry in a Time of Nation-Building* (Oxford, 2001), 254.
29. The arbitrariness of the connection is pointed out by Culler (*Poetry of Tennyson*, 238). Ricks succinctly describes the vulnerability of the poem's moral scheme (*Tennyson*, 157–8), and I gratefully take over some of his examples here.
30. Reynolds, *The Realms of Verse*, 256–7.
31. Culler, *Poetry of Tennyson*, 241.
32. Culler identifies five bare lines describing the golden age (ibid. 218).
33. Jordan, *Tennyson*, 168.
34. Ibid. 181.
35. Culler's description (*Poetry of Tennyson*, 228).
36. The anecdote is pulled out of the *Memoir* and its suggestiveness explored by John Bayley in 'Tennyson and the Idea of Decadence', in Hallam Tennyson (ed.), *Studies in Tennyson* (1981), 186–205, at 187.
37. H. A. L. Fisher's reminiscence, quoted in Philip Collins, *Reading Aloud: A Victorian Metier* (Lincoln, 1972), 4.
38. Bayley, 'Tennyson and the Idea of Decadence', 187.
39. Ibid. 192.
40. Eliot, *Selected Essays*, 332.
41. William Empson, *Essays on Shakespeare*, ed. David B. Pirie (Cambridge, 1986), 84.
42. A. S. Byatt, 'The Lyric Structure of Tennyson's *Maud*', in Isobel Armstrong, (ed.), *The Major Victorian Poets: Reconsiderations* (1969), 69–92, at 69.
43. Humbert Wolfe, *Tennyson* (1930), 32–3. *The Waste Land* often glances at *Maud*, in the nightmarish cityscape (ii. 202–14) and the 'handful

of dust' (ii. 241); and compare Eliot's opening lines with *Maud*'s injunction 'Mix not memory with doubt' (ii. 197).

44. J. B. Steane, *Tennyson* (1966), 100.
45. Eric Griffiths, *The Printed Voice of Victorian Poetry* (Oxford, 1989), 164.
46. See Ricks, *Tennyson*, 247. Alan Sinfield, *Alfred Tennyson* (Oxford, 1986), 7–8, 187 n. 11.
47. Isobel Armstrong, *Victorian Poetry: Poetry, Poetics and Politics* (1993), 279.

CHAPTER 4. GRIEVING

1. C. Alphonso Smith, *Repetition and Parallelism in English Verse: A Study in the Technique of Poetry* (New York, NY/New Orleans, LA, 1894), 32.
2. Sigmund Freud, 'Mourning and Melancholia', in *The Standard Edition of the Complete Psychological Works of Sigmund Freud*, ed. James Strachey et al. (24 vols.; 1953–66), xiv, 243–58, at 245, 244. Cf. the first chapter of Peter M. Sacks, *The English Elegy: Studies in the Genre from Spenser to Yeats* (Baltimore, MD, 1985); and F. E. L. Priestley, *Language and Structure in Tennyson's Poetry* (1973), 120–2.
3. Peter Levi once said, 'Elegy is a lament that has strayed from its pure origins' (*The Lamentation of the Dead* (1984), 9); and with classical analogies in mind, cf. Paul Turner, *Tennyson* (1976), 118–19.
4. W. David Shaw, *Elegy and Paradox: Testing the Conventions* (Baltimore, MD, 1994), 50.
5. Jerome Hamilton Buckley, *Tennyson: The Growth of a Poet* (Cambridge, MA, 1960), 127, 124.
6. E. D. H. Johnson, 'The Way of the Poet', in John Dixon Hunt (ed.), *Tennyson: In Memoriam: A Casebook* (1970; repr. Basingstoke, 1987), 188–99, at 198.
7. Alan Sinfield, *The Language of Tennyson's* In Memoriam (Oxford, 1971), 148. In his later book Sinfield is more interested in charting '[t]he awkwardness of the attempt at closure' *Alfred Tennyson* (Oxford, 1986), 119).
8. See Turner, *Tennyson*, 119.
9. Christopher Ricks, *Tennyson* (2nd edn.; Basingstoke, 1989), 209.
10. Hallam Tennyson denied with some emphasis that his father said any such thing: see Philip L. Elliott, *The Making of the* Memoir (2nd edn.; Lincoln, 1995), 20 n..
11. T. S. Eliot, *Selected Essays* (3rd edn.; 1951; repr. 1980), 333-4.
12. A. C. Bradley, *A Commentary on Tennyson's* In Memoriam (3rd edn.; 1910; repr., 1929), 22.
13. Isobel Armstrong, *Language as Living Form in Nineteenth-Century*

Poetry (Brighton, 1982), 186. Repetitions are resourcefully tracked by Sinfield, *Language of Tennyson's* In Memoriam, 150, etc.

14. 'Gute Nacht'; from Franz Schubert, *Winterreise (The Winter-Journey)*, ed. Revd Troutbeck ([n.d.]), 6–7.

15. Tennyson is cited in R., note to l. 8; and cf. Gordon N. Ray, *Tennyson Reads 'Maud'* (Vancouver, 1968), 39.

16. See Buckley, *Tennyson*, 109.

17. A. Dwight Culler, *The Poetry of Tennyson* (New Haven, CT, 1977), 159.

18. Ricks, *Tennyson*, 210.

19. I owe the reference to Christopher Ricks, *The Force of Poetry* (Oxford, 1984), 77.

20. Ricks, *Tennyson*, 216.

21. Priestley is good on the poem's invention of its own genre in *Language and Structure*, 122–5.

22. Cf. Matthew Campbell, *Rhythm and Will in Victorian Poetry* (Cambridge, 1999), 182.

23. *The Letters of Edward FitzGerald*, ed. Alfred McKinley Terhune and Annabelle Burdick Terhune (5 vols.; Princeton, NJ, 1980), i. 486; quoted in Ricks, *Tennyson*, 203.

24. Bradley, *Commentary*, 23, *et seq.*

25. J. C. C. Mays, '*In Memoriam*: An Aspect of Form', *University of Toronto Quarterly*, 35 (1965–6), 22–46, at 36.

26. G. K. Chesterton, *The Victorian Age in Literature* (1913; repr. 1947), 18.

27. Armstrong, *Language as Living Form*, 199.

28. For the elegiac 'reversal' or peripeteia, see Culler, *Poetry of Tennyson*, 149.

29. Alan Sinfield, '"That which is"': The Platonic Indicative in *In Memoriam XCV*', *Victorian Poetry*, 14 (1976), 247–52, at 252; and cf. Culler, *Poetry of Tennyson*, 182–4.

30. Ian H. C. Kennedy, '*In Memoriam* and the Tradition of Pastoral Elegy', *Victorian Poetry*, 15 (1977), 351–66, at 362.

31. Iris Murdoch, *Existentialists and Mystics: Writings on Philosophy and Literature*, ed. Peter J. Conradi (1997), 293.

32. 'The stern were mild when thou wert by, | The flippant put himself to school' (cx. 9–10). Cf. Graham Hough (referring to the evolutionary fantasy that comes at the poem's close): 'though it was generally agreed that Hallam was an exceptionally talented young man, I do not think that anyone, even Tennyson, could really suggest that he was a biological advance on *homo sapiens*' ('The Natural Theology of *In Memoriam*', *Review of English Studies*, 23 (1947), 244–56, at 253).

33. Robert Grant, *The Politics of Sex and Other Essays on Conservatism, Culture and Imagination* (Basingstoke, 2000), 112.

34. Eric Smith, *By Mourning Tongues: Studies in English Elegy* (Ipswich, 1977), 7. The whole discussion of elegy and pastoral is illuminating.
35. The best account of 'nature' in the poem remains Hough's 'Natural Theology'.
36. *The Notebooks of Samuel Taylor Coleridge*, ed. Kathleen Coburn et al. (5 vols.; Princeton, NJ, 1956–2002), i, entry 812.
37. Eric Griffiths, *The Printed Voice of Victorian Poetry* (Oxford, 1989), 127.
38. The matter is discussed in Turner, *Tennyson*, 118–19.
39. Kennedy describes the way the poem works 'to exploit the pastoral conventions while at the same time questioning their validity' ('*In Memoriam*', 352).
40. *Letters of FitzGerald*, i. 699; quoted by Ricks, *Tennyson*, 212.
41. *Letters of FitzGerald*, i. 486; quoted in Ricks, *Tennyson*, 203.
42. C. S. Lewis, *A Grief Observed* (1961; repr. 1978), 12.
43. Cited by Randall Jarrell: *Kipling, Auden & Co.: Essays and Reviews 1953–1964* (Manchester, 1981), 127.
44. See Griffiths, *Printed Voice*, 97-8 *et seq.*
45. John Bayley, 'Tennyson and the Idea of Decadence', in Hallam Tennyson (ed.), *Studies in Tennyson* (1981), 186–205, at 204.
46. John Bayley, *The Uses of Division: Unity and Disharmony in Literature* (1976), 15.
47. Mays, '*In Memoriam*', 26.

CODA. 'MODERN RHYME'

1. F. R. Leavis, *New Bearings in English Poetry* (2nd edn.; 1950; repr. 1971), 15.
2. H. M. McLuhan, 'Tennyson and Picturesque Poetry', in John Killham (ed.), *Critical Essays on the Poetry of Tennyson* (1960), 67–85, at 68, 71.
3. Elaine Jordan, *Alfred Tennyson* (Cambridge, 1988), 181.
4. As in Viktor Frankl's memorable account of release from a concentration camp: ' "Freedom" – we repeated to ourselves, and yet we could not grasp it. We had said this word so often during all the years we dreamed about it, that it had lost its meaning' (*Man's Search for Meaning* (4th edn.; Boston, MA, 1992), 95).
5. W. B. Yeats, *Autobiographies* (1955; repr. 1980), 489, 484.
6. Angela Leighton, 'Touching Forms: Tennyson and Aestheticism', *Essays in Criticism*, 52 (2002), 56–75, at 65.
7. Samuel Taylor Coleridge, *Biographia Literaria*, ed. James Engell and Walter Jackson Bate (2 vols.; Princeton, NJ, 1983), ii. 15.
8. Ibid. ii. 8.
9. I am much indebted here to John Bayley, 'Tennyson and the Idea of

Decadence', in Hallam Tennyson (ed.), *Studies in Tennyson* (1981), 186–205, esp. at 196–7.

10. T. S. Eliot, *On Poetry and Poets* (1957; repr. 1984), 29–30, 32.
11. Edward Lear, *The Complete Verse and Nonsense*, ed. Vivien Noakes (2001), 161.
12. Hugh Kenner, 'Some Post-Symbolist Structures', in Frank Brady, John Palmer, and Martin Price (eds.), *Literary Theory and Structure: Essays in Honor of William K. Wimsatt* (New Haven, CT, 1973), 379–93, at 380–1. R. identifies a legitimate source for 'Akrokeraunian' in Horace's *Odes*, and adduces Lear himself using the word in his *Journals of a Landscape Painter in Albania and Illyria* (1851) – in which Lear also illustrated the Peneïan pass.
13. Henry James, *The Middle Years* (1917), 90.
14. An opinion expressed at the end of 'Tennyson as a Humorist' (1950), a radio talk; now included on a BBC tape, *John Betjeman: Recollections from the BBC Archives* (BBC Worldwide, 1998).

Select Bibliography

EDITIONS

Standard Edition

The Poems of Tennyson, ed. Christopher Ricks (2nd edn., incorporating the Trinity College MSS; 3 vols.; Harlow: Longman, 1987). This supercedes Ricks's one-volume edition of 1969, as it is able to include readings drawn from the large holding of Tennyson manuscripts at Trinity College, Cambridge, reproduction of which had been long prohibited by the terms of Hallam Tennyson's 1924 bequest. With the exception of the early play, 'The Devil and the Lady', Ricks does not print Tennyson's dramatic works. There is a generously handy single-volume paperback abridgement of the second edition, *Tennyson: A Selected Edition* (Harlow: Longman, 1989), which contains all the major poems.

Other Tennyson Editions

Works, ed. Hallam Lord Tennyson (9 vols.; London: Macmillan, 1907–8). The 'Eversley' edition. This includes many of Tennyson's remarks about his poems: they are reproduced in Ricks's footnotes.
Poetical Works, Including the Plays (London: Oxford University Press, 1953). Often reprinted, latterly under the title *Poems and Plays*.
The Letters of Alfred Lord Tennyson, ed. Cecil Y. Lang and Edgar F. Shannon, Jr. (3 vols.; Oxford: Clarendon Press, 1982–90).

Facsimiles

Ricks, Christopher, and Day, Aidan (eds.), *The Tennyson Archive* (31 vols.; New York: Garland, 1987–93). An immense undertaking, which reproduces in facsimile, as far as possible, all Tennyson's poetical manuscripts.

Editions of Individual Works and Volume

Poems of 1842, ed. Christopher Ricks (London: Collins, 1968).

Idylls of the King: A Variorum Edition, ed. John Pfordresher (New York, NY: Columbia University Press, 1973). Gives variants between Eversley and the surviving manuscripts, proofs and earlier published versions.

In Memoriam, ed. Susan Shatto and Marion Shaw (Oxford: Clarendon Press, 1982).

Idylls of the King, ed. J. M. Gray (Harmondsworth: Penguin, 1983).

Maud, ed. Susan Shatto (London: Athlone Press, 1986).

Selections

Auden, W. H. (ed.), *Tennyson: An Introduction and a Selection* (London: Phoenix House, 1946).

Cecil, Lord David (ed.), *A Choice of Tennyson's Verse* (London: Faber, 1971).

Ricks, Christopher (ed.), *A Collection of Poems by Alfred Tennyson* (Garden City, NY: Doubleday, 1972).

Amis, Kingsley (ed.), *Tennyson* (Poet to Poet; Harmondsworth: Penguin, 1973).

Roberts, Adam (ed.), *Tennyson* (Oxford Authors; Oxford: Oxford University Press, 2000).

Some Other Works

The Writings of Arthur Hallam, ed. T. H. Vail Motter (New York, NY: MLA, 1943).

Lady Tennyson's Journal, ed. James O. Hoge (Charlottesville, VA: University Press of Virginia, 1981).

The Letters of Arthur Henry Hallam, ed. Jack Kolb (Columbus, OH: Ohio State University Press, 1981).

Palgrave, Francis (ed.), *The Golden Treasury*, ed. Christopher Ricks (Harmondsworth: Penguin, 1991). Not a text by Tennyson, but one much influenced by him, and an immense influence in its turn on nineteenth-century English taste. Ricks's Penguin edition records Tennyson's contribution in the notes.

BIBLIOGRAPHY

Beetz, Kirk H., *Tennyson: A Bibliography, 1827–1982* (Metuchen, NJ/ London: Scarecrow, 1984).

Day, Aidan, 'Tennyson', in Joanne Shattock (ed.), *The Cambridge Bibliography of English Literature*, iv. *1800–1900* (Cambridge: Cambridge University Press, 1999), cols. 675– 85.

Shaw, Marion, *An Annotated Critical Bibliography of Alfred*, Lord Tennyson (Hemel Hempstead: Harvester, 1989).

BIOGRAPHY

Allen, Peter, *The Cambridge Apostles: The Early Years* (Cambridge: Cambridge University Press, 1978). A good account of the culture of the 'Apostles'.

Allingham, William, *Diary* (1907; repr. Fontwell: Centaur Press, 1967). Contains the best anecdotes of Tennyson.

Bevis, Matthew (ed.), *Lives of Victorian Literary Figures: Volume Three: Alfred, Lord Tennyson* (London: Pickering and Chatto, 2003). An excellent selection of pieces by Tennyson's contemporaries.

Knowles, James, 'Aspects of Tennyson', *Nineteenth Century*, 33 (1893), 164–88.

Levi, Peter, *Tennyson* (London: Macmillan, 1993). Levi was not only a distinguished poet but also the biographer of Virgil and Edward Lear, each in his way a Tennysonian figure.

Martin, Robert Bernard, *Tennyson: The Unquiet Heart* (Oxford/London: Clarendon Press/Faber, 1980). The most comprehensive modern biography.

Page, Norman (ed.), *Tennyson: Interviews and Recollections* (London: Macmillan, 1983). Usefully gathers together many contemporary accounts.

Pinion, F. B., *A Tennyson Chronology* (Basingstoke: Macmillan, 1990).

Richardson, Joanna, *The Pre-Eminent Victorian* (London: Cape, 1962).

Ricks, Christopher, *Tennyson* (London: Macmillan, 1972; 2nd edn., Basingstoke: Macmillan, 1989). A life as well as a critical study.

Tennyson, Sir Charles, *Alfred Tennyson* (London: Macmillan, 1949). A fine biography, which first revealed the depression and despair of Somersby.

Tennyson, Hallam, *Alfred, Lord Tennyson: A Memoir by his Son* (2 vols.; London: Macmillan, 1897, sometimes reprinted in one volume). The *Memoir* remains the essential starting point, even though its discretion has often been criticized. (For a noble defence, see Christopher Ricks, *Essays in Appreciation* (Oxford: Clarendon Press, 1996), 172–205; and see also Philip L. Elliott, *The Making of the Memoir* (2nd edn.; Lincoln: The Tennyson Society, 1993).) Hallam Tennyson had privately printed a four-volume *Materials for a Life of A. T. Collected for my Children* (n.d. [c.1895]), which is only to be found in a few good research libraries.

—— (ed.), *Tennyson and his Friends* (London: Macmillan, 1911). Essays in reminiscence.

Thwaite, Ann, *Emily Tennyson: The Poet's Wife* (London: Faber, 1996). An absorbing and evocative account of Emily Tennyson.

CRITICISM AND SCHOLARSHIP

The following list is highly selective. For a fuller list of books and articles, the reader should consult Marion Shaw's bibliography.

Albright, Daniel, *Tennyson: The Muses' Tug-of-War* (Charlottesville, VA: University Press of Virginia, 1986).

Armstrong, Isobel, 'The Collapse of Object and Subject: *In Memoriam*', in *Language as Living Form in Nineteenth-Century Poetry* (Brighton: Harvester, 1982), 172–205.

—— *Victorian Poetry: Poetry, Poetics and Politics* (London: Routledge, 1993).

—— (ed.), *The Major Victorian Poets: Reconsiderations* (London: Routledge & Kegan Paul, 1969).

Auden, W. H., 'Tennyson', in *Forewords and Afterwords*, selected by Edward Mendelson (London: Faber, 1973), 221–32. Originally the introduction to *Tennyson: An Introduction and a Selection* (1946).

Bayley, John, 'Tennyson and the Idea of Decadence', in Hallam Tennyson (ed.), *Studies in Tennyson* (London: Macmillan, 1981), 186–205. A marvellously ramificatory account of the comedies of poetic self-consciousness in Tennyson.

—— 'The Dynamics of the Static', *Times Literary Supplement*, 3 Mar. 1978, 247.

Beer, John, 'Tennyson, Coleridge, and the Cambridge Apostles', in Philip Collins (ed.), *Tennyson: Seven Essays* (Basingstoke: Macmillan, 1992), 1–35.

Bradley, A. C., *A Commentary on Tennyson's* In Memoriam (3rd edn.; London: Macmillan, 1910).

—— *The Reaction against Tennyson* (English Association Pamphlet 39; Oxford: English Association, 1917); collected in A. C. Bradley, *A Miscellany* (London: Macmillan, 1929), 1–31.

Brooks, Cleanth, 'The Motivation of Tennyson's Weeper'; in John Killham (ed.), *Critical Essays on the Poetry of Tennyson* (London: Routledge & Kegan Paul, 1960), 177–85.

Byatt, A. S., 'The Lyric Structure of Tennyson's *Maud*'; in Isobel Armstrong (ed.), *The Major Victorian Poets: Reconsiderations* (London:

Routledge & Kegan Paul, 1969), 69–92.

Campbell, Matthew, *Rhythm and Will in Victorian Poetry* (Cambridge: Cambridge University Press, 1999). A subtle and readerly account, with many observations finely made of Tennyson.

Chesterton, G. K., *The Victorian Age in Literature* (London: Oxford University Press, 1913, often reprinted). Still full of tendentiously good things.

Christ, Carol T., 'The Feminine Subject in Victorian Poetry', *English Literary History* 54 (1987), 385–401.

—— *Victorian and Modern Poetics* (Chicago, IL: University of Chicago Press, 1984). A revisionary account that argues for the continuity of Victorian and modernist poetry.

Collins, Philip (ed.), *Tennyson: Seven Essays* (Basingstoke: Macmillan, 1992).

Cronin, Richard, *Romantic Victorians: English Literature, 1824–1840* (Basingstoke: Palgrave, 2001). Especially good on the political influences upon the earlier Tennyson.

Culler, A. Dwight, *The Poetry of Tennyson* (New Haven: Yale University Press, 1977). An encompassing and humane book.

Dean, D. R., *Tennyson and the Geologists* (Lincoln: Tennyson Society, 1985). A good account of Tennyson's troubled interest in contemporary developments in the earth sciences.

Dodsworth, Martin, 'Patterns of Morbidity: Repetition in Tennyson's Poetry', in Isobel Armstrong (ed.), *The Major Victorian Poets: Reconsiderations* (London: Routledge & Kegan Paul, 1969), 7–34.

Douglas-Fairhurst, Robert, *Victorian Afterlives: The Shaping of Influence in Nineteenth-Century Literature* (Oxford: Oxford University Press, 2002), esp. 182–269. An agile, accomplished, pleasureful book with fine things to say about Tennyson.

Eliot, T. S., '*In Memoriam*', in T. S. Eliot, *Selected Essays* (3rd edn.; London: Faber, 1951; repr., 1980), 328–38.

Griffiths, Eric, 'Tennyson's Breath', in *The Printed Voice of Victorian Poetry* (Oxford: Clarendon Press, 1989), 97-170. Criticism of immense elegance and insight.

—— 'Tennyson's Idle Tears', in Phillip Collins, *Tennyson: Seven Essays* (Basingstoke: Macmillan, 1992), 36–60.

Hair, Donald S., *Tennyson's Language* (Toronto: University of Toronto Press, 1991).

Hilton, Nelson, 'Tennyson's Tears: Idle, Idol, Idyl', *Essays in Criticism*, 35 (1985), 223–37.

Hough, Graham, 'The Natural Theology of *In Memoriam*', *Review of English Studies*, 23 (1947), 244–56.

Hunt, John Dixon (ed.), *Tennyson: In Memoriam: A Casebook* (London: Macmillan, 1970; repr. Basingstoke: Macmillan, 1987).

Jordan, Elaine, *Alfred Tennyson* (Cambridge: Cambridge University Press, 1988).

Joseph, Gerhard, *Tennyson and the Text: The Weaver's Shuttle* (Cambridge: Cambridge University Press, 1992).

Jump, John D. (ed.), *Tennyson: The Critical Heritage* (London: Routledge & Kegan Paul, 1967). An invaluable volume, which gathers the most important contemporary critical responses.

Kennedy, Ian H. C., '*In Memoriam* and the Tradition of Pastoral Elegy', *Victorian Poetry*, 15 (1977), 351–66.

Killham, John (ed.), *Critical Essays on the Poetry of Tennyson* (London: Routledge & Kegan Paul, 1960).

—— *Tennyson and The Princess: Reflections of an Age* (London: Athlone Press, 1958). A well-researched placing of the work in its political moment.

Langbaum, Robert, *The Poetry of Experience: The Dramatic Monologue in Modern Literary Tradition* (1957; repr., London: Chatto & Windus, 1972), esp. 87–93.

Lang, Cecil Y., *Tennyson's Arthurian Psycho-Drama* (Lincoln: Tennyson Society, 1983).

Leighton, Angela, 'Touching Forms: Tennyson and Aestheticism', *Essays in Criticism*, 52 (2002), 56–75. A finely suggestive essay about Tennyson's relationship with the idea of 'art for art's sake'.

McLuhan, H. M., 'Tennyson and Picturesque Poetry', in John Killham (ed.), *Critical Essays on the Poetry of Tennyson* (London: Routledge & Kegan Paul, 1960), 67–85.

Mays, J. C. C., '*In Memoriam*: An Aspect of Form', *University of Toronto Quarterly*, 35 (1965–6), 22–46.

Paden, W. D., *Tennyson in Egypt: A Study of the Imagery in his Earlier Work* (Lawrence, KA: University of Kansas Press, 1942).

Pattison, Robert, *Tennyson and Tradition* (Cambridge, MA: Harvard University Press, 1979).

Peltason, Timothy, *Reading 'In Memoriam'* (Princeton, NJ: Princeton University Press, 1985).

Priestley, F. E. L., *Language and Structure in Tennyson's Poetry* (London: Deutsch, 1973).

Rader, Ralph Wilson, *Tennyson's Maud: The Biographical Genesis* (Berkeley and Los Angeles, CA: University of California Press, 1963).

Reynolds, Matthew, *The Realms of Verse 1830–1870: English Poetry in a Time of Nation-Building* (Oxford: Clarendon Press, 2001), esp. 203–73. Impressively contextualized, closely read.

Richardson, James, *Vanishing Lives: Style and Self in Tennyson, D. G. Rossetti, Swinburne, and Yeats* (Charlottesville, VA: University Press of Virginia, 1988).

Ricks, Christopher, *Tennyson* (2nd edn.; Basingstoke: Macmillan, 1989). The best account of the poet, which reads the work beautifully and relates it to the life with great tact.

—— 'Tennyson', in *Allusion to the Poets* (Oxford: Oxford University Press, 2002), 179–216. An essay about Tennyson's allusiveness, first published as 'Tennyson Inheriting the Earth', in Hallam Tennyson (ed.), *Studies in Tennyson* (London: Macmillan, 1981), 66–104.

—— 'Tennyson's Methods of Composition', *Proceedings of the British Academy*, 52 (1966), 209–30. Partially repeated in Christopher Ricks, *Tennyson* (2nd edn.; Basingstoke: Macmillan, 1989), 281–94.

Robson, W. W., 'The Dilemma of Tennyson', in John Killham (ed.), *Critical Essays on the Poetry of Tennyson* (London: Routledge & Kegan Paul, 1960), 155–63.

Sedgwick, Eve Kosofsky, 'Tennyson's *Princess*: One Bride for Seven Brothers', in *Between Men: English Literature and Male Homosocial Desire* (New York, NY: Columbia University Press, 1985), 118–33; repr. in Rebecca Stott (ed.), *Tennyson* (Longman Critical Readers; Harlow: Longman, 1996), 181–96.

Shannon, Edgar Finley, Jr., *Tennyson and the Reviewers: A Study of his Literary Reputation and of the Influence of the Critics upon his Poetry 1827-1851* (Cambridge, MA: Harvard University Press: 1952).

Shaw, W. David, *Elegy and Paradox: Testing the Conventions* (Baltimore, MD: Johns Hopkins University Press, 1994). Contains a most suggestive discussion of Tennyson (esp. pp. 210–35), mindful of genre.

—— *Tennyson's Style* (Ithaca, NY: Cornell University Press, 1976).

Shaw, Marion, *Alfred Lord Tennyson* (Hemel Hempstead: Harvester Wheatsheaf, 1988). Among the most illuminating and sympathetic feminist accounts.

Sinfield, Alan, *Alfred Tennyson* (Oxford: Blackwell, 1986). An influential, revisionary reading: Tennyson as the embodiment of an ideologically motivated institution, 'Literature'.

—— *The Language of Tennyson's 'In Memoriam'* (Oxford: Blackwell, 1971).

—— 'Tennyson and the Cultural Politics of Prophecy', in Rebecca Stott (ed.), *Tennyson* (Longman Critical Readers; Harlow: Longman, 1996), 33–53.

Steane, J. B., *Tennyson* (London: Evans Brothers, 1966). An introduction in the 'Literature in Perspective' series. It is now seldom remarked; but F. W. Bateson thought it 'very clever', and it is a first-rate introduction.

Stott, Rebecca (ed.), *Tennyson* (Longman Critical Readers; London: Longman, 1996).

Tennyson, Charles, 'Tennyson as a Humorist', in *Six Tennyson Essays* (London: Cassell, 1954), 1–38.

Tennyson, Hallam (ed.), *Studies in Tennyson* (London: Macmillan, 1981).

Tucker, Herbert F., *Tennyson and the Doom of Romanticism* (Cambridge, MA: Harvard University Press, 1988). Clever, intricate, weighty. It is also worth consulting the article that forms the germ of the book, 'Tennyson and the Measure of Doom', *PMLA* 98 (1983), 8–20.

— (ed.), *Critical Essays on Alfred Lord Tennyson* (New York: Macmillan, 1993).

Turner, Paul, *Tennyson* (London: Routledge & Kegan Paul, 1976). Well attuned to classical echoes and influences.

The Tennyson Society (www.tennysonsociety.org.uk/tennyson/) annually publishes a consistently interesting journal, *Tennyson Research Bulletin* (1967–). The society issues, additionally, occasional papers and specialized monographs (some are listed above).

Index

Works are indexed under the names of their authors.